Beginning Arduino Programming

Brian Evans

Apress®

Beginning Arduino Programming

ISBN-13 (pbk): 978-1-4302-3777-8

ISBN-13 (electronic): 978-1-4302-3778-5

President and Publisher: Paul Manning
Lead Editor: Dominic Shakeshaft
Technical Reviewer: Ryan Owens
Editorial Board: Clay Andres, Steve Anglin, Mark Beckner, Ewan Buckingham, Gary Cornell, Jonathan Gennick, Jonathan Hassell, Michelle Lowman, James Markham, Matthew Moodie, Jeff Olson, Jeffrey Pepper, Frank Pohlmann, Douglas Pundick, Ben Renow-Clarke, Dominic Shakeshaft, Matt Wade, Tom Welsh
Coordinating Editor: Jessica Belanger
Copy Editor: Kimberly Burton
Indexer: SPI Global
Cover Designer: Anna Ishchenko

Distributed to the book trade worldwide by Springer Science+Business Media, LLC., 233 Spring Street, 6th Floor, New York, NY 10013. Phone 1-800-SPRINGER, fax (201) 348-4505, e-mail orders-ny@springer-sbm.com, or visit www.springeronline.com.

For information on translations, please e-mail rights@apress.com, or visit www.apress.com.

Apress and friends of ED books may be purchased in bulk for academic, corporate, or promotional use. eBook versions and licenses are also available for most titles. For more information, reference our Special Bulk Sales–eBook Licensing web page at www.apress.com/bulk-sales.

The source code for this book is available to readers at www.apress.com.

To Susan and Kori for making me laugh.

Contents at a Glance

Contents

About the Author

Brian Evans is an artist working in electronic media and Assistant Professor at Metropolitan State College of Denver, where he teaches multidisciplinary courses in art and design on topics that include spatial media, electronics, and 3D fabrication. Many of his classes use open-source hardware, including MakerBot or RepRap 3D printers and the Arduino electronics platform, in the creation of new works in art and design.

His work has been shown at the Los Angeles Municipal Art Gallery at Barnsdall Park, the Orange County Center for Contemporary Art, and the University Art Museum at California State University, Long Beach. Evans was a resident and contributor to the Grounding Open Source Hardware residency and summit at the Banff New Media Institute in Alberta, Canada, in 2009 and contributor to the Open Hardware Summit in New York, in 2011. He received an MFA at California State University, Long Beach, in 2008 and a BFA at Arizona State University in 2005.

About the Technical Reviewer

Ryan Owens graduated from Gonzaga University in Spokane, Washington, with a degree in electrical and computer engineering. He is a design engineer for SparkFun Electronics, where he creates new products and writes tutorials and project walk-through guides for all levels of embedded electronics. He also taught a handful of classes on beginning electronics and Arduino programming for SparkFun, where typical students range from children to IT professionals.

Acknowledgments

This book could not have been written without the endearing support, encouragement, and thoughtful intuition of my wife, Susan, my partner and best friend, thank you for all of your help. And to my daughter, Kori, who provided caring moral support for her Dad throughout this process. I must also acknowledge and thank my father, Arvin, who helped me out of a few binds and maybe even contributed to a few. I am also sincerely grateful for my friends and colleagues at Metropolitan State who have given me a home to grow as a professor and for encouraging me at the beginning of this project.

Many thanks and gratitude to Paul Badger for batting around ideas for this book early on; to David Mellis for answering all those stupid e-mails; and to Tom Igoe for the thoughtful and insightful dialog that we shared. This book is also hugely indebted to the active and generous community of makers who have made the Arduino platform what it is and who have freely shared so much of their hard work. I have taken inspiration and borrowed from many great sources and thank you all.

I, of course, need to thank the publisher, Apress, and acknowledge the amazing editorial team whose tireless work made this book what it is. This includes Frank Pohlmann for giving me this opportunity out of the blue, Jessica Belanger for keeping me on track, and James Markham for constantly putting me on my head. Thanks also to the technical reviewer, Ryan Owens, for his insight and feedback.

I must also thank my very creative and talented students who cut their professor a little slack when this project began and who give me new reasons every day to continue to do what I do.

Introduction

This book will help you to develop working source code for the Arduino microcontroller. In these pages, we will primarily concern ourselves with the software aspect of physical computing—designing code to work with physical objects that exhibit behavior or interactivity through software. Starting with the basic context of the Arduino platform to getting up and running with our first code, we will discuss the structure and syntax of Arduino's C-based programming language, looking at variables, control structures, arrays, and memory. This book will then go into many of the functions unique to Arduino development for controlling digital and analog input and output, timing, randomness, writing functions, and using many of the Arduino libraries for working with different kinds of hardware and communication protocols.

Arduino, like Processing before it, adopted the idea of a code sketchbook. We will carry on this metaphor as we talk about the process of sketching in code as an intuitive method for quickly testing out new ideas in code. Most of this book is written around this idea of developing programming skills through sketching. We will also provide some suggestions for new projects and hardware, new languages to try out, and ways to contribute back to the community. This book intentionally does not dwell too long on electronics theory, circuit design, hacking, or other specifically hardware-based practices, although we'll revisit the hardware side of things in our last chapter to provide a small foundation for physical computing.

This book in many ways picks up where the *Arduino Programming Notebook* left off, with even more in-depth discussions about the Arduino environment; simple, no-frills code samples; and clear, easy-to-read schematics and illustrations. The *Notebook*, a little PDF booklet, was my first experience writing about the Arduino and was never meant to be more than a brief guide for my students when I first introduced a class of 15 college art and design majors to the Arduino in 2007. Best laid plans and all, this little booklet has now been translated into Spanish, Russian, and Dutch (that I know of), is hosted in so many different places that it is impossible to keep track of, and it's been used in workshops and classes around the world. I haven't updated the *Notebook* over the last few years, and in all honesty I am not entirely sure what to do with it now, so hopefully this new book will fill a void and find a similar, widespread adoption that the little booklet has enjoyed all these years.

Who This Book is For

This book is written for the primary audience of the Arduino platform: artists, designers, students, tinkerers, and the makers of things. While you might have some programming experience that you want to bring to the Arduino platform, we will assume no prior knowledge of writing code. With that said, a healthy familiarity of the computer is helpful, as is the willingness and inquisitive curiosity to look beyond this book for certain answers.

The majority of Arduino users just want to get things done and often don't care about the little details—they just want their projects to work. I understand this, as I am one of those people. I first discovered programmable microcontrollers when I was an art student, and at the time, art school was not generally the most conducive environment for learning how to write code and wire up motors—at least it wasn't before the Arduino came along. Likewise, I was never one for a love of mathematics, which thankfully is not a prerequisite to deeply enjoy the process of writing code.

Reading This Book

Our process in each chapter will be to focus on some fundamental projects that build on the primary concepts presented in that chapter. For each project, we will begin with a project description and discuss the specific hardware needed for that project. We will also provide diagrams and illustrations for making these simple circuits and interfacing them to the Arduino board. As you read through each project, you should take notes and write in the margins—we won't be offended. Experiment, try new things, and see what happens.

The projects demonstrated in this book are meant to be prototypes, or fundamental proof-of-concept designs for a new device. We will adhere to a degree of minimalism, keeping to simple and easily obtainable hardware that supports the development of sophisticated written code. Once you have built the prototype, it can be incorporated into a final project later. We won't actually be doing that here so that we can focus on actually writing and developing code. Our examples will borrow and build on each other throughout the book, revisiting past examples when we need to as our understanding of writing code develops.

The intent with our code samples is to write compartmentalized or modular code wherever possible to allow for easy adaptability and future development. We will spend a lot of time developing our coding skills so that when it comes time to develop a new project independently, you will know where to begin. The sketches are meant to be fluid—you are encouraged to hack them—changing values, timing, pin assignments, ranges, and so on—until it no longer works. Then try to fix it. We will stick to a particular style of writing code in our samples, although we urge you to develop your own writing style that reflects the way you think and the way you want to see your code.

Wiring up the circuits for our projects is as simple and straightforward as possible, with little to no understanding of electronics necessary. As a way to reconnect our discussions of programming to the physical electronics used throughout the book, Chapter 12 will provide a brief review of some basic electronics, including how circuits work, reading schematics, and an introduction to soldering. If you find that you are struggling with hooking up the projects in the earlier chapters, you might want to jump to Chapter 12 for a refresher. Otherwise, this chapter will serve as a good summary that could help answer some questions you might not even know you had. While this might at first seem a little backwards, it has worked pretty well in my classes over the last few years.

Arduino 1.0

At the time of this writing, the Arduino developers are hard at work on a more stable, more efficient, and generally improved version of the Arduino software called Arduino 1.0. The final release version of Arduino 1.0 should be available right about the same time that this book is published. This is important because in the process of making things better, some things had to be broken. This means that some older code written under the alpha release of the Arduino software will no longer work on Arduino 1.0.

Conversely, the code in this book and images of the Arduino development environment have all been prepared using a beta release of Arduino 1.0 (`http://code.google.com/p/arduino/wiki/Arduino1`), so images of the Arduino software may appear different from the final version, some of the code in this book may not work on older versions of the software, and still other features of 1.0 were not yet fully implemented—so I couldn't write about them. There may also be other growing pains with this upgrade that we are not fully aware of at this time, so if an unusual problem crops up, then you might want to blame 1.0 and start there to figure out what's wrong.

Conventions

We will use several conventions in this book, including fixed width fonts in line to denote specific code examples, **bold text** highlights new concepts or definitions, and anything with a parenthesis after it—as in setup() or loop()—will denote something called a function. Anytime there is a block of fixed-width font separated from the main text, it is a multiline code example, as in the following:

```
// this is a mulitline
// code example
```

> **Note** Occasionally there will be areas separated as this sentence is, as a side note, general tip, or caution about something you will want to pay careful attention to.

Downloading the Code

The source code for this book is available from the Apress web site (www.apress.com) in the Source Code / Downloads section. If you are publishing examples that use code from this book, using attribution that includes the title, author, publisher, year, and ISBN is generally a nice thing to do.

CHAPTER 1

Getting Started

One of the keys to the Arduino's success is the minimal amount of time that it takes for a complete novice to move from opening the little box containing the Arduino interface board to having their first source code, also known as a sketch, up and running on that board.

The Arduino software development environment is free to download and use with no lengthy registration procedures or end-user agreements, and there is little to no setup to get the board running with your computer, regardless of the platform, working equally well on Mac, Linux, and Windows-based PCs. The Arduino web site at www.arduino.cc provides easy-to-follow "Getting Started" tutorials and whenever you get stuck there is always the active, vocal, and generally helpful Arduino community that is willing to share its knowledge. This low barrier to programming embedded electronics means it's possible to make lights blink in ten minutes flat with little to no prior experience.

This chapter will walk you through the history behind the Arduino platform, with an eye towards what makes the Arduino such a success story. We will look at some of the things that can be done with the platform and get you started on the right foot with a firm understanding of its possibilities. This includes a brief walk-through of that first ten-minute experience so that we can quickly move into some of our first projects in the next chapter. But first, let's start with a little background.

Arduino is for Makers

Arduino is a flexible programmable hardware platform designed for artists, designers, tinkerers, and the makers of things. Arduino's little, blue circuit board, mythically taking its name from a local pub in Italy, has in a very short time motivated a new generation of DIYers of all ages to make all manner of wild projects found anywhere from the hallowed grounds of our universities to the scorching desert sands of a particularly infamous yearly arts festival and just about everywhere in between. Usually these Arduino-based projects require little to no programming skills or knowledge of electronics theory, and more often than not, this handiness is simply picked up along the way.

Central to the Arduino interface board, shown in Figure 1-1, is an onboard microcontroller—think of it as a little computer on a chip.

Figure 1-1. *The Arduino Uno interface board, 2011*

This microcontroller comes from a company called Atmel and the chip is known as an AVR. It is slow in modern terms, running at only 16Mhz with an 8-bit core, and has a very limited amount of available memory, with 32 kilobytes of storage and 2 kilobytes of random access memory. The interface board is known for its rather quirky design—just ask the die-hards about standardized pin spacing—but it also epitomizes the minimalist mantra of only making things as complicated as they absolutely need to be. Its design is not entirely new or revolutionary, beginning with a curious merger of two, off-the-shelf reference designs, one for an inexpensive microcontroller and the other for a USB-to-serial converter, with a handful of other useful components all wrapped up in a single board. Its predecessors include the venerable BASIC Stamp, which got its start as early as 1992, as well as the OOPic, Basic ATOM, BASIC-X24, and the PICAXE.

Where all of these precursors are generally closed proprietary products and often require a single computer platform to use, the Arduino development environment is free for all to use and will run on just about any kind of computer that supports Java. The actual hardware board costs a mere USD $30 or EUR €22 and needs nothing more complex than a USB cable to get up and running. This affordable price, nearly half that of its closest competitor, and the board's durable design have led to numerous Arduino-like boards being stitched into embroidery (see Figure 1-2), embedded in pumpkins to be launched through the air by trebuchets, and even sent into outer space in weather balloons.

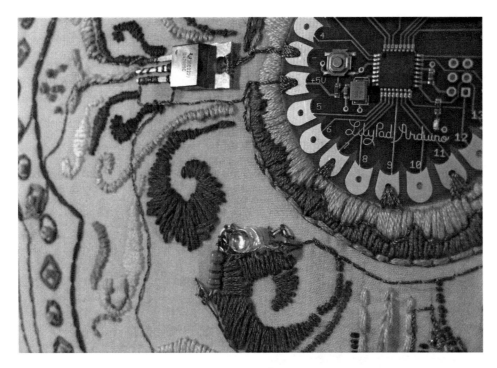

Figure 1-2. LilyPad Arduino embroidery, courtesy Becky Stern, sternlab.org

This at least tells us a little bit about what kind of person the Arduino was originally designed for and about the hardware used in its design, but these things alone do not begin to account for the huge degree of success enjoyed by the Arduino as a whole. To get a sense for this popularity, we need to look at the larger Arduino ecosystem and how some fairly divergent parts came together to create a movement.

The Arduino Ecosystem

The Arduino is not just one simple thing making it a little hard to define. It is a microcontroller platform, an open-source design that encourages modification and reuse, a community that has embraced and grown up around the Arduino, and a new crop of projects and devices that can trace their lineage to the Arduino and have in return contributed back to the development of various aspects of the entire Arduino ecosystem.

The Arduino Platform

The Arduino ecosystem begins with the Arduino platform, itself several layers of hardware and software working together to create a cohesive whole. We can start with the hardware interface board—that little, blue circuit board that you build into your projects. It has a fairly standard onboard microcontroller that can interact with the world around it by using its programmable inputs and outputs, as well as a USB port and controller for easily communicating with your computer. This USB connectivity and friendly sockets for hookup wires to easily plug in to, contribute to the high level of usability in the interface board design.

Equally important to this ecosystem is the Arduino development environment, a program based on the Processing development environment (http://processing.org) that you use to write, edit, compile, and upload your Arduino source code to the interface board. The Arduino team made the general assumption that people don't really care about the myriad of technical specifics involved with microcontroller architecture—they just want it to do something cool. With that in mind, the Arduino development environment wraps up some of the more techie parts of programming AVR microcontrollers into a nice, simple library of Arduino-specific commands that are easier to use and easier to understand, and built right into every sketch written for the Arduino. This development environment is so versatile, that an Arduino interface board is not even needed to use it. Instead, we can use the very same AVR microcontroller as is built onto the interface board, but in an entirely different device—such as the example shown in Figure 1-3 of a microcontroller on a breadboard that has been programmed with an Arduino sketch.

Figure 1-3. *Arduino compatible AVR microcontroller on breadboard*

Finally, we are brought to the Arduino bootloader, a little chunk of code residing on the microcontroller that allows it to be easily programmed with a simple serial connection rather than cranky, external hardware. As long as the bootloader has been programmed onto the microcontroller beforehand, we can use that chip in whatever device we choose, such as the breadboard in Figure 1-3, and still write code for it using the rest of the Arduino platform. It helps if we use one of the microcontrollers common to the Arduino, but this is not always a prerequisite, with many other Atmel microcontrollers working nearly as well with little or no modification.

Open-Source Hardware

The Arduino platform is itself pretty useful for microcontroller projects, but that alone is not enough to propel the popularity and widespread adoption of the platform. Instead of closing the design of the interface board and development environment, the entire Arduino project is deeply entrenched in the emerging practice of open-source hardware. Unlike open-source software, of which Linux is usually the often-cited example, open-source hardware seeks collaboration where physical objects are the outcome. It engages a distributed model of hardware development with contributors generally residing in different parts of the world. Rather than closed systems, open source projects allow an individual freedom to access the source files of a design, make improvements, and redistribute these improvements to a larger community.

The Arduino ecosystem fundamentally embodies this aspiration for openness in design, architecture, collaboration, and philosophy. You can see it for yourself as all of the design files, schematics, and software are freely available to download, use, modify, remake, and even resell. What started as a seemingly serendipitous decision to open the Arduino design and software to the greater community, spurred by the closing of the design school where the Arduino team was first formed, has lead to an entirely new movement in design. The practice of contributors having the liberty to use these designs freely (free as in speech) and with no obligation to buy anything (free as in beer) helps make the Arduino as endearing as a collection of silicon and copper can be. Not to mention that this creative feedback loop ensures that every inspired innovation derived from the Arduino platform is met with ever more imaginative uses for even more new things.

Community

Maybe even more important than the hardware platform itself, the Arduino community is most likely the single greatest cog in the Arduino machine. This community of makers has contributed to the Arduino ecosystem by developing code and libraries, designing new hardware, teaching workshops and classes, and sharing what they've made. The Arduino is now being taught in high schools, colleges, and universities everywhere and "Arduino Night" is a regular ritual at any of a number of hacker spaces around the world. People coming together around the Arduino, as shown in the image of a soldering workshop at Maker Faire in Figure 1-4, contributes to this global community that has made the Arduino such a success.

Figure 1-4. *Soldering Workshop, Maker Faire, San Mateo, CA, 2011, courtesy SparkFun Electronics*

Community engagement for a project like the Arduino is essential for the success or failure of the project. Fortuitous timing also helped in that the Arduino came to the scene at the same time that the return of the Maker and DIY movements also began again. This ever-increasing new crop of makers means that you never have to look hard to find willing co-conspirators to help on anything open source; whether it's through pockets of helpful individuals in the interweb or your neighborhood hacker space, help is never that far away.

Arduinoland

This community-driven research and development seems to have a magical effect on any project to come out of the wake of the Arduino, and this proverbial kingdom of mystical wonder is something I'm going to call Arduinoland. Maybe it's because the hardware design works, is open, and is hackable, or maybe it's because of a communal desire to build upon each other's work, but whatever it is, in Arduinoland, soldering iron marvels, difficult to nearly impossible to pull off in a garage just ten years ago, seem to happen every day. Anything from interactive electronic textiles, autonomous flying aircraft, networked beer keg refrigerators, photographic missions to near space, and immersive architectural installations have all sprouted from this open Arduino ecosystem.

Take the MakerBot CupCake CNC for example, a sub-$1,000, kit-based, plastic-extruding, 3D printer shown in Figure 1-5. Needing an electronics system to interpret codes sent from an attached computer to drive the positioning of the printhead and the temperature of the extruder, the MakerBot team built off the Arduino hardware platform and the development environment to create an open platform for building plastic objects.

Figure 1-5. MakerBot CupCake 3D printer with Arduino-compatible electronics

Or for all of those brown thumbs out there that can never seem to water their house plants when it's most needed, a team of New York University students developed a tweeting plant moisture meter called Botanicalls, shown in Figure 1-6. Based on the Arduino reference design, combined with an off-the-shelf Ethernet module and a simple moisture probe all wrapped up in a leafy-green circuit board, the Botanicalls device will post a tweet and blink an LED whenever the soil moisture of the plant falls below a certain threshold, letting its owner know that they should get out their watering can.

Figure 1-6. *Botanicalls Arduino-based tweeting plant water meter, courtesy Botanicalls*

These projects and many others have all benefited from the rapid development and reliable longevity brought to you by Arduinoland and the hard work put in by the Arduino team and community at large to create an open architecture that enables continued and accelerated growth and creativity.

Arduino is C… Mostly

In addition to the various aspects of the diverse Arduino ecosystem, we have the programming language of the Arduino platform, which is the central focus of this book. The core language used in the Arduino development environment is the C computer programming language first developed at the research institute of Bell Laboratories in the early 1970s for use with the UNIX operating system. C uses a procedural language syntax that needs to be processed by a compiler to map human-readable code to machine instructions. The long-standing popularity of C lends the Arduino some of its heritage, but the code that we are writing in this book is only mostly C.

Because there are aspects of the C language that look like it was written by dyslexic aliens, and with the language sometimes accused of being overly cryptic and difficult for beginners to pick up, the Arduino team has developed the standard Arduino library that provides a simple and targeted set of functions that make programming the Arduino interface board about as easy as it can get. Now, these libraries are themselves actually C++, itself a subset of the original C language, but we really don't need to go there.

What's important is that most of the code that we will write for the Arduino, including its syntax, structure, operators, control statements, and functions, remain fundamentally and functionally the same as C. What will be unique to the Arduino, however, are all sorts of functions that you will come to know and love, including `pinMode()`, `digitalWrite()`, and `delay()` that are specific to the standard Arduino library. For the purposes of this book, this basic framework of C combined with the additional Arduino library that is automatically a part of every sketch that we write, is what we will refer to as

Arduino C. To illustrate this point, Listings 1-1 and 1-2 provide two examples of the same source code to blink the onboard LED connected to digital pin 13.

Listing 1-1. *Blink LED with avr-libc*

```
#include <avr/io.h>
#include <util/delay.h>

int main(void) {
  while (1) {
    PORTB = 0x20;
    _delay_ms(1000);
    PORTB = 0x00;
    _delay_ms(1000);
  }
  return 1;
}
```

Listing 1-2. *Blink LED with Arduino*

```
void setup() {
  pinMode(13, OUTPUT);
}

void loop() {
  digitalWrite(13, HIGH);
  delay(1000);
  digitalWrite(13, LOW);
  delay(1000);
}
```

These two different listings show two functionally identical sketches, one written with the Arduino library and one written without. The really nifty thing here is that, if you want to geek out, the Arduino development environment is fully compatible and extensible using C/C++ code written using the avr-libc library, a subset of the standard C library, and the GCC compiler, both written for Atmel's standard 8-bit AVR microcontrollers. Listing 1-1 is written with avr-libc while Listing 1-2 is written using the Arduino library. They both are compatible with the Arduino development environment and can be uploaded the same way to the Arduino board. The first example also consumes a fifth of the amount of memory as the second example, coming in at 210 bytes as opposed to 1010 bytes.

What the Arduino example lacks in memory efficiency, however, it more than makes up for in usability and integration with the Arduino interface board. For example, referring to the digital pin that our LED is connected to as pin number 13 is generally easier for most people than the hexadecimal address 0x20 on PORTB. This simplicity is one the benefits to writing code using Arduino C. That is not to say that one is better than the other, but simply that this scalability and flexibility is an often-overlooked benefit of learning on the Arduino platform because it allows budding code-monkeys the opportunity to develop into ever more powerful architectures later. We will focus on programming the Arduino using the standard Arduino libraries, although if you want to know more, full documentation on the avr-libc library package can be found at www.nongnu.org/avr-libc/. While we are at it, it is also worth mentioning that it is even possible to program the Arduino interface board using other development environments more often associated with computer development, such as Eclipse, NetBeans, or any other development package that you are familiar with … or if you have an aversion to the color teal.

What's Needed

Now that we know why we are learning to write code and generally what this platform offers, we are going to need a little bit of hardware to complete the projects discussed in the rest of this book. Even though we will focus our discussions primarily on programming the Arduino, the hardware is what makes programming the Arduino so much fun. The best place to get started with prototyping electronic circuits with the Arduino is through one of the many starter kits available from various retailers for anywhere from $40 to $100 USD or about €30 to €70 EUR. SparkFun Electronics (www.sparkfun.com) offers the Starter Kit and Inventor's Kit; Adafruit Industries (www.adafruit.com) the Budget Pack or Starter Pack; *MAKE Magazine*'s Maker SHED (www.makershed.com) with either a Getting Started Kit or the Mintronics Survival Pack; or the Arduino Store's (http://store.arduino.cc) Workshop Kit. Figure 1-7 shows what this assembled kit might look like.

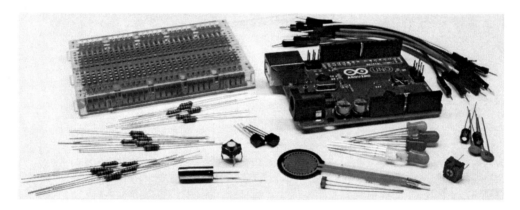

Figure 1-7. *Getting started hardware kit*

While each of these kits will have more or less what you need, Table 1-1 provides a simple shopping list of some of the specific hardware that we will use in the following pages, which you might want to purchase individually or at least check whether or not the kit you are considering contains these items. Prices are only approximate and are listed just to give you an idea on the costs.

Keep in mind that this is just a general list of recommended parts; feel free to purchase something different—as long as it's somewhat similar to what's listed—and to order from vendors of your choice. For example, rather than using an Arduino Uno, the standard Arduino interface board, maybe you're interested in wearables or e-textiles and would like to use a LilyPad Arduino instead. That's fine, just be sure to read up on the differences between the recommended hardware and your own on the Arduino Hardware page at http://arduino.cc/en/Main/Hardware. Likewise, many of the items on the list, such as resistors, are kind of like horseshoes in that close enough will usually get the job done. For a more detailed list that includes all the parts used in this book, refer to the expanded hardware list in the appendix at the end of this book.

Table 1-1. *Abbreviated Hardware List*

Part	Description	Price (US / EUR)
Arduino Uno	Microcontroller interface board	$30/€22
USB cable	A-B (often used for printers) for the Arduino Uno	$4/€2
Solderless breadboard	Either standard (400 tie points) or mini (170 tie points)	$6/€4
Hookup wire	Solid 22 AWG or pre-terminated M/M jumper wires	$7/€5
Light emitting diodes	Standard 5mm LEDs and common cathode RGB LEDs	$10/€7
Resistors	Handful each of 220, 330, 1K, 10K ohm ¼ watt or similar	$10/€7
Capacitors	A couple 1 and .1 microfarad capacitors of any variety	$4/€3
Analog sensors	10K ohm trimpot, 10K ohm photocell, TMP36 temp sensor	$4/€3
Switches	Miniature momentary pushbuttons and tilt switches	$3/€2
Transistors	2N2222 or 2N3904 NPN transistor or similar	$1/€1

This minimal list of hardware will get you through about half of the book with other specific components necessary for the more advanced projects. When required, information on additional parts will be provided at the start of the chapter or section. While detailed in each chapter, these projects will include the use of temperature sensors, force/flex sensors, light sensors, accelerometers, wind sensors, liquid crystal displays, stepper motors, hobby servos, and other sorts of hardware. Although, rather than mandate a hefty toolbox of equipment, the projects and code will be written with as much flexibility as possible to allow the use of other sensors or actuators, depending on what you have available and your own personal interests and project ideas.

To keep things simple, we will power the Arduino Uno from the USB port of our computer using a USB cable for each one of the projects in this book. Once we upload the programs to our boards, however, the program is permanently stored on the board just like a USB flash drive. We could (if we wanted) power the Arduino board from an external power source, such as DC power supply or battery, and not need the USB cable at all. For more information, refer to the section "Connecting & Powering Arduino" on the Arduino Playground at `http://arduino.cc/playground/Main/ArduinoCoreHardware`.

Getting Up and Running

By this point, you have a pretty good sense for what the Arduino is, its history, and some of what you can do with it. It's really exciting that with a few carefully written commands, which you will learn in the upcoming chapters, you can make things light up or move, sense the world around you, and generally make things more fun.

And now that you have some basic hardware in hand, including an Arduino interface board, it's time to get up and running. We need to do the following before moving on to the next chapter:

1. Download and install the Arduino development environment

2. Connect the Arduino board with a USB cable and install drivers

3. Launch the Arduino application and open the Blink example

4. Select your board and serial port

5. Upload your first sketch

Don't worry. It's not that difficult to get going. In fact, it's generally hard to go wrong, because it is nearly impossible to burn the house down or cut off an arm with an Arduino. And even if you wire up something wrong, it's probably okay because the Arduino board is a tough little guy and can take some abuse. So don't worry that you might mess something up. Of course, we are going to make some mistakes, but hopefully they will teach us something and we will become better programmers and makers because of it. So let's get on with it.

Installing the Software

First things first, you need to download and install the Arduino software. Because the Arduino Team is always making updates to the software, you should head to the main download page on the Arduino web site (http://arduino.cc/en/Main/Software), shown in Figure 1-8.

Figure 1-8. Arduino software download page

From here download and install the latest version of the software for your particular operating system. Full installation instructions are available on the Getting Started page at `http://arduino.cc/en/Guide/HomePage`. Linux can be a little tricky to get installed as of this writing, so be sure to carefully follow the instructions posted.

Connecting the Arduino

With the software installed, you should be able to connect your Arduino to the USB port on your computer using an A-B USB cable. The Arduino's power indicator LED will light up on the board, letting us know that it has power and is ready to go. With a brand-new Arduino Uno, the first time that it powers up, the pin 13 LED marked L will begin to blink rapidly, letting us know that the board has been fully tested. On Windows-based PCs or older Arduino boards, it is necessary to install a driver for the Arduino's onboard USB to Serial convertor, as shown in Figure 1-9. For the latest on how to install these drivers, be sure to follow the instructions on the drivers section of the Getting Started Guide at `http://arduino.cc/en/Guide/Windows#toc4`.

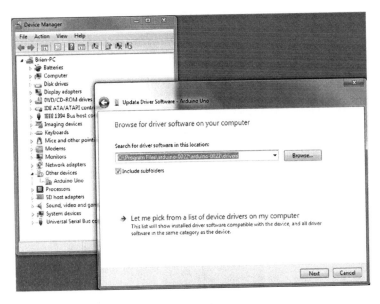

Figure 1-9. *Installing drivers on Windows 7*

Opening a Sketch

Now you can launch the Arduino development environment. This will bring up an empty window if this is your first time out. Open an example sketch by navigating to the File menu ➤ Examples ➤ 1.Basics and select the sketch named Blink, as shown in Figure 1-10. You should now see a very simple example sketch for blinking the onboard LED once every second.

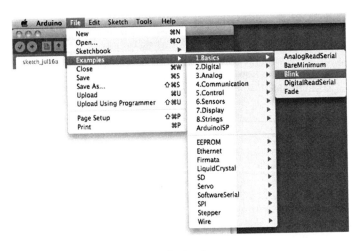

Figure 1-10. *Opening example sketch*

Selecting the Board and Serial Port

Before we can upload our sample sketch, we need to select the correct board type and serial port that the board is attached to on our computer. Setting the correct board can be done in the Tools ➤ Board menu by selecting Arduino Uno or one of the other corresponding board names, as shown in Figure 1-11.

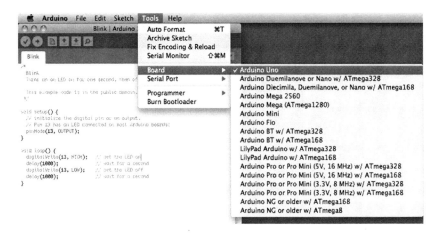

Figure 1-11. *Selecting board type*

Next, we need to choose the correct serial port under the Tools ➤ Serial Port menu, as shown in Figure 1-12. This port should be named COM3, or something similar, on a Windows PC; or something like /dev/tty.usbmodem or /dev.tty.usbserial on the Mac.

Figure 1-12. *Selecting serial port*

Uploading a Sketch

Once you have selected the proper board and serial port, it's time for the fun part. To upload a sketch onto the Arduino board, simply hit the Upload button on the toolbar, as shown in Figure 1-13. The onboard LEDs marked RX and TX will blink furiously and you will receive a message in the status bar that says, "Done uploading." That's all there is to it!

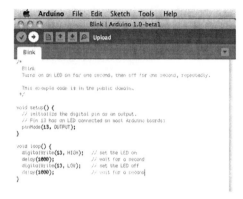

Figure 1-13. *Uploading a sketch to the Arduino board*

Summary

With all the installing, connecting, and uploading done and out of the way, you should now have a blinking LED on your Arduino Uno. That's not to say you already fully understand how it all works—because that would kind of defeat the entire purpose of this book. But now that we've got something to blink and know that we can make it work, we might as well jump into learning the basics of programming the Arduino with our first project. By jumping right into how the code works, we can move from hacking together lines of code that somebody else gave us to actually writing them ourselves.

CHAPTER 2

Sketching in Code

In the last chapter, we managed to get our first sketch up and running with the famous Blink sketch, otherwise known as the "Hello world" example. This is often a good place to start because it has a long-standing tradition as the first program to write when learning a new language. In the case of programming hardware, we generally use the LED to blink hello. While that is a good beginning, we want to quickly get to some of the more interesting aspects of Arduino C, beginning with the focus of this chapter: the fundamental mechanics and control structures of sketching Arduino code. Our first project, RGB Blink, will explore the basic structure, syntax, and functions necessary for controlling the output of a three-color LED, taking our blinking LED to the next level.

We'll start with a primer on what sketching means and how we can put the philosophy of sketching in code to use. As we will do throughout this book, we will then jump right into our project example and once you have this project wired up and the sketch uploaded to your Arduino board, we'll back up and further explain how the sketch works and discuss most of the elements used in the project. In this way, when we look at each of the individual concepts in the chapter, you'll already know how they were put to use. In this chapter, we'll have a look at the basic anatomy of our project sketch and discuss how and why Arduino C does what it does. Don't worry if it doesn't make a tremendous amount of sense in the beginning, just work through it and it should get clearer as you go along.

What's needed for this chapter:

- Arduino Uno

- 5mm RGB LED with common cathode

- 1x 330 ohm and 2x 220 ohm ¼ watt resistors or similar

- Hookup wires

- Solderless breadboard

What is Sketching in Code?

The idea of sketching in code is a way of thinking about writing code as a simple intuitive process, just like drawing in a sketchbook. In this way, an Arduino program is called a sketch and is saved in a folder called a sketchbook. Sketching means we can get our hands dirty and quickly try out a new idea. It is a skill available to all of us, not just artists and designers, and neither is it limited to pens, paper, pencils, or napkins.

So often, an idea in one of my classes begins with the simple words, "Wouldn't it be cool if ...?" Quickly sketching out these ideas serves as a way to conceptualize this moment of inspiration. Writing code can be just like this; it is after all a creative process used to solve specific problems. Sketching implies a sense of directness in the application of materials, like a pencil to a piece of paper. The Arduino development environment takes this same approach to making code as simple and direct as is possible. It is also why we will begin with simple sketches that quickly get you making something right away rather than bogging down in page after page of complex theory or algorithms.

When sketching in code, it's okay to write bad code. You won't hurt anything. As long as you get in there and start somewhere, as doing anything is always better than doing nothing. Making mistakes and learning what does work and what doesn't, is an important part of learning anything new. In our sketchbook, we will start with simple **source code**, the basic instructions that tell the Arduino what it should do, along with basic hardware, starting small and working our way through to more involved examples.

You should freely experiment with every example, changing values, and piecing things together in unexpected ways to see what happens. Don't be discouraged if it doesn't work the first time; stick with it and it will get clearer with time. Testing and iterations are important parts of successfully writing code. So, change existing code or write some new code to establish a basic framework and then verify that your changes compile correctly. Work in incremental steps one addition at a time as you add to this basic framework for your code so that when you finally have something substantial, you can load it on to the interface board to see what happens. If something didn't quite work as expected, all you need to do is undo that last incremental step. In this way it's a good idea when you make changes, to only change one thing at a time before verifying that it still works before moving on to the next change.

Project 1: RGB Blink

To really get started, we are going to use a nifty little component called a red-green-blue light emitting diode, or more simply an **RGB LED**. The RGB LED works off a similar principle as televisions and computer monitors. By using the same three colors of light that we are receptive to in our vision— specifically red, green, and blue—we can reproduce a vast array of colors through an additive color-mixing process. This form of color mixing should sound familiar from secondary school science, and is shown in the RGB color wheel in Figure 2-1. While it's a little harder to make out in a black-and-white book like this one, if you use your imagination you'll see that by combining two primary colors we end up with a secondary color. For example, add the color red to blue and we get magenta or if we add red and green we will get yellow. If we add all three primary colors together we will end up with white light.

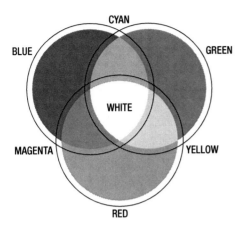

Figure 2-1. RGB color wheel

The particular LED we will be using is actually three separate LEDs—in the three primary colors of red, green, and blue—in one component package. Additionally, this LED is a common cathode type, meaning that the three LEDs share a common cathode pin, or connection to ground. This pin is the longest of the four pins coming out of the LED. We will connect each of the other three pins to the Arduino board through current limiting resistors, using hookup wires and a solderless breadboard.

To get an approximately equal or balanced output from each LED, we will use a 330 ohm resistor (ohm is a unit of measurement for resistance) connected to the red LED, or leg 1 of the RGB LED, and 220 ohm resistors to the other two, legs 3 and 4. If you don't have these resistors on hand, you can use the values 100 and 150 ohm or others that are close enough in value, anywhere between 100 ohms and 1 kilohm. If you use the same values for each color that's okay too, but each color's brightness might not be as closely matched. Some RGB LEDs are different from others so double-check the data sheet or product description as your mileage may vary. Refer to the following schematic and illustration for how to wire up this circuit.

Hooking It Up

For the projects in this book, we will follow a couple of diagrams that show in different ways how the hardware goes together. We begin with a **schematic**, like the one in Figure 2-2, which is basically a simple drawing that shows in the most direct way possible how to make a circuit with lines that connect simple, abstracted symbols for the electrical components. Where things get placed in a schematic is rarely where they end up in our actual physical circuit—it's just a way to show how one thing connects to another. Because schematics can be rather abstract, we will also include an illustration, like the one in Figure 2-3, showing one way that the finished circuit might look on the breadboard and how it connects to the Arduino board.

■ **Note** To find out more information on prototyping circuits, including how to read schematics and the symbols for different components, check out Chapter 12 later in this book.

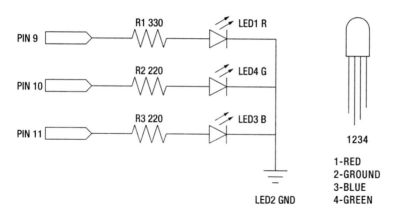

Figure 2-2. RGB Blink schematic

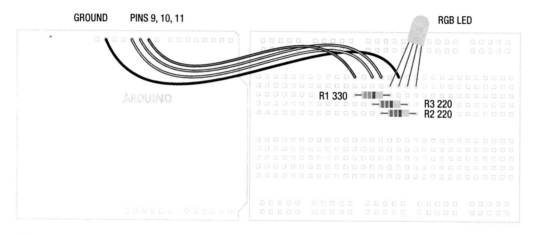

Figure 2-3. RGB Blink illustration

Uploading the Source Code

To get this circuit working, and to give us something to discuss, we are going to start with a simple sketch to change the color of our RGB LED from red to green to blue, continuously every second. If you look back to the Blink example from the last chapter, the code in Listing 2-1 should look fairly similar. Fundamentally, we are moving from using one LED to using three, turning each one on and off in a particular order. Once we start to understand this example, we will revisit it again with some more complex code.

Listing 2-1. RGB Blink Source Code

```
/* Project 1: RGB Blinky
   Uses a single RGB LED to cycle through three colors.
*/

void setup() {
  pinMode(9, OUTPUT);        // sets digital pins as outputs
  pinMode(10, OUTPUT);
  pinMode(11, OUTPUT);
}

void loop() {
  digitalWrite(9, HIGH);    // turns on red
  digitalWrite(11, LOW);    // turns off blue
  delay(1000);              // waits for 1 second
  digitalWrite(10, HIGH);   // turns on green
  digitalWrite(9, LOW);     // turns off red
  delay(1000);              // waits for 1 second
  digitalWrite(11, HIGH);   // turns on blue
  digitalWrite(10, LOW);    // turns off green
  delay(1000);              // waits for 1 second
}
```

Source Code Summary

Our first project sketch takes the Blink example that we uploaded in the first chapter and builds on it by adding the additional two colors available in our RGB LED, connected to pins 9, 10, and 11 rather than the built-in LED on pin 13, to blink each of the three colors in turn. As I will explain in this chapter, there are two groups of code in this sketch called functions grouped by matching curly braces, { }, each named setup() and loop()—ignore the keyword void for the time being. We use setup() to configure the state of input and output pins, as well as other actions that we only need to run once. Conversely, loop() will perform whatever actions are inside of it over and over again for an eternity, assuming limitless power as a prerequisite. Each line of code is executed inside a function, in order, from the top to the bottom. Inside the loop() function, when the last line of code is reached the function will repeat, beginning again with the first line of the loop() function.

Inside of each of these functions are statements that can include calls to other functions, such as pinMode(), digitalWrite(), and delay(). The function pinMode() is used to set a specific pin to either INPUT or OUTPUT. digitalWrite() is used to set the state of an output pin to HIGH or LOW, effectively used here to turn on or off an LED. The last function, delay(), does as it's named and delays the program for a specified number of milliseconds. We will spend the rest of our time together looking at these and other functions and statements that we will use when writing code for the Arduino platform, but first let's start with the basic structure of Arduino C.

The Structure of Arduino C

Our first project will provide an interesting backdrop for understanding what's going on with the basic structure of programming an Arduino sketch. This section will attempt to explain some of the larger points of how sketches are organized and generally work and will apply to every sketch that we might write, not just our previous example. We will get to more on the specifics of functions and statements, including their syntax and parameters, a little later.

To begin with, Arduino C follows a set of rules that govern syntax and structure and tell the interface board what to do. Some of these rules are inherited from C and others have been put into place by the Arduino development team to simplify usage for beginners. C is a top-down structural programming language, meaning that lines of code are executed in order from the top of the program until it reaches the end at the bottom. We will adopt this top-down method in our analysis of the sketch for Project 1 to discuss the major points of the Arduino programming syntax and structure, beginning with our first lines of code.

Using Comments

Looking at our first example, the first three lines contain a small descriptive block of text that we refer to as **comments**. Comments are areas of text that are ignored by the compiler, but provide useful notes and documentation that give us a little extra information about the sketch to make the code easier to understand for us humans. Use them to provide information about the project that the sketch is written for, about what certain variables do, what information a function needs to work properly, or what will happen if some part of the code is changed. Because comments take up no memory space on the Arduino board, they should be used generously throughout your sketch and are one of those good habits to have that should be adopted early on. Other people, including your future self, will be happy and thank you. Here's our example:

```
/* Project 1: RGB Blinky
    Uses a single RGB LED to cycle through three colors.
*/
```

This is an example of **block comments**. Anything in between the characters /* and */ are completely ignored and do not affect the outcome of the program. Block comments can be stretched across multiple lines, creating blocks of information, but need to be balanced with /* at the beginning to tell the compiler to ignore the following text until the compiler reaches the closing characters, */. The Arduino development environment conveniently changes comments to a grey color once they have been properly registered. This lets you know that you have entered comments properly or that you still need to close block comments (because your entire sketch suddenly became grey).

In addition to block comments, a second similar form of comments, called **line comments,** are used throughout the example sketch. Line comments are any line of text that begin with the characters // and automatically end with the next line of code. Unlike block comments, line comments do not need closing characters and are often used at the end of a statement to provide a little more information about what that line does. This is the case in our first line comment in the previous example, as follows:

```
// sets digital pins as outputs
```

Both types of comments are also pretty useful for disabling parts of a sketch for testing and debugging. Just "comment out" an offending line to see what happens in your code. It's also helpful to make a change in a part of the code but leave the old code in place using comments just in case you want to go back to it later. Take for example the following line:

```
digitalWrite(10, HIGH);
```

This statement could be disabled or otherwise ignored without deleting the line, by adding line comments in front of the statement as follows:

```
// digitalWrite(10, HIGH);
```

Alternatively, although not necessarily any clearer, the value could be changed using the following method:

```
digitalWrite(13 /*10*/, HIGH);
```

In this example, the value 10 is made into a comment using block comments in the middle of the line, and is, therefore, ignored by the compiler, but leaves it behind just in case you forget the old value. Once the integer value 10 has been hidden from the compiler, the integer 13 will become the new value for this statement. Keep in mind that whenever a section of code is commented out, it will only take effect the next time the sketch is uploaded to the Arduino board.

Line comments work for disabling single lines of code, but it would begin to be quite tedious to place line comments at the beginning of every line in a large block of code that needed to be temporarily ignored. Instead, place block comments around the whole section to be ignored, with /* at the beginning and */ at the end of the block of code to make the compiler ignore it.

■ **Note** This won't work if somewhere in your block of code you have another set of block comments, as it is not possible to nest block comments inside of one another. In this case, you might have to change the inner block comments to line comments or make some other modifications.

Comments are tremendously useful to the programmer and anyone reading your code, but they can sometimes get in the way, especially if you're trying to write a book. For this reason, after our initial project here, we will no longer comment our code on a line-by-line basis. Yes, that may sound a little like, "do as I say, not as I do," but I hope that it will make the discussion about particular concepts that much clearer without the added verbiage. If necessary to unpack a tricky line, we might add them in there for extra clarity.

Basic Functions

The C programming language is broken down into blocks of code called **functions** that form the main building blocks of any program. In this project we have two functions, setup() and loop(), each containing statements that do specific actions performed in order from top to bottom. As a requirement of the Arduino library, every sketch must at the very least contain both a setup() and loop() function in order to operate, even if they are empty. The following is technically a complete and working Arduino sketch, although it doesn't do much:

```
void setup() {
}

void loop() {
}
```

While we can and will create our own functions later in the book to handle certain tasks or consolidate blocks of code, if we intend to use one of these two functions we would need to use both of them. Since empty functions are rather boring, let's look at the following setup() function from our first project example:

```
void setup() {
  pinMode(9, OUTPUT);
  pinMode(10, OUTPUT);
  pinMode(11, OUTPUT);
}
```

Starting at the beginning, we specify the function's data type, in this case void, which is not terribly important for the moment, followed by the function's name, setup, an opening and closing parenthesis, ( ), and a block of code bounded on either side with opening and closing curly braces, { }. The three lines of code inside the curly braces are examples of statements used to set up the state of the digital pins on the Arduino interface board. Specifically, we're telling the Arduino that pins 9, 10, and 11 should be used as outputs and that we intend to use them a little later on in the sketch.

Of these two functions, the setup() function is called only once at the beginning of our sketch and is used for setting up various aspects of the Arduino board for running our code. A **function call** is another way of saying that the function, and all of the functions contained within it, is executed in the order they are listed. Examples of using the setup() function might also include establishing serial communications, making initial sensor readings, or running certain tasks that are only needed one time. This function will always run once, immediately after powering up or resetting the Arduino board.

Note Anytime we discuss a function in this book, we will use a pair of parenthesis after its name to help distinguish functions from things like variables. As an example, assignValue refers to a variable (more on these in a moment) where assignValue() refers to a function call.

The second function, loop(), makes it possible for your sketch to run continuously, and begins after the last statement in the setup() function has finished executing. Once the Arduino has completed its statements in order, reaching the end of the statements in the loop() function, it will, appropriately enough, loop back to the top of the loop() function and begin again, ad infinitum. Chances are this is where the bulk of your Arduino sketches will reside. Later in this book, we will investigate ways to manipulate the flow of the program and even demonstrate some methods for bouncing information back and forth between functions of your own creation.

Note When the Arduino runs a sketch, it starts at the top and works its way towards the bottom. This is called **program flow** and refers to the order that the statements are executed. Much like the way the loop() function continuously repeats when it reaches the end of its statements, there are other ways to modify the program flow, which will be discussed later.

Statements and Syntax

As mentioned earlier, nestled inside the curly braces of functions are lines of code called **statements**. Quite simply, these are the parts of the sketch that actually do something, such as calls to other functions, including those functions that are a part of the standard Arduino library, declaring and assigning values to variables, or performing arithmetic operations or comparisons. In our first project, anything in between the curly braces { } is a statement; take the following, for example:

```
digitalWrite(9, HIGH);
```

This line of code is a statement that calls one of the Arduino library's built-in functions named `digitalWrite()`, which is used to turn on or off one of the Arduino digital pins previously configured as an output. We pass this function two pieces of information that it needs to do its job: the number of the pin and the state that we want the pin to be in. These additional parameters, specific to each function, are called **arguments** and are found inside the left and right parenthesis, with multiple arguments separated by **commas**. In this example, we are telling the Arduino environment to turn on digital pin 9 of the Arduino interface board, as explained later.

There are two kinds of statements used in programming C: simple statements, including the most recent example, as well as compound statements. **Simple statements** include function calls, such as our earlier call to `digitalWrite()`, assignment statements, and arithmetic operations and are always terminated with a semicolon. **Semicolons** (;) are used to separate one simple statement from another so that the development environment can tell them apart. Forgetting to end a simple statement with a semicolon will result in one of the most common errors in the Arduino development environment. The following are a few examples of simple statements:

```
delay(1000);

digitalWrite(11, HIGH);

int myValue = 0;

myValue = 150 + 150;
```

Compound statements are made up of several lines of code that include other statements. Functions, such as `setup()` and `loop()`, are in effect compound statements. The `if` statement, covered in greater detail later in this book, is another form of a compound statement. A common example of the `if` statement would look like the following:

```
if (pin2 == HIGH) {
  digitalWrite(13, HIGH);
}
```

This statement will check the condition of the variable `pin2` and will perform the following enclosed statements, to turn pin 13 on, if the variable meets the defined condition, in this case if the state of pin 2 is equal to `HIGH`. In this example, we see that compound statements use **curly braces**, { }, to enclose one or more statements within it, creating a continuous block of code. Curly braces must be used in matching pairs and can encompass as many other statements, both simple and compound, as necessary.

While our example works fine, curly braces are only really needed by the structure of multi-line compound statements. If, as in the most recent example, the conditional statement only includes one other simple statement, the complex statement could be rewritten as a simple statement by removing the curly braces, as in the following syntax:

```
if (pin2 == HIGH) digitalWrite(13, HIGH);
```

This example is functionally the same as the one prior to it, although it saves us some real estate on our screen and debatably makes the code easier to read. To say it another way, curly braces are useful for enclosing multiple statements in one continuous block of code, creating a compound statement while simple statements use the semicolon at the end of each single line. Remember that simple statements inside of compound statements still need to end with semicolons.

In these examples, you have also seen the application of the **parenthesis**, ( ), to enclose arguments in a function or, as we will later see in more depth, for isolating arithmetic and comparison operations. Parentheses are used in pairs, so don't forget to close them off. The `loop()` function has nothing inside its parenthesis because no data is being passed to or from the function (more on this later). On the other hand, the example of `digitalWrite(9, HIGH)` passes two values to and from the `digitalWrite()` function, in this case the physical pin number on the interface board and its condition assignment. We have also used the parenthesis in separating a comparison operation in the case of `if (pin2 == HIGH)` where we are testing the condition of `pin2` against the constant `HIGH`. In arithmetic, parenthesis are also used to alter the order of operations as in `(2 +2) * 10`, although we will get to comparison and arithmetic operations in more detail momentarily.

Verifying and Uploading

Taking this concept of sketching to heart by tossing together some lines of code that we are still not fully up to speed on, we've got a sketch entered into the Arduino development environment and we think we have all the syntax and statements correct, but now what? In the last chapter, we blindy uploaded our first sketch full of confidence, but how do we know if the code we entered will work or not before uploading it to the Arduino board? To answer these questions, let's revisit uploading our sketch to the Arduino board, looking a little closer at the verifying and uploading process, including how to save your sketches and some of the common errors we might run into.

Verifying

As mentioned earlier, it is always a good idea to periodically verify a sketch that you're working on, just to make sure that you're on the right track, and even though this happens automatically before uploading a sketch to the Arduino board, it's a good idea to verify before uploading. To **verify** our code is to check that our code is correct and follows all the right syntactical rules that our sketches need to follow. We verify our sketch by hitting the Verify button in the top left of the toolbar in the Arduino development environment, as shown in Figure 2-4.

Figure 2-4. Verifying/compiling

Verifying will run the sketch through a process called **compiling**, where the development environment takes the Arduino C code that we have written and translates it into a binary format that the actual microcontroller will understand. If all goes well, a note will appear at the bottom of the window that says, "Done compiling," and you will be told the binary sketch size in bytes. If there is an error during the verification process, skip ahead and check out the section on common errors to see if you can figure out what went wrong. Once we have completed writing our sketch, verified it for errors, and everything completes successfully, we are ready to upload the sketch to the Arduino board; but before we do that, let's save our hard work.

Saving

Once you've got a working sketch that is ready to be uploaded to your Arduino board, or even if it is still in-progress, you should probably save your file frequently. To save a sketch, all we need to do is hit the Save button in the toolbar, as shown in Figure 2-5.

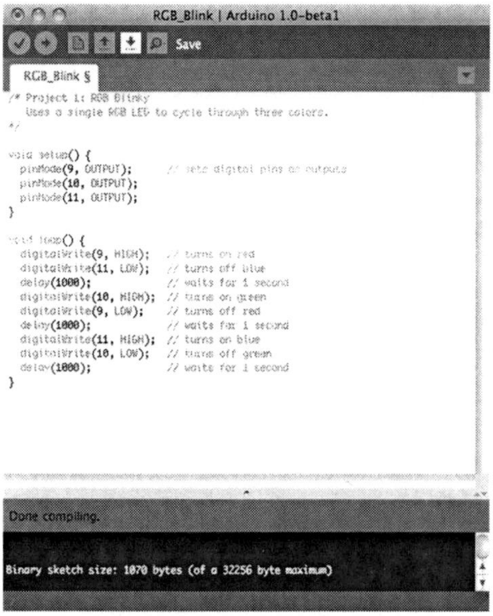

Figure 2-5. *Saving*

The Arduino development environment saves files in the default sketchbook folder named Arduino, usually found in your Documents folder. Sketch names must contain standard characters and numbers, however, they cannot begin with a number and cannot include a space character. Instead of spaces, we generally use the underscore (_) to separate words in a file name. The development environment also stores the file in a folder of the same name that it will automatically generate if the folder is not already there. Once saved, we can access our sketch from the File ➤ Sketchbook menu.

Uploading

Once our sketch is successfully compiled and has been safely stored in our sketchbook, we are ready to upload our sketch to the Arduino board by hitting the Upload button in the toolbar, shown in Figure 2-6.

Figure 2-6. *Uploading*

Pressing the Upload button will send a signal to the Arduino microcontroller that tells it that it needs to stop what it's doing and pay attention to the incoming code. At this point the LEDs marked RX/TX on the interface board will blink like mad, indicating that the code is being transferred to the board using serial communications through the transmitting (TX) and receiving (RX) of data using the built-in USB to Serial converter. When all is said and done, the notice bar will tell you when the upload is complete and your sketch will begin running momentarily.

Common Errors

You've just punched in your new sketch with eager anticipation to see that LED blink. You hit the Verify button, and after a long second or two, an error pops up. Now what?

If things didn't go as planned because of a compiler error, the notice bar will turn orange and sometimes give you a cryptic form of message, as seen in Figure 2-7, that basically tells you to go back and fix something.

Figure 2-7. *Compiler error*

This can be a little disappointing at first, but hang in there, I'm sure you'll figure it out. There are two general types of errors that we should be concerned with: hardware and syntax. Coming up are steps for troubleshooting these various error codes to help you get going again.

General **hardware errors** occur because something does not match the hardware you have or a connection isn't made correctly, as in the following example errors:

```
Serial port not found.
```

```
Problem uploading to board.
```

First, check that your board is connected to your computer and is indicating good power with a lit LED marked ON. With this verified, next check that the correct serial port and the proper board type have both been selected under the Tools menu. If the USB cable is not connected or the wrong serial port has been selected, the development environment will offer to connect using a different serial port. Sometimes a more serious hardware failure will generate similar errors and you will need to talk to your reseller to iron these problems out.

Other types of hardware errors might show up as something not working the way you think it should because of a bad connection. In our example project, you would expect the LED to first blink red, then green, and then blue; but yours doesn't light up red for some reason. This type of error comes from not wiring the components correctly, reversing the direction of certain parts like LEDs, or having the wires go to the wrong pins. This can be easily fixed by carefully going back over the hardware circuit, as shown in the schematic and illustration, to find out where something went wrong. It's even a good idea to have another pair of eyes look over it just in case they see something that you missed.

The second category of common errors are **syntactical errors** where you missed a semicolon, parenthesis, curly brace, or other character or form of syntax needed for the sketch to function properly, as shown in Figure 2-7 and the following examples:

expected ';' before…

expected ')' before…

expected '}' before…

The Arduino development environment will generally give you a pretty good idea where to look for this problem by moving the cursor near the problematic code and highlighting the code near where the error was found, so you can fix it by replacing the missing character before trying to verify the code again.

▓ **Note**   Remember that at the end of every simple statement a semicolon is needed to separate one statement from the next. Also, all parenthesis, curly braces, and block comments need to be matched in pairs.

Many syntax errors stem from Arduino C being case sensitive. In a **case sensitive** language, whether a letter is uppercase or lowercase must match exactly between what is entered and the syntax of the function, variable, or other statement being used. When writing Arduino sketches, there is a big difference between `pinmode()`, `pinMode()`, and `PINMODE()`—only one of these will actually work. The following are some examples of errors relating to case:

'pinmode' was not declared in this scope

'high' was not declared in this scope

These syntactical mistakes are examples of using the wrong case commonly when calling functions or using variables or constants. Look in the highlighted line of code for where you might have mistakenly typed `high` instead of `HIGH`, `output` instead of `OUTPUT`, `pinmode` instead of `pinMode`, or any other instances that are case sensitive.

No matter the error, just take a breath and think it through. I'm sure you will find it in no time. Writing code has a funny way of needing to be extremely logical and literal. If you are still having problems getting it going, you might turn to the generally helpful Arduino Forums at `http://arduino.cc/forum`.

Summary

Whew! That was a lot to get through for our first project, but we made it! We started with the philosophy of sketching in code; introduced our first project, including some diagrams and source code; discussed the structure of Arduino C, including using comments, the basics of Arduino functions, and working with statements and the elements of syntax; and then we wrapped things up by looking at compiling, saving, and uploading our sketches, as well as some common errors that might crop up once in a while.

That should have provided a nice overview of what goes into your typical Arduino sketch and given you a sense of how these various parts work together. It's really not that bad and the more you work with it, the easier it gets. Now before we get to some of the more advanced digital and analog functions available on the Arduino, we need to first cover a few more basics in the next couple of chapters. We will begin by revisiting our RGB Blink sketch from this chapter to see what we can do with it, while also talking about variables and the different kinds of data types available to us. Hang in there, I promise it'll get much more interesting once we get these basics out of the way.

Working with Variables

In our last project, there is nothing in the sketch except for our comments that helps us to identify which color LED is connected to which pin on the Arduino board, or, for that matter, what color we are turning on or off at any given time in the code. We would just have to remember that the number 9 in the line `digitalWrite(9, HIGH);` refers to the Arduino pin 9 that the red LED is connected to. Rather than trying to remember these things, because honestly we will forget or the next person we share our code with will have no clue, there is a better way to write our code using something called variables.

In this chapter, we will revisit the last project, pulling from our magic hat to create seven colors out of our three-color LED as a way to talk about the many uses for variables and how we can put them to work for us. We will also look at a few ways to manipulate variables using several different kinds of operators and how they work. For this new project, we will use the same hardware from the last chapter, but it might be a good idea to briefly mention them here again.

What's needed for this chapter:

- Arduino Uno

- 5mm RGB LED with common cathode

- 1x 330 ohm and 2x 220 ohm ¼ watt resistors or similar

- Hookup wires

- Solderless breadboard

Project 2: 7-Color Blink

If you'll remember the RGB color wheel in Figure 2-1 of the last chapter, we can mix red, green, and blue light to create millions of different colors. For our next project, we will take the simple three-color sketch from the last chapter and improve upon it by introducing simple color mixing to get seven colors, while pausing for a little longer on white for effect. This will give us an opportunity to introduce working with variables and demonstrate some basic operations, as well.

Hooking It Up

This project uses the very same hardware from the last chapter, as shown in Figures 3-1 and 3-2, which only make a repeat appearance here for convenience sake.

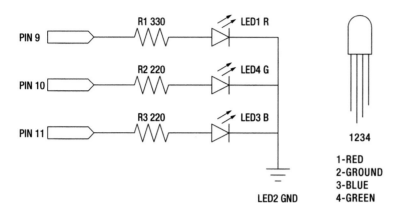

Figure 3-1. *7-Color Blink schematic*

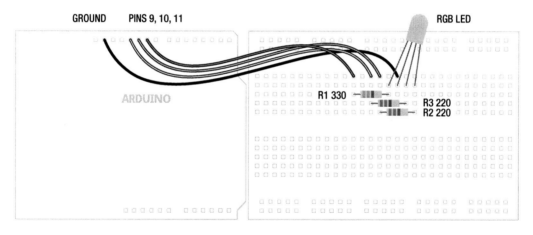

Figure 3-2. *7-Color Blink illustration*

Uploading the Source Code

The source code for this project in Listing 3-1 should look vaguely similar to our first project's code. It is a little longer now to create a sequence that will result in seven individual colors. We've also replaced the numbers 9, 10, and 11 with the variable names red, green, and blue, and added variables for the timing of the sketch. This will help us to read the code better and understand what exactly is going on.

Listing 3-1. *7-Color Blink*

```
const int red = 9;
const int green = 10;
const int blue = 11;

int time = 1000;
int multiple = 2;

void setup() {
  pinMode(red, OUTPUT);
  pinMode(green, OUTPUT);
  pinMode(blue, OUTPUT);
}

void loop() {
  digitalWrite(red, HIGH);      // red
  delay(time);
  digitalWrite(green, HIGH);    // yellow
  delay(time);
  digitalWrite(red, LOW);       // green
  delay(time);
  digitalWrite(blue, HIGH);     // cyan
  delay(time);
  digitalWrite(green, LOW);     // blue
  delay(time);
  digitalWrite(red, HIGH);      // magenta
  delay(time);
  digitalWrite(green, HIGH);    // white
  delay(time*=multiple);
  digitalWrite(blue, LOW);      // reset
  digitalWrite(green, LOW);
  time/=multiple;
}
```

Source Code Summary

To kick things off, we start our sketch with a block of code that defines each of the variables that will be used in our code. In this way we will know, for example, that the red LED is connected to pin 9 and the time delay between colors is 1000 milliseconds, or 1 second. If we wanted to change any of these values, to set different pin numbers for the RGB LED or to increase or decrease the delay time, we would only have to change the value in one single location, speeding up changes to the sketch and making it that much easier to understand. This will become more important later on when our sketches begin to do more interesting things with our variables, but for now let's look at the following first line of code in more detail:

```
const int red = 9;
```

This line declares that the first variable is named `red`; identifies the variable's data type as an integer, or `int`; and then tells the compiler that this variable should stay constant using the `const` modifier. Finally, this one line of code will also assign the numerical value 9 to the variable named `red`. In this way, the keywords `red`, `green`, `blue` are all variable names that we made up to identify the pin that each color of the RGB LED is connected to, while `time` is a variable to store the time period that each color stays on for, and `multiple` will be used to delay for a longer period on white just to give it a little emphasis.

Later in the sketch, we substitute the numbers that might be found inside the various statements with the variable names that we set up earlier so that every time that name is called, the compiler knows to look up the appropriate value. By using variables in our code, the following two lines will be functionally equivalent:

```
pinMode(red, OUTPUT);
```

```
pinMode(9, OUTPUT);
```

The rest of the code is just a slightly longer version of our last project sketch. In addition to red, green, and blue, you should now see yellow, cyan, magenta, and even white. Pretty nifty, huh? In addition to turning on and off each color of LED, we turn on two colors at the same time to make the intermediary colors, and all three colors to make white. Inside the `loop()` function, we begin with red, then add green to make yellow, turn off red to make green, add blue to make cyan, turn off green to make blue, turn on red to make magenta, and then turn on green to make white. At this point, we perform a compound operation to multiply the time delay with another variable called `multiple` to create a longer delay on the white color. We then reset our colors by turning off blue and green, leaving only red, perform another operation on the time delay to return it back to its original value, and then we start the loop all over again.

Now that we have seen variables in action, let's look at them in much greater depth to find out how we can put them to work for us.

What's a Variable?

The variables that we use in writing code are the very same variables that we learned about in school. Take the following equation for example:

$$a^2 + b^2 = c^2$$

I'm sure you've seen this before; it's the Pythagorean theorem and it's pretty useful for finding the length of one side of a right-angle triangle if we know any of the other two sides. The letters a, b, and c are the names for numerical data, in this case the letter c is used for the hypotenuse while a and b are the other two sides of the triangle. We can also call these letters variables. **Variables** are quite simply containers for information. In programming, variables have a **name** that tells us what data the variable might contain and they have a **type** that determines what kind of information the variable can hold, and finally they have a **value** whether we know what it is or not.

We can use variables to assign human-readable names for things like pin numbers or useful values. They can also be used to store numbers that constantly change while our code is actively running. This can be useful for setting up counters, performing calculations, or for passing new values to and from functions. To properly use a variable, we need to start with declaring the variable. After that, we should also talk about good variable names, the various types of variables, and a few other things related to working with variables.

Declaring Variables

When setting up a new variable, we need to at the very least determine two pieces of information: the variables data type and its name. This process is called **declaring** a variable where we will hold a place open in the Arduino's memory to store our information. Declaring a variable is as simple as indicating the data type followed by a unique name for the variable. The following are some examples of simple variable declarations:

```
int x;
```

```
int myVariable;
```

```
int time;
```

The sort of data that can be stored in a variable, and what can be done with it, is determined by the variable's **data type**. The data type that is chosen is very important later on when it affects what we can and cannot do with it. In the previous examples, we are declaring integer data types, signified by the int keyword, a useful data type for numerical data. After establishing the data type, we need a clear **variable name** that tells us in plain English what the variable does. As a general rule of thumb, it should be descriptive, but not overly cumbersome. Take the following examples:

```
int r;
```

```
int red;
```

```
int redLEDConnectedToPin9;
```

Each of these three variable names is technically correct, but naming our variable red instead of the letter r is generally easier to understand. Single-letter variable names, with a few exceptions, are often harder to read and make sense of; for example, a lowercase l (L) looks an awful lot like the uppercase I (I), or even the number 1 (1). The extreme case, redLEDConnectedToPin9, is generally too verbose and makes reading, as well as writing, the code somewhat tedious.

Where these previous examples simply declare the variable data type and variable name, it is also possible to assign a value to a variable when we declare it in a single statement. In our example sketch, we did this in the following line:

```
int red = 9;
```

Here we are declaring the variable named red as an integer data type and assigning the value 9 to that variable name using the assignment operator to be discussed shortly. While the Arduino compiler will still hold a place open in its memory for a variable even if we do not assign it a value, it is generally a good idea to assign a value in the variable declaration even if that value is 0.

Variable Names

We can name a variable pretty much anything we want, but there are a few rules we need to follow. First of all, function and variable names can only contain letters, underscores, numbers, or the dollar sign. Spaces or odd characters like the @ or & are not allowed and the first character cannot be a number. White space is not allowed inside a variable name, as generally when white space is allowed, you could have one space or hundreds and it wouldn't matter. This white space includes new lines from hitting the Return or Enter keys, or indents from the space bar or Tab key. Considering this, the variable names `myVariable`, `mYvAlUe`, `DELAY_TIME`, and `value1` are all valid names. Conversely, the variable names `1stValue`, `delay time`, and `time&money` are not valid names for a variable.

Now some of these names may not be the most readable, which is why many Arduino programmers have adopted certain naming guidelines or **conventions**. Naming conventions are generally controversial in programming circles, and they are not specifically required when defining your own unique names, but they can make code easier to read in the big scheme of things.

For example, we can have a variable name with multiple words but, because we cannot use spaces inside our variable name, we might want a way to separate each word to make the name easier to read. One possibility is to use an underscore between each word, as in `red_led_connected_to_pin_9`, a method usually favored by UNIX programmers. Instead, we will use the convention known as **camelback notation**, as in `redLEDConnectedToPin9`. Under this convention, the first letter of the first word will be lowercase while the first letter of each subsequent word will be capitalized with no space between each word. Take the following examples:

`variable`

`myVariable`

`value1`

`tiltSwitchValue`

It's really your choice how you name your variables and you will often see both types in other people's sketches, but we feel that camelback notation makes the code easier to read and matches the format the Arduino developers have decided upon for all of the built-in functions in the Arduino library. Likewise, it is the general convention that constants are sometimes written in all caps with underscores in between multiple words, as in the following examples, although we will not adhere strictly to this in naming our own constant variables.

`HIGH`

`INPUT`

`BLUE_LED`

■ **Note** Remember that the Arduino language is case-sensitive, so whatever style you adopt, you need to use it consistently throughout your sketch. This also means that any predefined variables or function names that are already a part of Arduino C must be used with exact capitalization.

One thing to keep in mind is that while there is no maximum or minimum length for variable names, extremely long names start to become rather tedious to type over and over. On the other hand, one-character names are often too cryptic. A few exceptions to this would be the lower case letter `i`, which is a commonly used variable to indicate an index along with the variable names `j` and `k`. Likewise, `a`, `b`, `c` or `x`, `y`, `z` are other sometimes used as short names, often when adding a longer name would not necessarily provide any more information.

Data Types

While there are many data types available to the Arduino, for the moment we will start with the numerical types that use either whole numbers or floating-point numbers. Numeric data types are available in two varieties: **signed** and **unsigned**. Unsigned variables will always contain positive values, whereas signed variables can express numbers with a negative value. Usually most data types default to signed data types, but can be changed using the unsigned variable qualifier described later.

The **integer** data type is Arduino's primary variable data type for storing numbers; it can be used to store numerical values between -32,768 and 32,767. These values need to be whole numbers such as 42, 28,000, or -32, and can not include values with decimal points. Integer-type variables consume 16 bits or 2 bytes of our available 32 kilobytes of program memory—why this is important will become clearer when we discuss memory in Chapter 8. Integer variables can be declared with the **int** keyword, as follows:

```
int myVariable;
```

If you look at enough examples of Arduino code, you'll start to see that integers are a commonly used data type. For the most part, we will stick with this convention except where it makes more sense to choose another data type. Part of the reason for carefully choosing the proper data type for the job is that all numerical data types, including integers, will roll over in one direction or another when they exceed the minimum or maximum capacity. So given the following example:

```
x = 32767;
x = x + 1;
```

The variable x will now contain the value -32,768, as the integer exceeded its maximum capacity and rolled over to its minimum capacity and started again there. Remember that this also works both ways—so if x = -32768; and the following line is x = x - 1; then x will be equal to 32,767.

As far as integers are concerned, there is only one value between 3 and 5, which is of course 4 because integers work in whole numbers. In contrast, **floating-point** numbers, expressed as the **float** data type, are capable of expressing fractions of a number using a decimal point and can be used to represent a multitude of values between 3 and 5, such as 3.14159, 4.25, or 5.0. Floats use 32 bits of memory and, like integers, can express values that are positive, negative, or zero. To declare a floating-point variable, we use the float keyword; and if assigning a value, we will also need to include a decimal point—even if the digit after the decimal point is 0. The following are two examples of float declarations:

```
float pi = 3.14159;
float circle = 360.0;
```

Because the Arduino lacks any dedicated hardware to manage floating-point math, floats are slow to process and may not yield the most accurate results. With only about 6 or 7 digits of precision, the expression z = 12.0 / 5.0 will yield 2.4000000953 instead of 2.4. While extremely helpful in certain situations, it is best to avoid floats where possible, especially in timing critical applications.

In addition to integers and floats, there are numerous other data types available on the Arduino. **Byte**, an 8-bit data type, can store values between 0 and 255. Unlike integers and floats, bytes are unsigned so that when a byte exceeds 255, it rolls over to 0. Bytes can be useful if we need to save some memory or are pretty sure we won't have a problem with data roll over.

```
byte dataPin = 11;
```

Other data types include the 32-bit **long**, which is the big brother of the integer, and the 1-bit **boolean** data type that only stores two values—either true or false. In Table 3-1 there are some of the various data types available to the Arduino platform, some of which we will cover in more depth later in the book.

Table 3-1. *Arduino Data Types*

Name	Size	Range
boolean	1 bit	true or false
byte	8 bit	0 to 255
char	8 bit	-128 to 127
int	16 bit	-32,768 to 32,767
long	32 bit	-2,147,483,648 to 2,147,483,647
float	32 bit	-3.4028235E+38 to 3.4028235E+38

Variable Qualifiers

As discussed earlier, variables will behave in certain ways based on the properties of their data type. By using **variable qualifiers**, it is possible to modify the behavior of certain variables in ways that will fundamentally change how we work with them. For example, the `const` or **constant** variable qualifier makes the value of a variable a read-only constant that cannot be changed once the value has been assigned. This could be useful in our sketch, so instead of the variable declaration reading as follows:

```
int red = 9;
```

We could write the line like this:

```
const int red = 9;
```

We use the `const` keyword at the beginning of a variable declaration to define a variable as a constant value to prevent us from inadvertently changing the variable's value later in the code. This is useful if we know that, as in the example, the pin number of the red LED will never change. If we attempt to assign a new value to the constant variable **red**, we will be reminded with a friendly compiler error. The constant qualifier is also useful for reducing the amount of memory that is needed by the code while it's running. Don't worry too much about that now; we will talk more about memory usage later in Chapter 8.

You might find examples of code that use the `#define` preprocessor directive instead of `const`, as in the line `#define red 9`. The constant qualifier is generally the preferred method of the Arduino development team over the `#define` preprocessor directive for defining constant variables. This is because the constant qualifier can be checked for errors and will follow all of the rules of variables, including variable scope defined momentarily, while not creating any potential conflicts with the Arduino library.

As briefly mentioned before, certain data types are either signed or unsigned. To modify the range of a few of the data types we could use the **unsigned** qualifier and the `unsigned` keyword, making them store positive-only values. This qualifier is beneficial for increasing the positive range of variables or for indicating to the reader of the code that the value expected will never be negative. For example:

```
unsigned int maxThreshold = 1024;
```

By placing the `unsigned` keyword in front of the integer variable declaration, the variable `maxThreshold` may now only store positive values in the range of 0 to 65,535. Table 3-2 provides a list of unsigned variable data types and their modified ranges.

Table 3-2. Unsigned Data Types

Name	Size	Range
unsigned char	8 bit	0 to 255
unsigned int	16 bit	0 to 65,535
unsigned long	32 bit	0 to 4,294,967,295

You will notice that an unsigned char has the same value range as the byte although, for this range of values, byte is the preferred data type. Also keep in mind that unsigned data types will roll over just like their signed brethren when they exceed their minimum or maximum values.

In addition to unsigned and const, there are other variable qualifiers that we will revisit in later chapters, as they are needed.

Predefined Constants

In addition to user defined constant variables, the Arduino development environment uses its own predefined constants. The first of these constants defines the Boolean logic states based on logical truth tables using two states: true and false. The `false` condition is easily defined as being 0 or sometimes off. On the other hand, `true` is, in many ways, anything other than false. In this sense, `true` could be 1, or 'on,' but it could also be 5, -42, or even 64,000. Unlike our other constants, `true` and `false` always appear in lowercase.

Our other pairs of constants, which you have already seen some of, are generally used as part of the Arduino's digital I/O capabilities and will be discussed in more depth in later. These constants define the operation of the digital pins as either `INPUT` or `OUTPUT` using the `pinMode()` function, or define the pin levels as being `HIGH` or `LOW`, roughly equivalent to pin states of +5 volts and 0 volts, or on and off respectively.

Variable Scope

While we have so far been discussing how variables are declared, where we declare variables is as important as how we declare them. The location of a variable declaration in the larger sketch determines where that variable can be used, or what is known as **variable scope**.

```
const int red = 9;
```

This variable from our previous example is declared outside the `setup()` and `loop()` functions at the beginning of the source code. This is known as a **global variable** and can be used by all functions in the sketch regardless of location. If, however, this variable was declared inside the `setup()` function, it would become a **local variable** and would be unavailable to `loop()` or any other functions. Local variables can also be used inside `for` loops, commonly as counters, where only that statement can use it and not the rest of the function. In fact, it is entirely possible for one variable name to be used in two different manners depending on where those variables are declared and used. However, if we attempt to access a variable outside of its scope, we will receive another one of those friendly reminders in the form of a compiler error letting us know where we went wrong.

Because writing code for Arduino C is a little different from normal C source code, specifically in our use of the setup() function to perform one time only tasks, we will often use global variables to define pin numbers, set up thresholds, or define constants, so that all functions in a sketch can use the same values. This would not generally be the case with code written for other platforms, but it works for us.

Using Operators

Now that we have thoroughly explored what the variables are, what can we do with them? To answer this question we need to examine various **operators**, which are special characters used to perform specific operations. For now, we will stick with simple assignment, arithmetic, and compound operators, and get into some others in the next chapter.

When we talked about declaring variables, we used the **assignment operator**, =, which looks just like the equals sign but isn't exactly the equals sign we know and love from algebra class. Take a look at the following example:

```
myValue = 255;
```

Here, the assignment operator is telling the compiler to take the value or expression on the right side of the operator and assign that value to the variable on the left side of the = character. In this case, we are taking the value of 255 and putting it into a variable we are calling myValue. Considering the following hypothetical code fragment:

```
int myValue, newValue;
myValue = 255;
newValue = myValue;
```

The first line declares two integer type variables on the same line. (Yes, I know this is ninja sneaky, but as long as we separate the variable names with commas, we can declare multiple variables with the same data type.) The second line then assigns the numerical value 255 to the variable myValue. Then in the third line, remembering that assignments work somewhat counter intuitively right to left, we assign the value of myValue to the variable newValue. In this case newValue will now also hold the value of 255. That should be crystal clear, right?

■ **Note** Because we can only declare a variable in the same scope once, we do not use the data type when assigning a value to a variable after the first declaration. If in the previous example we wrote int myValue = 255; instead of myValue = 255; we would have another compiler error.

Arithmetic Operators: +, -, *, /

With that out of the way, let's look at the simple arithmetic operators to add, subtract, multiply, and divide. To start with, let's say we wanted to add two numbers together and assign it to a variable; it would look something like the following:

```
myValue = 4 + 38;
```

Beginning on the right side, the Arduino will add 4 and 38 and assign the sum to the variable myValue, which now will equal the numerical value of 42. Likewise, since variables act just like the numbers that they store, they can be included in the equation as well.

```
myValue = 255;
newValue = myValue - 128;
```

After assigning the value 255 to myValue, the next line subtracts 128 from myValue and assigns the result to newValue that now contains the number 127. We can even do this using the same variable as in the following example:

```
myValue = 255;
myValue = myValue - 1;
```

Beginning with 255, 1 is subtracted from myValue and this new result, 254, is reassigned to the variable myValue. If we performed this second line 255 times in a row, we would **decrement**, or lower the value of myValue until it reached 0.

The values that we are performing these operations on are called **operands**. The data type of the operands determines the data type used by the operators with the largest type being used if they are of different types. Consider the following code fragment, which should be somewhat familiar from high school geometry:

```
float pi = 3.14159;
int diameter = 5;
float C;
C = pi * diameter;
```

In this case, the operator used to determine C ignores the fact that the variable diameter is an integer data type and, in the last line, we multiply the float variable pi (3.14159) to the integer variable diameter (5) and we end up with the floating-point value of 15.7079505920 assigned to the variable C. This shows that when one of the operands is of the float data type, floating point math is used for the entire calculation and, as a result, suffers from the usual drawbacks of large memory size and slow operation.

In this most recent example, the variable C was of the float data type and as a result could store the fractional value. If, however, both of the operands are of the same data type, the operation will be performed using that type regardless of the actual outcome, as follows, for example:

```
int myValue;
myValue = 9 / 5;
```

This statement divides 9 by 5; however, since myValue is an integer type variable, the resulting value assigns the lobbed off result of 1 to myValue rather than the actual value of 1.8 because integers can only contain whole numbers. Notice that this isn't rounding up or down but rather disregarding any fractional numbers after the decimal point.

Be careful about accidently dividing a number by zero, as in x = 9 / 0;. Rather than giving you a compiler error for something you should not be able to do, the Arduino compiler will instead spit out some rather odd and unexpected numbers.

Compound Operators: ++, --, +=, -=, *=, /=

In the previous examples, we needed two values for the operators to work their magic, as in the following statement:

```
myValue = 0;
myValue = myValue +1;
```

Instead, we could use compound operators that combine an arithmetic operation with an assignment operation, thereby only needing one variable statement to do what they do. These can be used to either **increment**, raise the value, or **decrement**, lower the value, using just one operator. The following is an example that increments myValue by 1 using the ++ character symbol:

```
myValue = 0;
myValue++;
```

This statement, functionally identical to the very last code example, increments the variable by 1 and reassigns the new value to the current variable name. In this case, the variable myValue now contains the numerical value 1. Likewise, we can decrement the value using the -- character symbol, as follows:

```
myValue--;
```

Here, myValue now contains 0 again. In these two examples, the compound operators ++ or -- only increment or decrement by a value of 1. If we wanted to increment or decrement a variable by a value greater than 1 we could use one of these compound operators: +=, -=, *=, or /=. For example if we wanted to increment myValue by 10 we could use the following statement:

```
myValue += 10;
```

This statement, again identical to the statement myValue = myValue +10; adds 10 to whatever value is assigned to myValue. Assuming that myValue contains the number 10, we can multiply it by a factor and reassign the new value using the following example:

```
myValue *= 1.5;
```

The variable myValue has now been increased to 15. Remember though, if we assume myValue is an integer, a further *= 1.5 would result in 22 rather than 22.5 because integers lob off anything after the decimal point.

We used compound operators in our recent project code to multiply two variables together to create a longer delay time for white, as in the following example:

```
delay(time*=multiple);
```

In this line of code, we multiply the value of the variable multiple by the current value of time, assign this new value back to the variable time, and then we delay for that amount. In this way we can change either of the initial values for these two variables at the beginning of the code without needing to hunt down each line in the sketch. Compound operators are also useful for counters and indices and especially help compact the code into a more readable form when we get to the for loop control structures later.

Order of Operations

When the math gets a little more complicated, it's good to know about the **order of operations**, or the order in which operators are processed in any given expression. For example, depending on the way an expression is evaluated, 3 * 5 + 10 could yield either 25 or 45 depending on whether we multiply 3 by 5 then add 10 or add 5 to 10 and multiply the result by 3. When we consult the order of operations, however, we find that multiplication always takes precedence over addition regardless of the order they appear in the expression; so the correct answer would be 25.

Alternatively, if we wanted 45 we could add parentheses to the expression making it now 3 * (5 + 10) to modify the order in which the expression is evaluated. In this case, parenthesis take precedence over every other operator, so 5 is added to 10 and that sum is then multiplied by 3 for the modified result of 45. Parenthesis may also be added to an expression not necessarily to modify the order of operations, but rather just to make things easier to understand. Take the following examples:

```
x = 5 * 5 + 5;     // assigns 30 to x
y = (5 * 5) + 5;   // assigns 30 to y
z = 5 * (5 + 5);   // assigns 50 to z
```

In the first line, the order of operations is followed to result in a final value of 30, which happens to be the same value for the second line because the parenthesis are only their aesthetically. The final line modifies the normal order of operations by bracketing 5 + 5 with parenthesis so that that part of the expression will take precedence. Here, the sum of 5 and 5 is then multiplied by 5 for a total value of 50.

Table 3-3 shows the normal order of operations ranked by highest precedence at the top and lowest at the bottom. We have covered some of these operators in this chapter, while others will be discussed later.

Table 3-3. Order of Operations

Symbol	Description	Examples
( )	Parenthesis	(x+y)*z
++ --	Increment, decrement	x++, y--
* / %	Multiplication, division, modulus	x * 1.5
+ -	Addition, subtraction	y + 10
< > <= >=	Less than, greater than comparisons	if (x < 255)
== !=	Is, is not equal to	if (x == HIGH)
&&	Logical AND	if (x == HIGH && x > y)
||	Logical OR	if (x == HIGH || x > y)
= += -= *= /=	Assignment and compound assignments	x = y

Consulting the chart, you can see that division will always happen before addition and subtraction will happen before assignment. There's also some other things thrown in there, but we will get to these before too long.

Summary

In this chapter we introduced some concepts that we will continue to build on in the rest of the book, focusing on the use of variables, including operations and assignments. It is important to remember that variables are only declared once in a particular location, or scope, and that when performing operations or making assignments, whatever value is on the right of the equals (=) sign will be attributed to the variable on the left. Also remember that the operators we discussed in this chapter can be used to increment, decrement, or perform other arithmetic and compound operations, which are performed in a specific order of operations. In the next chapter, we will take this information and use it to alter our program's flow and learn how the Arduino can make decisions using various control structures, such as the `if` statement and `for` loop.

CHAPTER 4

Making Decisions

In the last chapter, we explored variables and how to declare them, their data types, assigning values, and performing simple operations using them. In this chapter, we will put the variables to work with some fundamental structures that the Arduino uses to make decisions and perform repetitive operations. This could include reading a switch or sensor and doing something based on its input, performing one or a set of operations for a defined number of times or until a different condition is met, or performing a range of operations depending on a range of conditions.

Our next project, Tilt Blink, adds a tilt switch to our RGB LED to form the basis for the rest of the chapter's in-depth discussions of the various statements for making decisions, such as the `if`, `for`, and `switch` statements and other control structures. We've also changed our code some, just to make things more interesting.

What's needed for this chapter:

- Arduino Uno

- 5mm RGB LED with common cathode

- Rolling ball tilt switch or other mechanical switch

- 1x 330 ohm , 2x 220 ohm, and 1x 10 kilohm ¼ watt resistor or similar

- Hookup wires

- Solderless breadboard

Project 3: Tilt Blink

For this project, we are building on our 7-Color Blink project from the last chapter with the addition of a simple tilt sensor. Let's say we want to quickly blink through the seven basic colors when our device is tilted or shaken, but otherwise turn off the LEDs when it's left alone. The tilt switch we are using to make this happen is a small metal tube with two wires coming out the bottom. Inside is a small metal ball that, when flat makes contact with the two wires closing the switch, but when tilted, the ball rolls away— opening the switch. This will be our way to turn on and off the RGB LED. Alternatively, any number of mechanical switches could be used instead if you can't find a tilt switch.

Hooking It Up

For this project, we are adding a simple circuit for the tilt switch (or other type of mechanical switch) to work as a very basic sensor. In this circuit, when the switch is open, a resistor connects the input pin to ground, providing a LOW signal. When the switch is closed it creates a connection to +5v, providing a HIGH signal. We will use these two states to light up our LED. Figures 4-1 and 4-2 show how to wire it up.

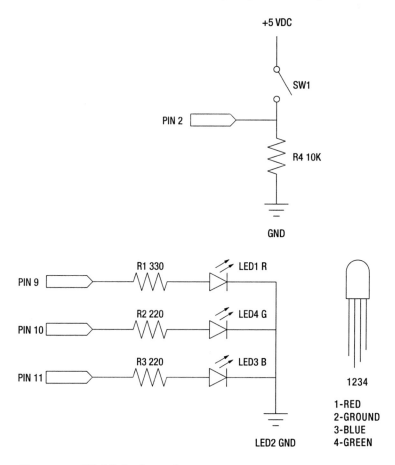

Figure 4-1. *Tilt Blink schematic*

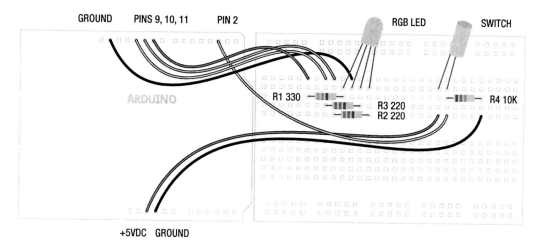

GROUND   PINS 9, 10, 11   PIN 2   RGB LED   SWITCH

ARDUINO

R1 330   R3 220   R4 10K
R2 220

+5VDC   GROUND

Figure 4-2. Tilt Blink illustration

Uploading the Source Code

In our last project, we managed to cycle through seven different colors with our LED in a fairly simple and straightforward manner. And that's generally a good thing, except when you start to try to do two or more things at once like cycling through different colors all the while waiting for a tilt switch to be triggered. In the last example, it would take 8 seconds to make it through all of the colors once. In that amount of time we could have easily missed a switch being triggered because our code was not smart enough, or fast enough, to do two things at once. In our source code for this project, shown in Listing 4-1, we have attempted to solve this by speeding things up a bit, reducing our time between readings from 8 seconds to a half of a second. We've also compartmentalized our code a bit more, introducing many of the concepts that I will explain further in this chapter.

Listing 4-1. Tilt Blink Source Code

```
const int rgb[] = {9,10,11};
const int time = 250;
const int switchPin = 2;

void setup() {
  for (int i=0; i<3; i++) pinMode(rgb[i], OUTPUT);
  pinMode(switchPin, INPUT);
}

void loop() {
  int newPin = 0;
  int oldPin = 0;
```

```
   int bounce1 = digitalRead(switchPin);
   delay(25);
   int bounce2 = digitalRead(switchPin);

   while ((bounce1 == bounce2) && (bounce1 == LOW)) {
     oldPin = newPin;
     newPin++;

     if (newPin == 3) newPin = 0;

     digitalWrite(rgb[oldPin], HIGH);
     delay(time);
     digitalWrite(rgb[newPin], HIGH);
     delay(time);
     digitalWrite(rgb[oldPin], LOW);

     if (newPin == 0) {
       for (int i=0; i<3; i++) digitalWrite(rgb[i], HIGH);
       delay(time);
       for (int i=0; i<3; i++) digitalWrite(rgb[i], LOW);
     }
     bounce1 = digitalRead(switchPin);
     delay(25);
     bounce2 = digitalRead(switchPin);
   }
   for (int i=0; i<3; i++) digitalWrite(rgb[i], LOW);
   delay(25);
}
```

Source Code Summary

This sketch looks dramatically different from our last one, so let's take it one step at a time to see how it works beginning our summary at the top with variable declarations. We start with the following three, constant, global variables that we will use throughout our sketch:

```
const int rgb[] = {9,10,11};
const int time = 250;
const int switchPin = 2;
```

The variable rgb[] is actually a special type of variable called an array that will be explained fully in Chapter 8. It contains the three pin numbers for our RGB LED (9, 10, 11) and each position in the array can be accessed by an index number (0, 1, 2). The variable time is used for the delay between each color—we speed it up here to make it more interesting. Finally switchPin is the pin that our tilt switch is connected to.

We use our setup() function to set the mode for each of the I/O pins that we are using, as follows:

```
for (int i=0; i<3; i++) pinMode(rgb[i], OUTPUT);
pinMode(switchPin, INPUT);
```

The first line uses a little trick with a for loop to step through each index of the array to configure each pin as an output. The next line establishes the input pin for our switch.

One of the challenges of quickly stepping through all seven colors is that we need to alternate between one color on, and then two colors on, and then back to one, moving through a specific sequence. For example, if we start with red, then we need to add green to make yellow, and then turn off red to leave green. To keep track of these alternating colors, or pin numbers, we set up two local variables in our loop() function:

```
int newPin = 0;
int oldPin = 0;
```

We'll come back to these variables in a moment. The next thing we need to do is to read the state of the switch to see if it has been triggered or not. The challenge here is that because switches are mechanical devices, whenever a switch is triggered, the metal contacts inside the switch have a tendency to "bounce," creating false or multiple triggers. To get around this, we can very quickly read the state of the digital input twice with a short pause between each reading and compare the results. If the two readings are the same, chances are pretty good that the switch has indeed been triggered. If not, it's probably a false reading. This is called **debouncing**. To do this we use the following:

```
int bounce1 = digitalRead(switchPin);
delay(25);
int bounce2 = digitalRead(switchPin);
```

In this section of code, we declare a variable called bounce1 and assign it the value of the switch reading, pause for a very short amount of time, 25 milliseconds, and then declare a second variable called bounce2 and assign it the value of a second reading. That's just enough time to ensure a good reading from the switch. We can then compare these readings in a while loop:

```
while ((bounce1 == bounce2) && (bounce1 == LOW)) {
```

For as long as both readings are the same, and they are both LOW (the tilt switch is normally closed so it only opens, creating a LOW signal in our circuit when the switch is tilted) the following code in the while loop will continuously run. Once the switch has been triggered, we begin the process of quickly blinking through each of the seven colors. To do this we bring back the following two variables:

```
oldPin = newPin;
newPin++;
```

What these two lines do is to assign the old value of newPin to oldPin and then increment newPin by 1. This way newPin is always one value ahead of oldPin. From the declaration of these two variables earlier, each start at 0, oldPin stays at 0 while newPin becomes 1. These values will be used as the index in the array and correspond to pin numbers for the RGB LED, so index 0 is pin 9, index 1 is pin 10, and index 2 is pin 11. Each time through the loop these numbers will increment by 1. If newPin ever reaches 3, an index that does not exist, this line will reset newPin to the value 0, as follows:

```
if (newPin == 3) newPin = 0;
```

This might make more sense when we look at the following business end of this loop:

```
digitalWrite(rgb[oldPin], HIGH);
delay(time);
digitalWrite(rgb[newPin], HIGH);
delay(time);
digitalWrite(rgb[oldPin], LOW);
```

Each time through the `while` loop, we will start with turning on the old pin, delay, then turn on the new pin, delay, and finally turn off the old pin. This is what will allow us to not only make the primary colors, but also the intermediate colors, as well. The one color that will not work this way is white. To get around that we use the following block of code:

```
if (newPin == 0) {
  for (int i=0; i<3; i++) digitalWrite(rgb[i], HIGH);
  delay(time);
  for (int i=0; i<3; i++) digitalWrite(rgb[i], LOW);
}
```

This `if` statement will turn on all of the colors of the LED to make white, delay, and then turn them all off, using that neat little trick from earlier to step through each pin in a `for` loop. This happens so fast that it simply appears that each color turns on or off at the exact same time.

The last thing to do in our `while` loop is to check if the state of our switch has changed at all by running our debounce code again, and if the state has changed, the `while` loop will exit. Finally, the last thing in our sketch is a line to make sure that all of the colors are off if the switch has not been triggered, and then we add a short delay just to make sure our readings stay in line.

Now, much of that may or may not have made a whole lot of sense. Don't worry too much about that for now because we will spend the rest of the chapter trying to explain how these control structures work in much greater depth. You might want to come back to this and see if it makes more sense after reading through the rest of this chapter.

Comparative and Logical Operators

Conditional statements like the `for` loop and `if` statement discussed in this chapter use comparison and logical operators to test for conditions. **Comparative operators** are used to compare the left side of an expression against the right side to produce a value of true or false. With this piece of information, the Arduino can use it to make decisions depending on the type of control structure being used. So if you wanted to test whether or not a variable held a particular value, you might use an expression like the following:

```
myValue == 5
```

Here we use the `==` comparative operator to test if the variable or value on the left of the operator is equal to the variable or value on the right. In this case, the expression would return as true if `myValue` contained the value 5, and false if it did not. You should note that we use the phrase "is equal to" instead of "equals". This helps us to differentiate the comparison operator (`==`) from the assignment operator (`=`), with the former referred to as "is equal to" and the later "equals".

Table 4-1 lists other comparative operators that we will discuss in greater depth and provide examples for in this chapter and beyond.

Table 4-1. Comparative Operators

Symbol	Description	Is true if...
==	is equal to	the left side is equal to the right side
!=	is not equal to	the left side is not equal to the right side
<	less than	the left side is less than the right side
>	greater than	the left side is greater than the right side
<=	less than or equal to	the left side is less than or equal to the right side
>=	greater than or equal to	the left side is greater than or equal to the right side

Comparative operators work great if needing to compare two values against each other, but you might need to make some more complex logical comparisons. In this way, you could use a **logical operator**, for example, to make two separate comparisons, and only do something if both comparisons are true. Consider the following example expression:

```
myValue >= 10 && myValue <= 20
```

This expression uses the **logical and** (&&) operator, returning true if and only if the conditional statements on both the left and the right are true. In this case, this statement will be true if `myValue` contains a value greater than or equal to 10 and less than or equal to 20. This creates a range of numbers between 10 and 20 that could be true.

Conversely, the **logical or** (||) operator will return a value of true if either of the conditional statements on the left or right is true. Take this following example:

```
myValue < 10 || myValue > 20
```

This line would only return true if `myValue` contained a value that was less than 10 or greater than 20, excluding the values from 10 through 20.

The final logical operator is the **not** (!) operator. This one is a little different from the others in that it works on only one operand and returns true only if the expression is false. Take the following example:

```
!myValue
```

This line will return true only if `myValue` is false or contains the numerical value of 0.

Comparative and logical operators are going to play a crucial part in the Arduino decision-making process. Table 4-2 provides a quick reference of the logical operators to refer back to.

Table 4-2. Logical Operators

Symbol	Description	Is true if...
&&	logical and	both expressions are true
||	logical or	either expression is true
!	logical not	the expression is false

Control Statements

Up until this chapter, our source code has been relatively straightforward. The Arduino microcontroller reads the lines of code in our sketches from the top of the code until it reaches the end at the bottom, and, when there are no more commands to execute, will bounce back to the top of the `loop()` function and start over again. The order or direction in which code is executed is called **program flow** and the ability to alter this order of executing commands is something called **flow control**.

There are two kinds of statements available in Arduino C for controlling program flow: **conditional** statements that make decisions based on whether or not a condition is true and **iterative** statements that perform things a certain number of times or until a condition becomes false. Conditional statements that include the `if` and `switch` statements selectively perform certain actions based on the state of a condition. Iterative statements that include the `for` and `while` statements are often called loops because, just like our `loop()` function, they will loop to the beginning of the statement and repeat their code when a condition has been met.

If

The `if` statement is the simplest of the control structures and is among the most prominent method for Arduino decision making. It will perform a block of code if a specific condition is met. The basic syntax for an `if` statement looks as follows:

```
if (condition) {
  statements
}
```

Following the keyword `if`, a pair of parentheses encloses a conditional expression. If we wanted to test a certain variable to see if it is equal to the value 5, we would begin the statement like the following:

```
if (myValue == 5)
```

In this example, if `myValue` is equal to 5, the statement would execute any following simple statement or block of statements enclosed by curly braces. If the condition is not met, in that they return the value false, then the following statement(s) will be ignored and are not executed.

A common use for the `if` statement is to read the state of a digital pin and perform an action based on its condition. As a hypothetical example, this could look something like the following:

```
tiltSwitch = digitalRead(switchPin);
if (tiltSwitch == HIGH) digitalWrite(13, HIGH);
```

This is a simple example that reads the value of `switchPin` assigning that value to the variable `tiltSwitch` and then tests the condition of `tiltSwitch`. If `tiltSwitch` is equal to the constant `HIGH`, then it will call the `digitalWrite()` function to change the state of the digital pin 13 to `HIGH`, which would have the effect of turning on the pin 13 LED on the Arduino interface board. Notice that this is another example of a simple statement that does not require curly braces.

If we wanted the LED to only turn on when the switch is activated and to remain off the rest of the time, we would use an `if...else` statement. Take the following example:

```
tiltSwitch = digitalRead(switchPin);
if (tiltSwitch == HIGH) digitalWrite(13, HIGH);
else digitalWrite(13, LOW);
```

Like the previous example, this statement will turn on the LED if the switch has been activated, however, by using the else keyword it is possible to turn off the LED the rest of the time. Essentially, if the condition is true, only the first statement will be executed and if it is false, only the second statement will be executed. In plain English, this statement would be similar to saying

```
"If the switch is on then turn on the LED, otherwise turn off the LED."
```

So far, our `if` statements have been checking for a specific condition using the `==` (is equal to) operator although any of the comparative or logical operators as shown could be used instead. Take for example, the following:

```
if (myValue >= 10 && myValue <= 20) {
  statements
}
```

This `if` statement will check for a range of values, only executing the following statements if the value of `myValue` is somewhere between 10 and 20.

```
if (!myValue) {
  statements
}
```

This sample uses the `!` (not) operator so that the enclosed statements will only be executed if the variable `myValue` is false, which also corresponds to `0` or `LOW`, but we will get to that a little later in the next chapter.

For

The `for` statement, or `for` loop, is an iterative statement that allows the Arduino to repeatedly execute lines of code in a loop a specified number of times. What makes the `for` loop unique is that it is based on a counter, or a specific variable that is incremented each time the loop is repeated. This counter is even quite useful, as the counter itself can be used just like any other variable by statements that reside inside the loop, as you will see in later examples. The basic syntax of a `for` loop follows:

```
for (declaration; condition; increment) {
  statements
}
```

The `for` loop begins with three statements that include: variable declaration, conditional statement, and incremental statement. Of these, the first is the counter variable declaration or initialization and is run only once the first time through the loop. The second statement is the conditional statement using comparative operators just like those found in the `if` statement and is tested each time through the loop.

If the condition remains true, the following code bracketed by the curly braces will be executed. If, however, the condition returns false, the for loop will end. The third and final statement increments the counter variable each time the enclosed block of code is executed.

Let's say we wanted to blink an LED five times quickly, we could use a for loop similar to the following:

```
for (int i = 0; i < 5; i++) {
  digitalWrite(13, HIGH);
  delay(250);
  digitalWrite(13, LOW);
  delay(250);
}
```

In this sample code, the first time through the for loop, we declare an integer type variable to serve as our index or counter and assign it the value 0 in this statement:

```
int i = 0;
```

Each time through the loop, the conditional statement will be checked to see if the condition remains true. Take, for example, the following:

```
i < 5;
```

In this statement as long as i is less than 5, the enclosed statements will be executed, turning on pin 13, waiting for 250 milliseconds, turning pin 13 off, then waiting another 250 milliseconds.

Each time through the loop, after all of the statements within the curly braces have been executed, the variable i is incremented, in an increment statement:

```
i++;
```

In this case we add 1 to the value of i and reassign this new value back to i so that each time through the loop i increases by 1. Remember the compound operator i++ is functionally identical to i = i + 1. In this way, i starts at 0 the first time through the loop, incrementing 5 times each time through the loop until its value is no longer less than 5, consequently ending the loop. In our project code, an example of the for loop in action includes the following example:

```
for (int i=0; i<3; i++) pinMode(rgb[i], OUTPUT);
```

Here, we are using a local variable i declared inside the loop to be used as a counter and assigned the value 0. For as long as i remains less than 3, expressed in the conditional statement i<3;, the code following the for statement will be executed. The for loop will then repeat three times, and each time the pinMode() function will be executed, setting a pin, as defined by the rgb[] array, as an output. Because we only needed a single simple statement to be executed, the curly braces are not required.

You can also see that we have used the counter i to increment the position of the array rgb[] being referenced. After that statement has been executed, the counter i will be incremented by one. Once i has reached the value 3, the for loop will terminate and proceed with the standard program flow to the following line of code.

While

The for statement is fairly common to Arduino programmers, but there are other ways to structure iterative loops. Where the if statement executed a statement once if a condition was met, and the for loop cycles through a specified number of times, the while statement, or while loop, is used to continuously execute a statement so long as the condition remains true. The basic syntax of a while statement looks like the following:

```
while (condition) {
    statements
}
```

Using the while statement, we could rewrite the previous for loop example to blink an LED five times in the following manner:

```
int i = 0;
while (i < 5) {
    digitalWrite(13, HIGH);
    delay(250);
    digitalWrite(13, LOW);
    delay(250);
    i++:
}
```

The first line, int i = 0; declares the index variable and assigns the value 0. The program flow reaches the while statement and compares the value 5 to the variable i, with the first time evaluating as true. The enclosed statements are then executed, which includes the line i++; used to increment the value of i at the end of the block of code.

When the end of the statements is reached, it loops back to the conditional statement of the while loop and if the condition remains true, the following statements are executed all over again. If, however, the condition is false, then the while loop ends and control passes to the following statements in the program.

So with the for loop, why would you need the while loop? If the previous example was all you were ever going to do with it, then no there is really not much use for it. However, if you think of the while statement more as a continuous if statement, then it becomes quite useful in the right situation. From our project code, we needed to do one thing over and over again while the switch remained triggered and to prevent the continuation of normal program flow until that condition is no longer met. In other words, as long as the switch was triggered in our project example, we wanted to continue to cycle through each of the seven colors until such time as the switch was no longer triggered.

A simpler way to write this code would be something like the following:

```
while (digitalRead(2) == HIGH) digitalWrite(13, HIGH);
```

In this example, for as long as the digital input on pin 2 is equal to HIGH, if for example a switch has been activated and is on, then the while loop will continue to keep pin 13 on, or HIGH, and will never exit the loop. Only when the conditional expression digitalRead(2) == HIGH returns false will the next following line of code be executed.

Do

Like the for statement, the while statement evaluates its condition before executing its block of code so that if the condition is not met, its code will never run. Sometimes it would be nice to always run the enclosed code at least once before evaluating its condition and for that we would use the do statement, or do loop. The do loop is like a modified while statement in that it executes a line or lines of code and then tests for a condition at the end of the loop rather than the beginning before deciding to loop to the beginning again or not. The following is the basic syntax for a do loop:

```
do {
 statements
} while (condition);
```

Rethinking the last code sample, we might want to make sure that the LED is off if the switch is off before continuing on with the rest of our sketch. Using the do…while loop we could write the statement like the following:

```
do digitalWrite(13, LOW);
while (digitalRead(2) == LOW);
```

In this sample, no matter the condition, the do statement will turn off the LED on pin 13 at least once and then test the input pin 2. While the expression digitalRead(2) == LOW remains true, the do loop will repeat infinitely, keeping the LED off. When the condition is no longer true, the do loop will exit and return to normal program flow.

Switch

The switch statement is like a really nifty version of the if statement in that it can execute one or more blocks of code, depending on a range of conditions. Basically, the switch statement compares the value of an expression against a list of cases executing whatever code begins after that case when a match is found. switch is a fairly powerful and complex control structure so we will only scratch the surface here, revisiting it in later chapters when we can better apply it. The basic syntax of the switch statement follows:

```
switch (expression) {
  case constant:
    statements;
  case constant:
    statements;
  default:
    statements;
}
```

The number of cases can be as many as you need (or have the memory for), but each one should have a unique constant or single-byte character following it—variables like myValue are not allowed as a case. After the colon that defines the case, we can have a block of code that is executed when that case is true. The default case allows for code to be executed when a specific case has not been previously specified.

To get a better idea for how the switch statement works, let's say we want to modify the early LED blink sketch using the switch statement so that when the tilt switch is activated, the LED will stay on rather than blink. To do that we could use the following code sample:

```
switch (digitalRead(2)) {
  case 0:
    digitalWrite(13, LOW);
    delay(1000);
  case 1:
    digitalWrite(13, HIGH);
    delay(1000);
}
```

Beginning with the expression following the `switch` statement, we will read the state of the digital input pin 2. If the tilt switch is activated then the pin will read as `HIGH`, which if you remember is basically equal to the value 1, and the code for case 1 will be executed. If the tilt switch is not activated it will read as `LOW` or 0, so the code beginning with case 0 will be executed until the end of the `switch` statement. This will also include the code following `case 1` because the normal program flow did not reach the closing curly brace yet.

What this means is that, assuming the `switch` statement is the only code in our `loop()` function, when the tilt switch is off, the LED will blink on and off every 1 second but when the tilt switch is on, the LED will stay on and not turn off again until the tilt switch is turned off.

Break

The `break` statement can be used inside other control statements to immediately end the loop or statement. If we borrow our five-blink sample from before, we could add an `if` statement followed by the `break` statement to exit out of the loop if a switch is activated. This would look like the following:

```
for (int i = 0; i < 5; i++) {
  if (digitalRead(2) == HIGH) break;
  digitalWrite(13, HIGH);
  delay(250);
  digitalWrite(13, LOW);
  delay(250);
}
```

Normally, in this example the `for` loop will complete its cycle five times before continuing on with the rest of the program. The additional line `if (digitalRead(2) == HIGH) break;` will check the status of pin 2 and if it is equal to `HIGH`, from a switch being activated, the break statement will cause the `for` loop to quit immediately and program control will resume with the next line of code after the `for` loop.

To go back to the earlier example for the switch statement, if rather than the LED blinking when the switch is `LOW`, we could use the break statement to break out of the switch statement by adding the `break` keyword at the end of case 0, like in the following modified example:

```
switch (digitalRead(2)) {
  case 0:
    digitalWrite(13, LOW);
    delay(1000);
    break;
  case 1:
    digitalWrite(13, HIGH);
    delay(1000);
}
```

Using `break`, when the code for case 0 has been executed, the statement is broken and program flow continues with the code after the end of the `switch` statement. With the modified code, we should be left with an LED that is on when the switch is on and off when the switch is off. The added bonus with the `break` statement is that it gives us the ability to have a loop that is conditional on multiple factors or behaviors. This is also effectively a way to end any loop structure through external sources.

Continue

The continue statement does not exit or quit an iterative loop like break does, but rather it skips over any remaining statements inside the loop and goes on to the next repetition of the loop. The continue statement only works on iterative statements like the for, while, and do loops and can be used among other things to skip odd or even numbers in a for loop. For example, if we had five separate LEDs connected to the Arduino on pins 9 through 13 and wanted to turn on and off only the odd number LEDs in sequence, we could use something like the following:

```
for (int i = 9; i <= 13; i++) {
    if (i % 2 == 0) continue;
    digitalWrite(i, HIGH);
    delay(500);
    digitalWrite(i, LOW);
    delay(500);
}
```

In the line of code, if (i % 2 == 0) continue;, we have added a conditional test based on the modulus operator in i % 2 so that if the number in the loop is an even number, it will evenly divide by 2 leaving a 0 remainder. If that condition is true, the continue statement will skip any further instructions inside of the loop and head back to the increment component of the for statement and resume normal operation.

In this example we also started our for loop with the value 9 (i = 9), incrementing i by 1 each time through the loop (i++), so long as i is less than or equal to 13 (i <= 13) for a total of five possible iterations. We are also using the indexing variable to correspond to a specific digital pin by using i in the statements like digitalWrite(i, HIGH);. In the end, the even numbers will be ignored and the LEDs connected to pins 9, 11, and 13 will turn on and off in sequence.

Summary

In this chapter, we explored all manner of ways in which the Arduino can alter the standard top-to-bottom program flow using various methods to make decisions and perform repetitive actions. You should have a basic understanding of how to make decisions using conditional statements and how to perform repetitive tasks in iterative statements, or loops. Of course, we will continue to work with these concepts in later discussions, building out from our foundational understanding of how we can structure Arduino sketches. But for now, that about wraps up the discussion of the generally more C-based structural programming syntax.

From here, we will discover more of the uniquely Arduino aspects of programming the Arduino microcontroller board that specifically relate to sensing and controlling the physical world. These are the parts of the Arduino library that make Arduino C unique. This is going to be the really fun stuff.

CHAPTER 5

Digital Ins and Outs

So far in our discussion of programming the Arduino microcontroller, we have generally glossed over the physical interactions of turning things on and off and sensing the world around us that make programming microcontrollers so much fun. Now it's time to fix that. Programming a microcontroller can be rather unique because of its ability to easily turn on and off motors, lights, and other actuators, as well as read from switches and sensors. This is possible on the Arduino Uno by using its 20 input and output (I/O) pins, each having different functions that can be configured in software—including input, output, analog to digital conversion (ADC), and analog output, more accurately called pulse width modulation (PWM)). This chapter will take as its focus the various digital input and output functions available and how to interface the needed hardware to make them work.

What unifies the functions and code in this chapter as being digital is that they all have only two different states: on or off. We have actually already used the Arduino's digital I/O from the very beginning of this book and briefly introduced digital input in the last chapter using a very simple form of a digital sensor in the basic rolling ball tilt switch. Other forms of digital input include pushbuttons, mat switches, magnetic or reed switches, thermostats, passive infrared motion detectors, and oh so many more. We can use digital output to turn on not only LEDs but also to make sound, create movement with motors or solenoids, and even control larger devices using transistors and relays.

We will start with an introduction of the electrical properties of the Arduino's I/O pins, followed by a new project called Noisy Cricket, and then we will move into a thorough examination of the digital functions and how we can incorporate them into our code.

What's needed for this chapter:

- Arduino Uno

- Passive infrared motion detector

- Piezoelectric speaker

- Momentary pushbutton or switch

- 10 kilohm ¼ watt resistor or similar

- Hookup wires

- Solderless breadboard

Arduino I/O Demystified

The Arduino interface board has a single row of connectors or pins on each side of the board. These are used mostly for inputs, outputs, and power. Figure 5-1 shows a simple illustration of the Arduino Uno interface board. Your board might be a little different.

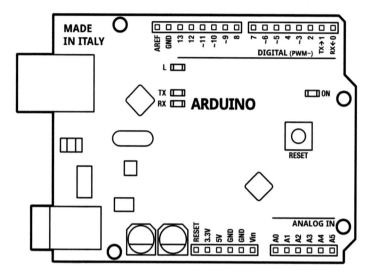

Figure 5-1. *Arduino illustration*

As shown in Figure 5-1 and printed on the interface board, there are 14 pins on one side of the board marked Digital that are numbered from 0 to 13. Of these, two are used for serial communications through USB for programming, debugging, and other forms of communication. These pins are numbered 0 and 1, and are marked RX <- and TX -> respectively. Anything connected to these pins may affect or be affected by serial communications. Pin 13 has a resistor and LED (marked L) connected to it on board so that it can be used for testing, diagnostics, and other forms of blinking. Six of the digital pins can also act as analog outputs using pulse width modulation (PWM). These are pins 3, 5, 6, 9, 10, and 11 on the Arduino Uno and are marked on the interface board with the tilde symbol (~). On the other side of the board are six additional I/O pins labeled as Analog In, numbering A0 through A5. These pins are connected to the microcontroller's analog to digital convertor (ADC) for interpreting incoming analog signals, although they can also be used as additional digital inputs and outputs.

Each I/O pin operates on a range of 0 to +5 VDC, or volts direct current. A range of 0 to +2V is said to be off or LOW while anything over about +3V is said to be on or HIGH. Generally, a circuit connected to one of the Arduino I/O pins needs to have a high or positive side connected to power (+5 VDC), some form of load, and a low or negative side connected to ground (GND). How a circuit is physically connected to the Arduino or in which direction determines how the I/O pin can be used and which side of the circuit is connected to the Arduino. Each pin can either **source**, or provide a positive biased current, or **sink**, to provide a negative biased current, up to 40 milliamps each. Typically, most Arduino circuits are designed so that they source current, as shown in Figure 5-2, although there are times where sinking current is necessary, as shown in Figure 5-3.

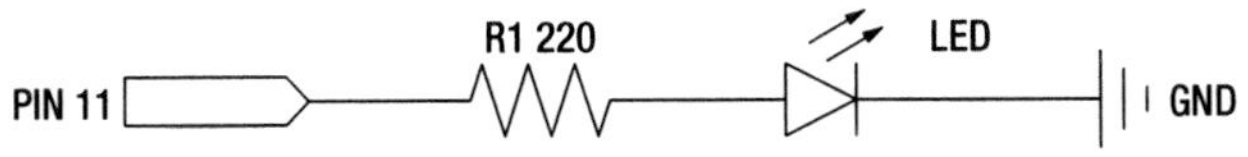

Figure 5-2. *An example of sourcing current*

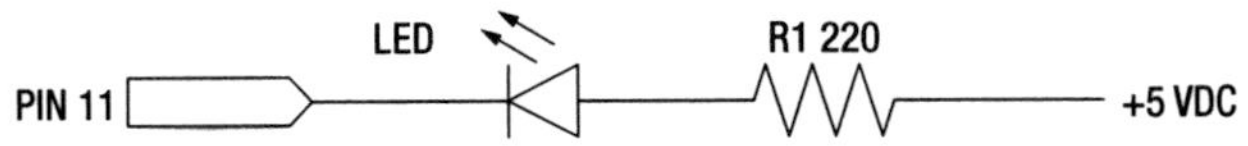

Figure 5-3. *An example of sinking current*

In comparing these two schematics, you should notice there is a difference in whether or not one side of the drawing is connected to +5 VDC or to GND and that this connection affects the direction of the LED. LEDs and a few other components are **polarized**, meaning that they only work in one direction, or with the correct polarity. By sourcing current, the Arduino I/O pin acts as source for +5 volts, providing a high-side positive supply of current. On the other hand, by sinking current, the Arduino I/O pin acts like a connection to ground, providing a low-side or negative current.

While each pin can provide about 40 milliamps of current, this is just about enough juice for one or two LEDs to work on each pin safely. Drawing more than 40 milliamps or exceeding +5v on any pin may either damage the microcontroller or the connected device. To safeguard against this happening, it is generally a good idea to connect output pins to other devices using one of two components, the first of which is a **current limiting resistor** used to drop or limit the current needed by the device. Playing it safe, a 1 kilohm resistor is a common value for current limiting for general applications, although we can get away with less resistance, as with our earlier LED schematics where we used a 220 ohm resistor to get more brightness out of the LED without damaging anything. Alternatively, we could use **transistors** or other switching components to switch larger current loads, like motors, solenoids, or strings of LEDs that exceed the maximum 40 milliamps of current and/or operate at voltages greater than +5v.

▨ **Note** While it is possible to damage the microcontroller from connecting things wrong, it is a surprisingly tough little chip and is fairly hard to completely ruin. More often than not, it will be okay after removing power to it and disconnecting the offending circuit. Sometimes, however, it is possible to end up with a dead pin that will no longer work, but only in catastrophic situations will the entire chip release the magic smoke.

It is important to remember that any time our circuit has a connection to ground that this must be common to the Arduino and every connected device or things will behave very erratically. What this means is that the ground pins of the circuit must somehow connect to the ground pins on the microcontroller. Likewise, any time we use a pin for an input that is not actually connected to anything, it is called a **floating pin** and we will get seemingly random and strange results as the pin picks up electrical interference and noise from the surrounding environment or from nearby circuits.

Project 4: Noisy Cricket

As a means to explore the uses of the Arduino's digital pins and to discuss the different digital functions, we are going to look at a new project: the Noisy Cricket. This project will make quite an annoying racket when left alone, but it will quickly hush up when someone gets near it—just like a real cricket. We will use a simple and inexpensive motion sensor as a trigger, although a tilt switch, mat switch, or any other simple on or off sensor will do. Wire the whole thing up and power it from a battery, then go find a hard-to-reach place for the cricket to call home and see how many people you can drive insane with it!

Hooking It Up

This circuit can be as simple or complex as you want to make it. We will go with the easy route, using an inexpensive, passive infrared (PIR)motion detector. We are somewhat partial to the ones from Parallax or Adafruit, listed in the appendix at the end of this book, for their ease of use and connectivity. A PIR motion detector is really good at detecting a change in the nearby ambient infrared temperature usually caused by the movement of warm-blooded creatures like us. It needs three connections: +5 VDC, GND, and OUT, however, double-check the sensor's technical specifications to make sure the correct connections are made to the right pins. The output pin is usually configurable and can provide a logic level HIGH when motion is detected and LOW otherwise. Alternatively, you could stick with the tilt sensor circuit from earlier or some other form of digital switch or sensor.

For the speaker, we are using a piezo buzzer, which uses a piezoelectric crystal coupled with a small diaphragm to make sound. Some piezo speakers are polarized and will have a side marked '+' that should be connected to the Arduino output pin. Instead of a piezo, a more conventional small, simple 8 ohm speaker like you would find in an electronic toy or alarm clock could also work with a 100 ohm series resistor placed between the output pin and the speaker. Figures 5-4 and 5-5 show how all of this goes together.

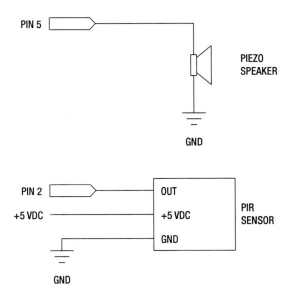

Figure 5-4. *Noisy Cricket schematic*

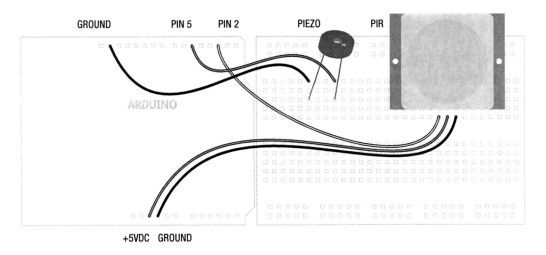

Figure 5-5. Noisy Cricket illustration

Uploading the Source Code

The code in Listing 5-1 should bring life to our noisy cricket while at the same time show off some of the complex behaviors that can be achieved by simply turning a pin on and off. This sketch is built around the idea of adding behavior to the chirp so there is a whole block of variables that can be changed to affect its character, which we will explain more fully in our summary.

Listing 5-1. *Noisy Cricket Source Code*

```
const int speakerPin = 5;
const int sensorPin = 2;

const int highChirp = 20;
const int lowChirp = 14;

const int chirpCycle = 70;
const int chirpPause = 8;
const int numChirps = 10;
const int midChirp = 150;
const int skittish = 5000;

void setup() {
  pinMode(speakerPin, OUTPUT);
  pinMode(sensorPin, INPUT);
}

void loop() {
  while (digitalRead(sensorPin) == LOW) {
    for (int i=1; i<=numChirps; i++) {

      for (int j=1; j<=highChirp; j++) {
        digitalWrite(speakerPin, HIGH);
        delayMicroseconds(chirpCycle * 10);
        digitalWrite(speakerPin, LOW);
        delayMicroseconds(1000-(chirpCycle * 10));
      }

      digitalWrite(speakerPin, LOW);

      if (i == numChirps/2) delay(midChirp);
      else delay(lowChirp);

    }
    if ((random(chirpPause)) == 1) delay(random(200,1000));
    else delay(midChirp);   }
  delay(skittish);
}
```

Source Code Summary

While at first glance there seems to be quite a lot going on in this sketch, if we take the time to break it down into its various parts, it's fairly easy to understand. Let's start with the block of variables and what they do.

```
const int speakerPin = 5;
const int sensorPin = 2;
```

These first two lines define which pins are connected to which device. In this case, we have connected the PIR motion detector to pin 2 and the speaker is connected to pin 5.

```
const int highChirp = 20;
const int lowChirp = 14;
```

Crickets chirp fairly fast. These second two lines set up the length of time (measured in milliseconds) that the chirp is on, using the variable highChirp, and off, using the variable lowChirp. With our numbers, the chirp will be on for a little bit longer than it is off, giving the chirp a more natural irregularity.

```
const int chirpCycle = 70;
const int chirpPause = 8;
const int numChirps = 10;
const int midChirp = 150;
const int skittish = 5000;
```

These five variables are what give our little cricket its character. The variable chirpCycle is used in a block of code that will give the chirp a higher frequency of sound than if we simply turned the pin on. chirpCycle refers to the duty cycle that the pin is on for every 1 millisecond, measured in a percentage or 70% , in our example. Increasing or decreasing this percentage will affect the pitch of the sound generated. chirpPause is used after the main chirp sequence to give the cricket a 1 in 8 chance of pausing for a longer time than normal. In our chirp sequence, numChirps determines the number of chirps in a cycle. The value 10 works for a good cricket sound but increasing or decreasing this will create a cricket that is more or less active. midChirp represents a brief pause measured in milliseconds in the middle of the chirp cycle. The final variable, skittish, is how long the cricket will stay quiet after movement has been detected. Next, we move on to our setup() function:

```
pinMode(speakerPin, OUTPUT);
pinMode(sensorPin, INPUT);
```

After all of the variables have been defined, our setup() function will set each of the I/O pins according to whether we intend to use them as inputs or outputs. More on this later, so let's move on to our loop() function.

```
while (digitalRead(sensorPin) == LOW) {
  for (int i=1; i<=numChirps; i++) {
```

The first line of our loop() function reads the state of the sensor pin and as long as it remains LOW, meaning that movement has not been detected, the second line will begin the chirp cycle for as many chirps that have been specified.

```
for (int j=1; j<=highChirp; j++) {
  digitalWrite(speakerPin, HIGH);
  delayMicroseconds(chirpCycle * 10);
  digitalWrite(speakerPin, LOW);
  delayMicroseconds(1000-(chirpCycle * 10));
}
```

This entire block of code is a replacement for turning on the speaker pin once. So why use five lines of code instead of one? The reason is to create a higher pitch sound by turning on and off the pin at a higher rate of speed, or frequency. This for loop will cycle through once each millisecond for a number of times specified by highChirp. This will have the effect of sounding like a solid tone for as long as specified, in this case 20 milliseconds since highChirp is equal to 20.

While we have used the delay() function previously, albeit with little explanation, delayMicroseconds() is another type of delay that appropriately enough measures time in microseconds rather than milliseconds. This means that delay(1) and delayMicroseconds(1000) are equal to the same amount of time. Using our chirpCycle of 70%, delayMicroseconds(chirpCycle * 10) will delay for 700 microseconds after the pin is turned on and delayMicroseconds(1000-(chirpCycle * 10)) will delay for 300 microseconds when the pin is turned off.

Next up, we need to turn off the speaker for either a longer delay midway through the chirp cycle, or for a short delay the rest of the time. The following two lines will check to see if we've hit the midway point or not:

```
digitalWrite(speakerPin, LOW);

 if (i == numChirps/2) delay(midChirp);
 else delay(lowChirp);
```

So far these lines of code have the effect of chirping five times in quick succession with only a slightly longer delay before chirping another five times. Once in a while it might be nice to toss things up a bit.

```
if ((random(chirpPause)) == 1) delay(random(200,1000));
    else delay(midChirp);
```

And these two lines do exactly that. As specified by chirpPause, we are providing a random chance of 1 in 8 that the cricket might pause for a breath of air that might last between 200 and 1000 milliseconds, or 0.2 up to 1 second in length. To accomplish this we are using the random() function that will be discussed in a later chapter.

```
delay(skittish);
```

Finally our last line of code in the loop() function is only ever reached when the PIR motion detector senses movement and sends a signal of HIGH to the Arduino. At this point, the cricket will wait for 5 seconds before checking to see if there is movement again. If someone remains too close to the cricket, it will stay quiet until they go away—and after running the cricket for any length of time I'm sure you will try to keep it quiet as much as you can.

Digital Functions

Now that we've seen the digital functions in action, let's look at each of them individually in greater detail to better understand how they work.

pinMode()

Before we can put the other digital functions to work, we first need to let the Arduino know how we plan to use its digital I/O pins. To do this, we use a function called pinMode() to set up which pin we are going to use and how we intend to use it. Its syntax is fairly simple, as follows:

```
pinMode(pin, state)
```

Inside the parenthesis of the function are two values separated by a comma. The first value is the number of the pin that we are setting up. This could be a number or variable with the value ranging from 0 to 13 or A0 to A5 (if using the Analog In pins for digital I/O) corresponding to the pin number printed on the interface board.

The second value is the state that we need for the pin to work with our circuit and can include either of two predefined constants: INPUT or OUTPUT. Using INPUT in a pinMode() function will place the pin in a state of high impedance, where the pin is configured to receive an incoming signal yet places very little load on the overall circuit. This is good for reading sensitive inputs without affecting the sensor in any way. A digital input pin is only sensitive to two values, HIGH and LOW.

By using OUTPUT, the digital pin is placed in a state of low impedance and can, therefore, source or sink a respectable current, considering the size of such a little chip, of 40 milliamps to other circuits. This is enough current to brightly light up an LED while providing little resistance to the rest of the circuit.

In this project, we use pinMode() two different ways:

```
pinMode(speakerPin, OUTPUT);
pinMode(sensorPin, INPUT);
```

The first line sets the speaker pin to an OUPUT state so that we can connect and power a small external speaker. The second line establishes the sensor pin as an INPUT, making it ready to receive signals from a low power sensor or other input.

For every digital I/O pin that we need to use, we must first establish its mode once in the program, usually done in the setup() function. This can get a bit tedious if we plan to use all 14 digital pins as outputs. Instead, we can use a for loop as shown in previous examples to set up each pin as an output, like in the following example:

```
for (int i=0; i<14; i++) pinMode(i, OUTPUT);
```

This line is a simple for statement used to repeat a line of code a total of 14 times, placing each digital pin into an OUTPUT mode. This could come in handy and save you some typing if you're trying to hook up 14 LEDs to one Arduino.

digitalWrite()

Once we have a pin established as an OUTPUT, it is then possible to turn that pin on or off using the digitalWrite() function. Its syntax follows:

```
digitalWrite(pin, state)
```

There are two statements that are used with this function that include pin number and state. Just like pinMode(), this could be a number or variable with the value ranging from 0 to 13 or A0 to A5. The second statement is the state of the output pin that corresponds to the two predefined constants: HIGH and LOW.

HIGH is the state of sourcing current and provides a connection to +5 VDC. LOW, the default of any output pin, is the state of sinking current, providing a connection to ground. If the circuit is configured similar to Figure 5-2, where the output pin is configured to source current for a circuit, setting the pin HIGH is basically turning the circuit on, while setting the pin LOW turns it off. This would be reversed if the circuit is more like Figure 5-3 and the output pin needs to sink current in order to turn on the circuit. This is why in this book we will generally stick to sourcing current in our circuits so that HIGH will most likely mean "turn something on."

Just like we did with the pinMode() function, it is possible to turn on or off all of the pins using a for loop. Take the following code sample:

```
for (int i=0; i<14; i++) digitalWrite(i, HIGH);
delay(1000);
for (int i=0; i<14; i++) digitalWrite(i, LOW);
delay(1000);
```

By substituting i in `digitalWrite(i, HIGH)` with the current iteration of the loop, this source code will turn on all 14 pins in order so quickly that it will appear that they all come on simultaneously. The rest of the code pauses for 1 second, turns each of the pins off, then pauses for another second. If you connected a series resistor and LED to each pin, then this code would blink all 14 LEDs on and off every second. To create a more interesting pattern, we could rewrite the sample like the following:

```
for (int i=0; i<14; i++) {
  digitalWrite(i, HIGH);
  delay(1000);
}
for (int i=13; i>=0; i--) {
  digitalWrite(i, LOW);
  delay(1000);
}
```

The first for loop will turn on each of the 14 pins individually, pausing for 1 second between each one, starting with pin 0 and ending with pin 13, until all of the pins are on. The next loop begins with pin 13 and ends with pin 0, turning off each pin individually with a 1 second pause in between each one until none of the pins are on.

digitalRead()

With a digital pin configured as an INPUT, we can read the state of that pin using the `digitalRead()` function. Its syntax is fairly basic, as follows:

`digitalRead(pin)`

Here, we specify the pin number of the INPUT pin using either a variable or a numerical constant. What we do with this reading depends on maybe two different ways to use this function. The first is to assign the state of the pin to a variable. The second is to use the function in the place of a variable. For example, if we take the following statement:

```
sensorState = digitalRead(sensorPin);
if (sensorState == HIGH) digitalWrite(ledPin, HIGH);
```

In these two lines of code, `digitalRead()` is used to read the input pin and this reading is assigned to a variable. The next line performs a conditional test on the variable and if this variable is equal to HIGH, then it will make an output pin HIGH. We could rewrite these lines of code in one functionally identical line instead, as follows:

`if (digitalRead(sensorPin) == HIGH) digitalWrite(ledPin, HIGH);`

This somewhat compact line of code uses the `digitalRead()` function in the place often occupied by a variable, so that if the reading of the sensor pin is equal to HIGH, then the rest of the line is executed.

State Changes

Because there are only two conditions possible when reading or writing digital inputs and outputs—high and low—we can use this predictability to detect a **state change**, where a pin changes from high to low or low to high, or even to count these changes. To detect a state change on a digital input, we don't actually need to know the precise state that the pin is in. Rather, we only need to know when a pin has changed from one state to another.

To do this, we need a way to compare the pin's current state with the state of the pin the last time we read it. If we check an input and it's high but the last time we checked it was low, then the button has been pressed. On the other hand, if we check an input and it's low but last time we checked it was high, then the button is no longer being pressed. By looking for this change, what we are doing is called **edge detection** because really all we are looking for is that specific moment or edge when the state changes from one condition to another.

Let's back up for a second and take a look at a very simple pushbutton circuit, as shown in Figures 5-6 and 5-7. This circuit will use the built-in LED on pin 13 (not shown) and add a momentary pushbutton on pin 2, which only stays closed or on when the button is actively being pressed. This will provide a good basis for our further discussion on state changes.

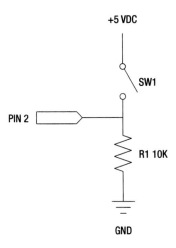

Figure 5-6. Pushbutton schematic

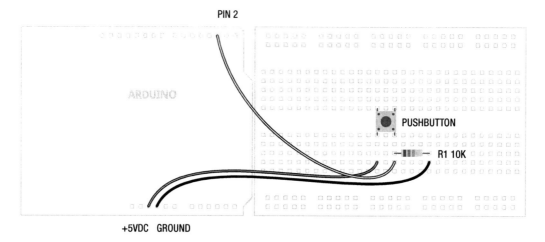

Figure 5-7. *Pushbutton illustration*

Toggle

With this wired up, we can now try out a few examples of source code that will use this circuit to detect state changes. Beginning with the code in Listing 5-2, this example will toggle the state of the LED each time the button is pressed.

Listing 5-2. *State Change Example 1*

```
const int switchPin = 2;
const int ledPin = 13;

int state;
int lastState;
int ledState;

void setup() {
  pinMode(ledPin, OUTPUT);
  pinMode(switchPin, INPUT);
}

void loop() {
  state = digitalRead(switchPin);
  if (state != lastState) {
    if (state == HIGH) {
      if (ledState == HIGH) ledState = LOW;
      else ledState = HIGH;
    }
    lastState = state;
  }
```

```
    digitalWrite(ledPin, ledState);
    delay(20);
}
```

This example uses two variables, `state` and `lastState`, to keep track of the state of the input pin at any given time. A third variable, `ledState`, is used to toggle the state of the LED. In this way, when the button is pressed the first time, the LED will turn on, press the button a second time and the LED will turn off, press the button a third time, the LED will come back on, and so on. Let's unpack the code a bit before moving to the next example, beginning with the first line in the `loop()` function.

```
state = digitalRead(switchPin);
```

This line reads the input from the pin connected to our push button and assigns its value to the variable state.

```
if (state != lastState) {
```

Our first of three conditional statements, this line is what this whole sketch hinges on. It checks to see if the current state is different from the state last time it checked. By using the `!=` operator, this line in English is like saying, "If the current state is not equal to the last state then execute the following lines." Notice, it doesn't actually matter at this point what the exact state is of the pin, only that it's different.

```
if (state == HIGH) {
```

This line will check to see what the state actually is so that the state of the LED can be changed accordingly in the next two lines.

```
if (ledState == HIGH) ledState = LOW;
else ledState = HIGH;
```

This `if…else` statement will either change the state of the LED to `LOW` if it was `HIGH` last time or `HIGH` if it was already `LOW`. This statement doesn't actually turn on or off the LED, but we will get to that in a moment.

```
lastState = state;
```

This line is the counterpart to the statement, `if (state != lastState)`, and is responsible for changing the current state of the input pin to the old state before we assign a new value to the variable state.

```
digitalWrite(ledPin, ledState);
delay(20);
```

These last two lines will set the `ledPin` to whatever `ledState` is equal to, either turning on or off the LED. The very short 20 millisecond delay is there just to slow things down enough so that the sketch reads one press of the push button as opposed to multiples.

Counting

Our last example toggled the LED on and off whenever the button was pressed. But what if you want the LED to turn on only once every five button presses? To do that we need to set up a counter that will count the number of presses. Listing 5-3 shows one way that this could be done.

Listing 5-3. *State Change Example 2*

```
const int switchPin = 2;
const int ledPin = 13;

int state;
int lastState;

int buttonCounter = 0;

void setup() {
  pinMode(ledPin, OUTPUT);
  pinMode(switchPin, INPUT);
}

void loop() {
  state = digitalRead(switchPin);
  if (state != lastState) {
    if (state == HIGH) {
      buttonCounter++;
    }
    lastState = state;
  }
  if (buttonCounter % 5 == 0) {
    digitalWrite(ledPin, HIGH);
    delay(20);
  } else digitalWrite(ledPin, LOW);
}
```

In this example, we have replaced the `ledState` variable with a `buttonCounter` variable to count the button presses. Instead of toggling the LED state, we are adding up each button press in this `if` statement:

```
if (state == HIGH) {
  buttonCounter++;
}
```

This will add one to the variable `buttonCounter` each time the input pin goes high. Then we need a way to test to see if we have hit five presses or not.

```
if (buttonCounter % 5 == 0) {
    digitalWrite(ledPin, HIGH);
    delay(20);
  } else digitalWrite(ledPin, LOW);
```

This final conditional statement does just that, by testing if the remainder of `buttonCounter` divided by 5 is equal to 0. If so, we know that the button has been pressed five times and the Arduino can turn on the LED. For any other number, the LED will remain off.

Modality

The process of **modality** is where a device, receiving information from a user through sensors and inputs, is expected to perform multiple actions based on that input. In our last example, the interaction was fairly simple, with a button being pressed five times to trigger the activation of the LED. What if we wanted multiple actions to occur based on multiple types of input? To do this we could use the `switch` statement and a counter based on the last example. Listing 5-4 is one possibility.

Listing 5-4. *State Change Example 3*

```
const int switchPin = 2;
const int ledPin = 13;

int state = 0;
int lastState = 0;
int buttonCounter = 0;

unsigned long startTime = 0;
unsigned long interval = 500;

void setup() {
  pinMode(ledPin, OUTPUT);
  pinMode(switchPin, INPUT);
}

void loop() {
  state = digitalRead(switchPin);
  if(state != lastState) {
    if (state == HIGH) {
      buttonCounter++;
      startTime = millis();
    }
  }
  lastState = state;

  if(startTime + interval < millis()) {

    switch (buttonCounter) {
    case 1:
      digitalWrite(ledPin, HIGH);
      delay(interval);
      digitalWrite(ledPin, LOW);
      delay(interval);
      break;
```

```
    case 2:
      for (int i=0; i<2; i++) {
        digitalWrite(ledPin, HIGH);
        delay(interval/2);
        digitalWrite(ledPin, LOW);
        delay(interval/2);
      }
      break;
    case 3:
      for (int i=0; i<3; i++) {
        digitalWrite(ledPin, HIGH);
        delay(interval/3);
        digitalWrite(ledPin, LOW);
        delay(interval/3);
      }
      break;
    case 4:
      for (int i=0; i<4; i++) {
        digitalWrite(ledPin, HIGH);
        delay(interval/4);
        digitalWrite(ledPin, LOW);
        delay(interval/4);
      }
    }
    buttonCounter = 0;
  }
  delay(20);
}
```

Admittedly, we are jumping ahead a little bit using some time functions that we will not cover in detail until Chapter 7, but this is a pretty neat example of creating modes of behavior based on a range of input conditions. In this case, we can push the button up to four times in a half-second interval and the LED will blink a number of times equal to the number of button presses. No button presses, or button presses that exceed four, will be ignored—not exactly the best case for interaction design but it works for our example.

While still fundamentally building off of the last two examples, the challenge with this type of problem is that the button presses need to happen within a certain time frame or the Arduino will sit there counting button presses forever. To make this work, we have added two unsigned long variables, startTime and interval, and are using the millis() function, explained in more detail later, that will provide us with a time stamp when the first button is pressed. Adding a known interval to this initial time stamp will allow us to determine if a sufficient interval has passed, in this case a half second.

Once this interval has been passed, the code proceeds to the switch statement that compares the variable buttonCounter to four different cases. Each case corresponds to how many times we want to blink, beginning with 1 blink in case 1 and working its way up to 4 blinks in case 4. After the LED has been blinked, we use the break statement to exit the switch statement to prevent unwanted blinks. In this example, we decided to keep the total number of blinks all to within 1 second by using the interval variable in the delay, dividing it by the number of times we want it to blink.

Moving on from here, we could continue to add cases to the switch statement and make a game out of how many times the button can be pressed in the interval time. We could also provide some sort of feedback when we don't receive the input that we want to receive, letting the user know that they should try again.

Summary

Finally getting to some of the fun stuff, this chapter introduced the input and output pins available on the Arduino interface board and the various functions to work with digital I/O. You've got a feel for how to set up a pin depending on how we intend to use it, the couple of ways that an input pin can be read, and some different methods to write to an output pin. Digital I/O is the bread and butter of embedded electronics and we will continue to return to it throughout the rest of this book.

For now though, we are going to move on to analog I/O. Whereas digital I/O is black and white, on or off, analog I/O opens up a world of grays, giving us an entire range of values between on and off. How far away is another person or a wall, how bright is it in the room, what's the relative humidity right now, how much does something weigh or how much force does it exert—these are all some of the questions that can be answered using the appropriate analog sensors. As a way to discuss the various analog functions at our disposal, our next project will explore how to make a fan spin based on someone's breath from a sensor's input. So let's keep going.

CHAPTER 6

Analog In, Analog Out

The Arduino interface board, just like most other computers, is a digital system that operates on binary values: 1 and 0, on and off, true and false. What if we wanted to know not just whether it was hot or cold outside but rather *how* hot or cold it was? Or instead of turning an LED on or off, maybe we want to dim or even fade an LED? To do this we need to either convert an analog reading into something that the Arduino can understand or, vice versa, approximate an analog output using digital signals. Where a digital signal has two possible states, an analog signal has many. Because we are dealing with electrical signals, digital states on the Arduino are usually considered to be 0v for LOW or off and +5v for HIGH or on. Analog signals on the other hand might represent any voltage between 0 and +5 volts, infinitely more than just on and off.

This chapter will specifically address the available hardware and the functions that we need to use them, in order to read, interpret, and output analog signals. We will discuss how a digital microcontroller can use both analog and pseudo-analog signals—pseudo-analog signals are signals simulated by digital means—converting and manipulating these signals as needed. We will look at a project called Telematic Breath that takes advantage of both reading and writing analog signals, followed by a more in-depth discussion of the various analog functions and how they work. We will also look at a way to "see" the analog input as the Arduino sees it, wrapping up the chapter with methods for mapping these values to more usable forms.

What's needed for this chapter:

- Arduino Uno
- Modern Device MD0550 wind sensor
- 2N2222 or 2N3904 NPN transistor or similar
- 5 volt DC brushless fan 50mm × 50mm or similar
- 10 kilohm CdS photocell or similar
- 10 kilohm and 1 kilohm ¼ watt resistors
- Hookup wires
- Solderless breadboard

Analog Demystified

To get our heads around the concept of what analog is, we should compare the difference between analog and digital signals beginning with Figure 6-1.

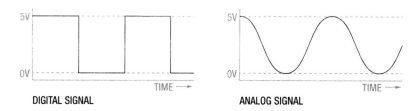

Figure 6-1. *Digital versus analog signals*

Looking at these two graphs that show the effect of the different signals types over time, you can see that where a digital signal abruptly shifts from high to low, an analog signal can gradually move through a multitude of steps in between these two extremes. This varying, or analog signal, is what we can use to determine how cold it is, how much pressure is being exerted, or to change the brightness of a light or the speed of a motor. In order for the digital microcontroller that likes 1s and 0s to be able to input and output analog signals we need to use some additional hardware built onto the chip to convert or interpret these signals for us.

In order to receive an analog input, we need to use the microcontroller's **analog to digital converter**, usually called an A/D converter or ADC, to convert a continuous analog voltage applied to one of the analog pins into a digital integer proportional to the amount of voltage at that pin. This is a specialized bit of hardware that is connected to 6 of Arduino's general I/O pins, marked on the board as A0–A5. The Arduino ADC has a 10-bit resolution, meaning that it will return a linear value from 0 to1023 corresponding to 0v and +5v respectively. With this resolution, the Arduino ADC can read levels of voltage down to 4.88 millivolts per level. Keep in mind, however, that where an analog signal is a continuous signal, the ADC will only take a single reading at the very instant that the function is called.

Because it is a digital device, the Arduino is actually incapable of providing a true analog output. Instead, it approximates an analog signal by turning on and off a pin very quickly in a process called **pulse width modulation** (PWM). This happens so fast it is nearly imperceptible to the eye, instead looking like a dim LED or a slow motor. The hardware that does this is connected to pins 3, 5, 6, 9, 10, and 11 on the Arduino Uno and has an 8-bit resolution, meaning that values between 0 and 255 will simulate voltages between 0v and +5v. While not a smooth continuous analog signal, by alternating the amount of time that the pin is on, or its **pulse width**, in relation to the time off, it will emulate an analog signal. The average voltage created by quickly alternating between on and off is called the **duty cycle** as illustrated in Figure 6-2.

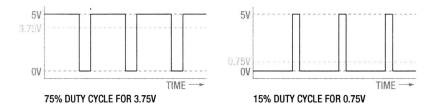

75% DUTY CYCLE FOR 3.75V   15% DUTY CYCLE FOR 0.75V

Figure 6-2. Pulse width modulation duty cycle

Figure 6-2 shows how a PWM signal that is on, or +5v, for 75% of the time and off, or 0v, for 25% will simulate an analog voltage of +3.75v. This would be referred to as a 75% duty cycle. Likewise, a duty cycle of 15%, where the pin is on for 15% of the time and off 85% of the time, would result in only an average of +0.75v. This is how we can use PWM to give an LED the appearance of fading or with the right hardware to change the speed of a motor. Now that we have a handle on how analog works on the Arduino, let's look at our next project.

Project 5: Telematic Breath

In our fifth project, we will sense and re-create or "broadcast" a breath or gentle breeze from one location to another using a simple wind sensor and a small fan. Breathe on the sensor and the fan will spin at a speed that correlates to the force of your breath. In this way, applying the data from an analog sensor to the speed of a fan will provide a very tangible experience of transmitting data from one source to another.

Hooking It Up

While the hardware is a little more complex than previous projects, it's not really all that bad, with a total of four components. We have specified a very particular sensor and fan at the beginning of this chapter to complete this project, although just about any analog sensor could be used in place of the wind sensor and about any other DC fan, motor, solenoid, or other actuator could be used to substitute the fan. Likewise you might change out the transistor for another switching device like a relay or MOSFET, detailed later in Chapters 11 and 12.

This particular wind sensor is a low-cost thermal anemometer developed by Paul Badger at Modern Device to measure wind speed. Specifically, it measures the electricity needed to maintain a specific temperature on a heating element as the wind changes. This sensor is remarkably sensitive and can detect the slightest breath. We will couple this with a fan to re-create the wind speed input by controlling the speed of the fan through PWM.

The fan we chose will run on +5v DC, but it exceeds the current available to the Arduino's output pins, so to power it safely, we need to use a small transistor to switch the bigger load. The transistor we are using is the 2N3904, although the 2N2222 is pin compatible and you could even substitute any of a number of other similar devices. The 2N3904 has 3 pins labeled e, b, and c—for emitter, base, and collector respectively. These names refer to what each pin does: emitter is connected to ground; collector to the negative side of the load, in this case the black wire on the fan; and base connects to a series resistor and to the PWM pin on the Arduino.

It is possible to use a higher voltage fan, say +12v DC, using a transistor to switch it on and off. To do this you need to connect a higher voltage power supply into your Arduino and instead of connecting the positive or red wire to +5v, you would connect it to a pin on the Arduino interface board labeled Vin. Just be sure to be careful as you wire up the circuit shown in Figures 6-3 and 6-4, taking it slow and double-checking everything to make sure you get the pins correct on the sensor and the transistor, and you will be fine.

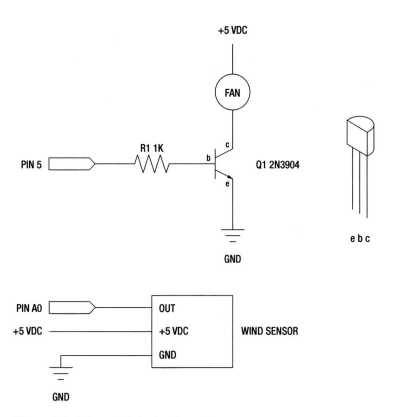

Figure 6-3. *Telematic Breath schematic*

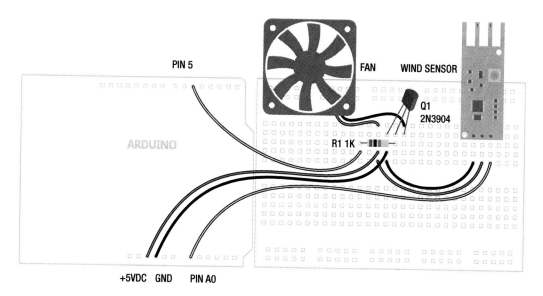

Figure 6-4. *Telematic Breath illustration*

Uploading the Source Code

After the crazy source code in the last chapter, this sketch will seem tame in comparison. Although while there is not much length to the code, there are a lot of new things going on that we will spend the rest of the chapter trying to explain. So let's get the circuit wired up, upload the source code in Listing 6-1, and see what it does.

Listing 6-1. *Telematic Breath Source Code*

```
const int fanPin = 5;
const int sensorPin = A0;

const int minReading = 25;
const int maxReading = 400;
const int fanStart = 100;

int analogValue = 0;

void setup() {
  Serial.begin(9600);
}

void loop() {
  analogValue = analogRead(sensorPin);
  analogValue = constrain(analogValue, minReading, maxReading);
  analogValue = map(analogValue, minReading, maxReading, 0, 255);
```

```
    Serial.print("analog value = " );
    Serial.println(analogValue, DEC);

    if ((analogValue > minReading) && (analogValue < fanStart))
    analogWrite(fanPin, fanStart);
    else analogWrite(fanPin, analogValue);

    delay(250);
}
```

Source Code Summary

Like nearly all of our sketches, we begin this one with a declaration of variables for the pins that we will use, giving them descriptive names. In this case, fanPin and sensorPin.

```
const int fanPin = 5;
const int sensorPin = A0;
```

Our next block of variables pertain to some general thresholds that relate to our sensor readings and what it takes to get the fan spinning.

```
const int minReading = 25;
const int maxReading = 400;
const int fanStart = 100;
```

The first variable minReading can be adjusted to reflect the minimum reading that our sensor is providing. Likewise, maxReading is used for the same purpose on the other end of the spectrum. This is, after all, a telematic breath, not telematic gale-force wind. To make the sensor even more sensitive, you might try a smaller value for maxReading, like 200. The last variable, fanStart, is the minimum value that it takes to get our particular fan up and spinning. Yours may be different.

```
int analogValue = 0;
```

Our last variable is the container we will use to store and manipulate our analog value obtained from reading our analog input pin.

```
void setup() {
  Serial.begin(9600);
}
```

The setup() function is a little sparse in this sketch. I think I can hear you now: "Hey, wait, isn't something missing?" The short answer is not really, because the analog functions make use of very specific hardware in the Arduino microcontroller, there is no need to set them up using the pinMode() function inside our setup() function. If we try to send an analog signal to a pin that isn't made for it, it simply won't work exactly as expected. So then all we are left with is a function that begins a communication protocol that we can use to let the Arduino talk to us.

```
analogValue = analogRead(sensorPin);
analogValue = constrain(analogValue, minReading, maxReading);
analogValue = map(analogValue, minReading, maxReading, 0, 255);
```

The first three lines of the loop() function are where the magic happens in this sketch. The first line obtains a numerical value from the analog input pin correlating to the voltage our sensor is putting out, which should indicate a general presence of a breath. The second line lobs off unusable values at either end of the spectrum that don't really work for us. In other words, this line limits our activity to the "sweet spot" of the sensor, making it as sensitive as we can get it to a gentle breeze. The third line takes this larger value and remaps it to a more useable range for output to our fan.

```
Serial.print("analog value = " );
Serial.println(analogValue, DEC);
```

These two lines can be used to see what values we are working with using something called the Serial Monitor, explained in more detail later in this chapter. Seeing these values is helpful in adjusting the thresholds defined at the beginning of the sketch.

```
if (analogValue > minReading && analogValue < fanStart)
analogWrite(fanPin, fanStart);
else analogWrite(fanPin, analogValue);
```

Now we reach the business end of the sketch—the part that actually does something. Our fan needs a little kick to get it going at first, so the first line checks to see if we have an analog value that we should do something with, but that might be too low for the fan to work with. In our case, we found that the value 100 is about the lowest number to guarantee that the fan would spin. So if that's true, we will send the minimum number to start the fan out to the output pin.

Otherwise, if the value is greater than or less than our fanStart and minReading values, we will send that value straight out to the output pin. If it's a small number, the fan will most likely not spin. If it's a bigger number, it will spin with greater speed up until it hits the ceiling at 255, which is full on.

```
delay(250);
```

Finally, our last line of code ends with a simple delay() just to slow things down some. Basically, it takes a little bit of time to get the fan up to speed, so a quarter-second pause is good for that. Now what does it all mean?

Analog Functions

The analog functions are a little different from the digital ones. First, as we discussed earlier, they do not need to be set up using pinMode() beforehand. Second, we are dealing with integer numbers that range from 0 to 255 or 0 to 1023, rather than digital states like HIGH and LOW, so we need to keep that in mind while working with them. So anyway, let's proceed onward with a discussion of the analog functions.

analogRead()

The counterpart to the digitalRead() function, analogRead() is equally as simple at first. Its syntax follows:

```
analogRead(pin)
```

When we call this function, we need to specify the analog pin that we are reading data from, in the format of A0–A5. The "A" is placed in front of the pin number to remind us that we are using one of the analog input pins, also marked on the board A0–A5. The reading returns a 10-bit value with a range of integers from 0 to1023 corresponding to the input voltage on the pin.

Also like the digitalRead() function, what we do with this value depends on the context in which we use the function. This includes assigning the reading to a variable to be used later in the code or to use the function in place of a variable. A common usage of this function to assign a value to a variable would appear as follows:

```
sensorValue = analogRead(A0);
```

Or we might use the function inside another. Say for instance, we wanted our pin 13 LED to blink slowly when it was dark and quickly when there was light. With a light sensor connected to pin A0, our code could look as follows:

```
delay(analogRead(A0));
```

Here we will delay for the amount of time as specified by the integer received from analog input pin A0 in an amount from 0 to a little over 1 second. To extrapolate this into a full code example, have a look at Listing 6-2.

Listing 6-2. *analogRead() Example*

```
int analogValue = 0;
int ledPin = 13;

void setup() {
  pinMode(ledPin, OUTPUT);
}

void loop() {
  analogValue = analogRead(A0);
  digitalWrite(ledPin, HIGH);
  delay(analogValue);
  digitalWrite(ledPin, LOW);
  delay(analogValue);
}
```

This is the basic blink sketch, except now the LED will blink slowly when an analog sensor provides a low-voltage reading and blink quickly when the sensor provides a higher voltage reading. This works by adding an analogRead() statement that assigns an analog value to the variable analogValue that we use as a length of time in the delay() function. What analog sensor is used for in this example is up to you, but our wind sensor from our project would work great. So, now that we can read these values, let's look at how can we output analog values.

analogWrite()

The function analogWrite() will allow us to access the pulse width modulation hardware on the Arduino microcontroller. The basic syntax for this function follows:

```
analogWrite(pin, duty cycle)
```

In using this function we need to give it two pieces of information. The first is the pin number, which can only include one of the following pins on the Arduino Uno: 3, 5, 6, 9, 10, and 11. These are marked as PWM on the interface board. Other versions of the Arduino may have fewer or more PWM pins available, so double-check your hardware's documentation. The second bit of information is the duty cycle expressed as an 8-bit numerical integer ranging between the values of 0 and 255. The value 0 corresponds to off or 0% duty cycle and 255 is basically full on or 100% duty cycle. Any value in between these two endpoints provides a corresponding duty cycle approximating an analog output.

It is a common practice to express the duty cycle value using a variable instead of a constant value. One way that we could do this would be to use a for loop, as in the following code sample:

```
for (int i=0; i<=255; i+=5) {
  analogWrite(5, i);
  delay(20);
}
```

This sample code uses a for loop to increment a counter, i, in steps of five beginning with 0 and ending with 255. This value expressed as a variable is then output to PWM pin 5 using analogWrite() followed by a brief 20-millisecond delay. If connected to an LED, this would have the effect of starting with the LED off and gradually increasing brightness until the LED was at full brightness. Likewise, if we used our fan circuit, the fan would start at off and increase in speed until it is spinning at full speed.

We could even combine analog output with analog input, as in the following simple sketch in Listing 6-3.

Listing 6-3. *analogWrite() Example*

```
int analogValue = 0;
int ledPin = 5;

void setup() {
}

void loop() {
  analogValue = analogRead(A0) / 4;
  analogWrite(ledPin, analogValue);
  delay(20);
}
```

This simple little sketch is the most basic form of our source code for the project, although if you try it you'll see it doesn't work quite as well. This code simply takes an analog reading and routes that value to an analog output. Again, there are no statements needed in the setup() function because we are using only analog functions.

One challenge that we face when using a value from an analog input and sending it to an analog output, is that the analogRead() function returns a value in the range of 0 to 1023, while analogWrite() only works with values in the range of 0 to 255. To get around this, when assigning the value to the variable analogValue in the first line of this most recent loop() function, we take the reading from analog pin A0 and divide this by 4 before assigning to our variable. All should work fine because 1024, the total number of possible values in a 10-bit reading, divided by 4 will result in 255, which is the maximum number of values that we can use in the 8-bit PWM function.

Now depending on the sensor we are using on our analog input, this may not result in either the most accurate or the prettiest results. To fix this, we will need to make use of some techniques and functions, some of which were used in our project earlier, to find out what our readings actually are and increase their accuracy, beginning with the next analog function and proceeding on through the rest of the chapter.

analogReference()

By using the analogRead() function, the Arduino assumes a voltage range of between 0v and +5v. Increasingly though, more and more sensors are using lower operating voltages from +3.3v to as low as

+1.8v, and as a result, will only return values up to their maximum operating voltages. The Arduino interface board, however, has a convenient pin called AREF located near digital pin 13 along with a function called analogReference() to give the Arduino's ADC a reference voltage other than +5v. This function will effectively increase the resolution available to analog inputs that operate at some other range of lower voltages below +5v. The syntax for this function follows.

analogReference(type)

The function is only called once in a sketch, but must be declared before analogRead() is used for the first time, making it a suitable candidate for placing in the setup() function. The type specified relates to the kind of reference voltage that we want to use. There are three possible reference voltage types on the Arduino Uno to be used for analogReference(), as listed in Table 6-1.

Table 6-1. *Analog Reference Types*

Type	Description
INTERNAL	Selects an internal reference voltage of +1.1v
EXTERNAL	Selects the external voltage reference connected to the AREF pin
DEFAULT	Returns to the default internal +5v voltage reference

While there are many reasons and methods for using a different voltage reference, many of these get very complex very quickly. The one we are most interested in providing is an external +3.3v reference when we use an accelerometer sensor to detect movement, discussed in greater detail in a later chapter. In order to get accurate readings from this sensor, we will make the following statement once at the beginning of our source code:

analogReference(EXTERNAL);

We will then need to connect the AREF pin to the output pin labeled 3.3V using a jumper wire. This will use the Arduino's Uno secondary onboard voltage regulator to provide an accurate external analog reference of +3.3v. With this setup, it is important to call the analogReference() function before the analogRead() function, or it is possible to short the internal and external voltages—perhaps damaging the microcontroller. Finally, it is also important to remember to never connect the AREF pin to a voltage source greater than +5v because it could also damage the microcontroller.

Analog Serial Monitor

So far, we have made the general assumption that the readings we are receiving from the analog input pins are providing a range of values from 0 to1023, but this is rarely the case, as you can see in our opening project's source code. The reason for this is that every sensor is a little different and will provide a varying range of voltages depending on what they are sensing. In order to better understand the range of values that a particular sensor is providing, we need to create a sketch to give us some visual representation of the values reported by the ADC. Before getting to that, let's back up again and look at a simpler analog sensor, as shown in Figures 6-5 and 6-6.

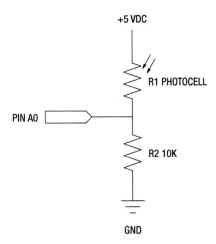

Figure 6-5. *Photocell schematic*

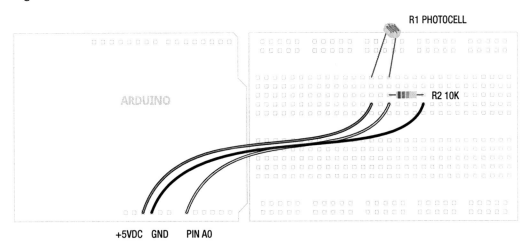

Figure 6-6. *Photocell illustration*

This schematic uses a variable resistor known as a photocell or light dependant resistor that changes its resistance based on how much or how little light reaches it. Photocells will have a maximum specified resistance for its darkness state and a minimum resistance at full light. For best results, the pull down resistor should match the maximum resistance of the photocell, although this is not mission critical. With this simple schematic wired up, we can use it to sense how light or dark it is in our environment. The question remains, how do we know what range of values our little light sensor is giving us?

Reading Analog Values

To find a solution to this problem, we can write a little code to read the values coming from the microcontroller's analog inputs, using several new functions that are part of the Serial library, itself part of the standard built-in Arduino library. Serial is used by two digital devices to talk to each other and is loosely related to a collection of communication protocols that includes USB. We've actually been using serial communications since the very beginning to upload our source code to the Arduino interface board. Now, using the following code in Listing 6-4, we can use the Serial Monitor included in the Arduino programming environment to actually "see" the values that the ADC is reading.

Listing 6-4. Analog Serial Monitor

```
const int analogPin = A0;
int analogValue = 0;

void setup() {
  Serial.begin(9600);
}

void loop() {
  analogValue = analogRead(analogPin);
  Serial.print("analog value = " );
  Serial.println(analogValue, DEC);
  delay(125);
}
```

This little sketch borrows quite a bit from our project sketch from before. It will read the value from analog pin A0 and send that value back to our computer using some of the functions that are a part of the Serial library. In order to see what the Arduino has to say, we need to use the Arduino Serial Monitor to listen to the interface board.

Using the Serial Monitor

The Serial Monitor is accessed through the button at the far right of the toolbar, as shown in Figure 6-7.

Figure 6-7. *Accessing the Serial Monitor*

After clicking the Serial Monitor button, a new window will open and begin displaying anything that it happens to be receiving from the serial connection to the Arduino interface board, as shown in Figure 6-8.

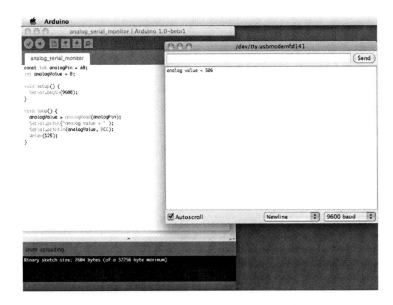

Figure 6-8. *Serial Monitor window*

Inside the Serial Monitor window, we have a large central white space that displays whatever information it receives from the serial port. We also have a text entry area at the top that would allow us to send data out to a serial device. Along the bottom of the window is a check box to enable the Autoscroll feature, an option for the end-of-line character when sending data from the Serial Monitor, and a setting for the speed of the communications between the two serial devices. While we will discuss serial communications in much greater depth in Chapter 10, now that we have the code uploaded to the interface board, and the Serial Monitor is open, let's briefly look at how our code works.

How It Works

To get the Serial library working with the Arduino interface board, and for it to send data through the hardware serial port, we need to first establish the communications speed between the two devices using the `Serial.begin()` function. This is generally done inside the `setup()` function, as was shown in our example code with the following line:

```
Serial.begin(9600);
```

Here, we tell the Arduino board at what speed to establish communications; in this case, our communication speed has been set to 9600 bits per second (bps or baud), a fairly common communication speed for these purposes. Basically, this helps the two digital devices agree on how fast they are going to talk to one another and this matching speed setting should also be selected in the Serial Monitor.

The text in the main window in Figure 6-8 that displays "analog value = 506" is created by the following two lines of code in the `loop()` function:

```
Serial.print("analog value = " );
Serial.println(analogValue, DEC);
```

The first line uses the `Serial.print()` function to tell the Arduino to send down the serial connection the characters "analog value = " with the double quotations signifying that the string of text should be displayed exactly as written. The second line uses the function `Serial.println()`, which is very similar to the first, but inserts a line return after it has sent its information so that the next time we send up a value it will start on the next line. This line will display the current value of the variable `analogValue` in decimal format (`DEC`).

That's about all there is to this simple little sketch. Now, with an analog sensor wired up to pin A0, the source code uploaded to the Arduino, and the Serial Monitor up and running, we should see a long list of analog values being updated every eighth of a second. This is pretty useful for what we are going to do with these values next.

Mapping Values

Once we see what kinds of values our analog sensor can give us, we can then decide what to do with those numbers. Sometimes we might want to drive a PWM pin using the analog input and so will need to change from a 10-bit value to an 8-bit one. Maybe instead of receiving values that we think we should get, like 0 to 1023, we get something more like 12 for the lowest number and 861 for the highest. It's even possible that although we have all these numbers, all we want to do are a few simple things depending on certain thresholds being reached. To make these unwieldy numbers more manageable, we can use several Arduino functions to map the values we get to the values that we want. Let's keep the photocell wired up and look at these functions in more detail.

map()

Previously, to convert from a 10-bit value to an 8-bit one, we simply divided the analog reading by 4 and applied that value to our analog output. An alternative method would be to use the `map()` function, which appropriately enough, is one of the more useful functions for mapping sensor values. There are several ways that it can be used, but let's look at its syntax first.

```
map(value, fromLow, fromHigh, toLow, toHigh)
```

The way it works is that we pass the function a total of five values, beginning by first defining the value that we want to map. This is most often a variable, but could also be a call to another function. It should be a whole number integer value, as floating-point math is ignored after the decimal point. The second and third values are the low and high values that we are beginning with expressed as constants or variables. This is where the Analog Serial Monitor comes in handy, allowing us to better plan for the values coming from our sensors. Finally, the fourth and fifth values are the new low and high values that we want to map the old values to. A good example of this is using `map()` to convert a 10-bit reading to an 8-bit value, as follows:

```
analogValue = map(analogValue, 0, 1023, 0, 255);
```

This statement will take the value from the variable `analogValue` with expected values that begin at 0 and go up to a maximum of 1023, and map these values to the new values of 0 to 255. This line effectively converts a range of values from 0 to1023 to 0 to 255. That's pretty handy for driving an analog output with an analog input.

Another thing that comes up frequently is the need to reverse a range of values. For example, using the code in Listing 6-3, the LED gets brighter when the light in the room is brighter. What if we wanted the LED to get brighter when it actually gets darker in the room? To do this we would need to reverse the range of values so that instead of outputting 0–255 we would flip it to 255–0. The `map()` function can be used to do exactly that.

```
analogValue = map(analogValue, 0, 1023, 255, 0);
```

By flipping the last two values, we are functionally flipping the values that we plan to use from the analog input. We can also use the `map()` function to set up ranges or thresholds of values that can trigger different events. This works well with the switch statement, just like the following code fragment:

```
analogValue = map(analogRead(analogPin), 0, 1023, 1, 3);
  switch (analogValue) {
    case 1:
    ;
    case 2:
    ;
    case 3:
    ;
  }
```

In this fragment, we are taking an analog reading and boiling it down to three possible states. Think of it as near, not too far, and far away; cold, warm, and too hot; dark, just right, and bright. What we do with those three states, I leave up to you.

constrain()

While the `map()` function is useful for changing the start and end values of a variable, it does not limit them to only those values. Leaving values outside of the `map()` function might be handy if we only want to map a small part of a range of values, but leave the rest of the possible values intact. If, though, we wanted to force the values to a very specific, limited range instead, we could use the `constrain()` function. The syntax for this function follows.

```
constrain(value, min, max)
```

The first value is the value that we want to constrain to a specified range. This can be specified as any data type and is not only limited to whole-number integers. The next two values represent the minimum and maximum values in the range.

So hypothetically speaking, if after analyzing our data, looking at the ranges returned by our sensor we find the minimum reported values average around 10 and the maximum tops out at around 900, we could constrain these values before remapping them to a new range. Take the following example code:

```
analogValue = constrain(analogValue, 10, 900);
analogValue = map(analogValue, 10, 900, 0, 255);
```

This code would limit the readings to anything between 0 and 900, ignoring any stray readings that exceed this minimum or maximum, followed by remapping `analogValue` to a more useable range of 0 to 255. Likewise, this same code could be used to, say, ignore readings from a proximity sensor that detects something that is far away, or a light reading beyond a level normally experienced.

Summary

This wraps up the basics behind some of the fun stuff that can be done in an analog world that consists of more than just on and off. You should have a pretty good grasp on how to read an analog sensor, and use these readings to change the brightness of an LED or adjust the speed of a motor. We also talked about how to see these numbers and once you know what they are, how to manipulate them into forms that are more useable for one purpose or another. For a little more information on this subject, you might also check out some of the example analog sketches included with the Arduino programming environment.

For now we are going to move on to a more advanced discussion of functions that includes some functions we haven't discussed before; writing and using custom functions; and a special kind of function that will allow us to stop what we are doing in a sketch and do something else all together. These can be pretty useful as we develop a deeper understanding of writing code. We will, of course, continue to return to both digital and analog functions throughout the rest of the book because they are not only fundamental to what we are doing, but entirely essential.

CHAPTER 7

Advanced Functions

So far we've covered not only the structure and syntax of programming Arduino's C-based programming language, but we've also examined many of the Arduino library's basic functions for reading and writing to digital and analog input and output pins. In this chapter, we will build on this foundation to catch up with some of the more advanced topics surrounding functions, including a look at a few functions that we haven't had the opportunity to cover so far in this book. We'll also cover how to write our own functions, including how functions work, as well as how to use a special kind of function called an interrupt service routine that works with the Arduino's hardware interrupt pins.

Let's begin with a discussion of the timing functions, such as `delay()` and `millis()`, followed by the functions for generating random numbers, before looking at our next project, Ambient Temps. We will then discuss writing and using your own functions followed by a second project, HSB Color Mixer, to demonstrate hardware interrupts in action.

What's needed for this chapter:

- Arduino Uno
- BlinkM MinM smart LED
- TMP36 temperature sensor
- 1 microfarad electrolytic capacitor or similar
- 10 kilohm trimpot or linear potentiometer
- 10 kilohm ¼ watt resistor or similar
- Momentary pushbutton or switch
- Hookup wires
- Solderless breadboard

Timing Functions

Because the Arduino's microcontroller can move fairly quickly, at least relative to what we can perceive, it is often necessary to make use of various delays to slow things down. We have already briefly mentioned some of the functions and techniques used for slowing things down, but this section will go into them in greater detail and provide some examples of why you might look at other methods for creating a delay beyond the standard Arduino functions.

delay()

From the very beginning with our first Blink sketch, we have made use of the `delay()` function to create a short pause in the middle of a program. There's really not a whole lot to the function, but there are some things we need to be aware of. The syntax for the function follows.

`delay(time)`

Time is specified in milliseconds, where a delay of 1000 milliseconds equals 1 second, 2000 milliseconds equals 2 seconds, and so on. This value can be expressed as a constant or variable in the unsigned long data type. Yes, that means as an unsigned long, it is theoretically possible to express a delay of 4,294,967,295 milliseconds, or roughly seven weeks long. In the interest of full disclosure, I have not personally verified this.

The delay time period needs to be expressed in a positive or unsigned value, or the `delay()` function will freak out and do things you would not expect, like rolling over a negative number to a really large positive number—and then you find yourself waiting seven weeks to find out. Likewise, you might, possibly through an arithmetic operation, specify a time delay that is equal to the expression 60 * 1000 in an attempt to create a delay that is 1 minute long. Because both of these values are expressed as signed integer constants, the result of 60 * 1000 is not 60,000 as you might expect, but rather something like -5, 536. This is a little glitch in how these values are processed—because both are signed integers, the result is also expressed as a signed integer.

Since now is as good of a time as any, let's look at how to fix this problem by forcing a specific data type using an integer formatter to get a result more compatible with our function. Table 7-1 provides several integer formatters that pertain to this discussion.

Table 7-1. *Integer Constant Data Type Formatters*

Formatter	Example	Description
"u" or "U"	255u	Forces constant into an unsigned data type
"l" or "L"	1000L	Forces constant into a long data type
"ul" or "UL"	32767ul	Forces constant into an unsigned long-data type

Given our example of wanting to create a hypothetical delay of 60 seconds, or 1 minute, through the expression 60 * 1000, we would need to force one of these constants into a long data type to keep the value in the positive range by tacking on the L formatter, as in: `60 * 1000L`. Because one of the values in this expression is now of the larger, long-data type, results from this expression will remain in the long data type, giving us the value of 60,000 that we were looking for.

Now that we are somewhat aware of problems with excessive delays created by the wrong data types, we can move on to using counter variables in place of integer constants to create a changing delay period. Take the following code sample:

```
for (int i=250; i>0; i-=5) {
  digitalWrite(13, HIGH);
  delay(i);
  digitalWrite(13, LOW);
  delay(i);
}
```

```
for (int i=0; i<250; i+=5) {
  digitalWrite(13, HIGH);
  delay(i);
  digitalWrite(13, LOW);
  delay(i);
}
```

This sample code uses multiple for loops to vary the speed at which the LED on pin 13 blinks. Beginning with a quarter second on and a quarter second off, the first for loop will decrement the counter variable i until it hits 0. Using this variable in our delay() function, we can speed up and slow down how quickly the LED blinks.

delayMicroseconds()

Rather than a long delay, we can use the delayMicroseconds() function to delay for a much shorter time like we did in Chapter 5. As with delay(), there is not much to its syntax, as follows:

```
delayMicroseconds(time)
```

Unlike delay(), time here is specified in microseconds, or millionths of a second, where a time period of 1000 microseconds would equal 1 millisecond or 0.001 of a second, 10,000 would equal 10 milliseconds or 0.01 of a second, and so on. While the value for time is specified as a long integer, it is only known to work up to a maximum delay value of 16,383. Likewise, delays below 3 microseconds don't work reliably either. Instead, use the delay() function for reliable operation for anything over a few thousand microseconds.

Like we did in the Noisy Cricket project to create a different tone, it is possible to use delayMicroseconds() to create a low-tech PWM for pins without PWM available to them. Take the following sample code:

```
digitalWrite(13, HIGH);
delayMicroseconds(100);
digitalWrite(13, LOW);
delayMicroseconds(900);
```

By turning on and off the pin very quickly it is possible to simulate a dim LED, just as we did with PWM except that this time it is on pin 13. In this sample code, in the time span of 1 millisecond, we turn on the LED for 100 microseconds and off for 900 microseconds for a 10% duty cycle resulting in a fairly dim LED.

So that's two simple methods for creating a delay using the built-in Arduino functions; however, the problem with delay functions in the Arduino library is that nothing else can run while the delay is in effect. Imagine a while loop that cycles through for as many milliseconds as we specify and does nothing else other than check the current time until the delay time has passed. Of course, that's not entirely true as some hardware-based functions will still function normally including PWM, hardware serial, and hardware interrupts. Regardless, there is no reason for the Arduino just sitting there doing nothing when we can use it for other things. To create a delay without a delay function we can use something called a hardware timer.

millis()

Inside the microcontroller on the Arduino board there are three on-board hardware timers that work in the background to handle repetitive tasks like incrementing counters or keeping track of program operations. Each of these timers is already being used in one capacity or another, usually for handling hardware PWM and system timing. The millis() function makes use of one of these hardware timers to keep a running counter of how many milliseconds the microcontroller has been running since the last time it was turned on or reset. Because this function uses a hardware timer, it does its counting in the background with no impact on the flow or resources of our source code. The millis() function should look familiar from Chapter 5, where we used it to count button presses.

There is no additional syntax or parameters for the millis() function. By calling the function, it returns a value in milliseconds that can be used like any other variable as part of a conditional test, to perform arithmetic operations on, or assigned to other variables. Because this function returns a value in an unsigned long data type, it will overflow, or reset to 0, in about 50 days. It can also create strange problems if an expression is performed on it using other data types like integers. To make use of the millis() function, we might write a line of code like the following:

```
unsigned long startTime = millis();
```

In this example, we declared a variable called startTime as an unsigned long data type and assigned the current value of millis() to this variable. This way we can keep track of the starting time of some statements or event that might need to be compared to later. Because the delay() function stops all other code from running for the entire time period of the delay, we can keep track of time using millis() to avoid using the delay() function. In way of example, Listing 7-1 provides an alternative blink example that uses millis() instead of the conventional delay().

Listing 7-1. *Blink Without delay()*

```
const int ledPin = 13;

int state = LOW;

unsigned long startTime = 0;
unsigned long interval = 500;

void setup() {
  pinMode(13, OUTPUT);
}

void loop() {
  if (startTime + interval < millis()) {
    state = !state;
    digitalWrite(ledPin, state);
    startTime = millis();
  }
}
```

This example code can be combined with other things—like reading switches or sensors, or turning on motors or other actuators, or creating a pattern of LED flashes all operating at different intervals—and because it does not use a delay() function, everything else in the sketch will continue to work. In our example, it does this by keeping track of the amount of time that the Arduino interface board has been on and compares this to an interval. If the interval has passed, then it will toggle the state of the LED and write that state to the LED pin—alternating between HIGH and LOW each time through the compound statement. Let's take a look at the following few lines of the code:

```
unsigned long startTime = 0;
unsigned long interval = 500;
```

This declares our counter and interval numbers in the unsigned long data type to avoid any weirdness with performing arithmetic or comparison operations using the millis() function.

```
if (startTime + interval < millis()) {
```

This line starts our counter by adding our interval to the start time and checking to see if this value has been exceeded by the time recorded by the millis() function. If millis() is the larger number, then the allotted time has passed and we should execute the enclosed statements. If the interval hasn't passed then we will skip this block of code and continue on to the rest of the sketch, which for this example is empty.

```
state = !state;
digitalWrite(ledPin, state);
startTime = millis();
```

Inside the if statement, these three lines begin by toggling the state of the LED so that if it starts as LOW it will now be HIGH and vice versa. The second line outputs whatever state we are on currently to the LED pin. Then we end the block of code by starting our timer over again, assigning the current time to our new start time.

By having multiple intervals and multiple start times we could theoretically have multiple or even staggered "delays" happening simultaneously with no real impact to any of them. As neat as this is, this technique is not necessarily a better delay() because there will be times when disabling inputs or otherwise stopping the normal program flow is necessary, or if the added complexity is simply not worth it. Debouncing a switch in code, as shown earlier, is one good example where it is necessary to stop reading the inputs for a very brief time just to make sure the signal received was the intended signal.

micros()

Where the millis() function returns the current operating time in milliseconds, the micros() function does the same, but in microseconds. This could be used in exactly the same manner as millis(), just on a much smaller scale, effectively returning the value 1000 for every 1 that millis() would return.

Unlike millis(), micros() will overflow, or reset back to 0, every 70 minutes or so. It also only has a resolution of 4 microseconds on the Arduino Uno, meaning that every value returned by the micros() function will be a multiple of 4.

Random Functions

Armed with a decent grasp of how to handle the Arduino delay functions, as well as an advanced method for creating a delay without one, let's look now at some ways to make things less precise with a little randomness. Up to this point, our timing has been fairly straightforward: turn on the LED, wait for 1 second, turn off the LED, wait for another second, and so forth. Each of our delays has been specified to a relatively accurate degree of precision so that a delay of 1000 milliseconds will be reasonably sure to give us a delay of 1 second. But what if we wanted a delay that was somewhere between 250 and 1000 milliseconds and not only that, but this value changed somewhat randomly every time it is accessed?

This is possible using a couple of the advanced Arduino functions for generating randomness. At least these functions generate something of a form of semi-randomness, which is kind of, sort of randomness. Let's now look at how we can use the random functions in our sketches as a form of timing and for some other uses, as well.

random()

The random() function returns a semi-random number up to the parameters specified. If no parameters are specified, it will return a value in the signed long data type, with a range of -2,147,483,648 to 2,147,483,647. Its syntax follows:

```
random(min, max)
```

The first parameter, if expressed, is the minimum possible value expected from the random() function. This value will be included in the possible outcomes. Likewise, the second value would be the maximum value expected. This value, however, will be excluded from the possible outcomes. So, to generate a random number with 10 possible values you could use the following statement:

```
int randomNumber = random(0, 10);
```

The possible values will include the integers 0 through 9. If this were all we wanted to do, it would be simpler to only specify the maximum value like the following:

```
int randomNumber = random(10);
```

This last statement is functionally the same as the previous one. It is even possible to receive negative random values, although if no minimum has been specified, the random() function will assume a value of 0 for its minimum value. As an example of creating a random delay, Listing 7-2 takes our blink without delay example and adds a single line to create some unpredictability.

Listing 7-2. Random Blink Without Delay

```
const int ledPin = 13;

int state = LOW;

unsigned long startTime = 0;
unsigned long interval = 500;

void setup() {
  pinMode(13, OUTPUT);
}

void loop() {
  if (startTime + interval < millis()) {
    state = !state;
    digitalWrite(ledPin, state);
    startTime = millis();
    interval = random(250, 1001);
  }
}
```

While we start with an interval of 500 milliseconds for the first time through our code (inside the `if` statement), we have added this line at the bottom:

```
interval = random(250, 1001);
```

This will generate a random delay between a quarter second and 1 second by assigning a random value between 250 and 1000 to the variable interval, even though we do not always need to assign the random value to a variable for it to work. Instead, because the function works in a similar way as `millis()` in that it returns a value to the place in the program where it was called, we can use it in place of a variable. Take the following code fragment:

```
for (int i=0; i<=255; i+=5) {
  analogWrite(5, i);
  delay(random(50));
}
for (int i=255; i>=0; i-=5) {
  analogWrite(5, i);
  delay(random(50));
}
```

In this sample code we fade an LED connected to pin 5 up to full brightness and back to off again with a random delay between each step in brightness. By placing the `random()` function with a specified maximum of 50 inside of the `delay()` function, each iteration through the `for` loop will pause for a random time period between 0 and 49 milliseconds.

Generating random numbers in our sketches has so many possible uses that we are only scratching the surface here. One last possibility before we look at how we can make our semi-random numbers a little better, is using the random function to choose one of several possible outcomes using a `switch` statement. Take this modified code fragment borrowed from the last chapter:

```
randomNumber = random(1,4);
  switch (randomNumber) {
    case 1:
    ;
    case 2:
    ;
    case 3:
    ;
  }
```

In this fragment, we generate a random number that includes the possible values 1, 2, and 3 and assign that value to the variable `randomNumber`. Referencing this variable in the `switch` statement will allow for one of three randomly chosen possible outcomes to be chosen depending on the value that was generated.

randomSeed()

Now because our random numbers are only semi-random, the `random()` function doesn't produce the most random numbers—depending, of course, on how you look at it. That's because the Arduino microcontroller—being a stubborn little computer that is fairly deterministic—uses a set formula to create a sequence of values that, while a fairly long sequence, only *appears* random and will inevitably repeat. It also means that each time you power on the Arduino interface board or give it a reset, the random() function will begin with the very same numbers every time. That can be a little predictable. To take this predictability out we need to use the randomSeed() function with a syntax as follows:

randomSeed(value)

By feeding the randomSeed() function a seed value, we can kick off the random generation at a more unexpected point somewhere in the depths of the random sequence. This seed value can be either an integer or long data type while the initial call to the randomSeed() function often happens in the setup() function although this is not entirely necessary. So, consider the following single line statement:

randomSeed(42);

This line is a reasonable example of using randomSeed() to start the sequence off in a little different direction than it would without it. However, with a fixed seed value, in this case the integer 42, the sequence will still repeat exactly the same each time the sketch is ran. This can be occasionally useful, but to make things even more random we can use a reading of a disconnected, or floating, analog pin as our seed value. An example of this would be the following line:

randomSeed(analogRead(A0));

Remember earlier in this book when we discussed how a floating pin is a bad thing? In this case the odd gibberish that we get from reading an unconnected analog input pin is just the thing we need to increase the "randomness" of our random numbers. By placing the analogRead() function inside of the randomSeed() function, and pointing it to an unconnected analog in pin, A0 in this case, we will get a more arbitrary starting point for our random sequence. This also has the benefit that every time the sketch starts over by turning on or being reset, or simply the next time we call the function in the same manner, we will usually get completely different results. Remember, though, that in order for this to function properly, the pin must be disconnected from any circuitry.

Note As of the summer of 2011, the Arduino Uno interface board is available in an SMD edition that features a smaller surface mount version of the ATmega328 microcontroller chip. A little undocumented bonus of this version of the chip is that it has an additional two ADC pins, A6 and A7. While these pins are not accessible on the Arduino pin headers, we can still use them for seed values because they are not connected to anything. The next time you need to use this function, try randomSeed(analogRead(A6)); if you have this version of the board.

That wraps up a few additional functions that we have not previously been able to talk about in a sufficient depth. As you probably have noticed, we use delays of one form or another a lot in our example code and randomness can come in handy on occasion. Let's move on from using built-in Arduino functions to writing our own by looking at our next project, which is followed by a discussion of writing and using functions.

Project 6: Ambient Temps

This project will provide a visual indication of the ambient temperature in our immediate location by pairing a simple temperature sensor with an RGB LED. You might want to embed this project in a glass jar, a lamp, or other object. When it gets hot, our LED will fade to a deep red color; when it's cold, a deep blue color; and when the temperature is about right, the LED will change to green, with all of the colors possible between the two extremes. To make this work, we are going to need more complex color-mixing than we have done previously with seven colors. Rather than make our lives more difficult than they need to be, we will replace our RGB LED with the BlinkM MinM smart LED for this project. The BlinkM is an RGB LED, like we have previously used, that has been coupled with a small Arduino-like microcontroller with some secret software, or firmware, that has been preloaded on the device. This means that the BlinkM is capable of handling all of the color mixing for us using, at least in our example, the Hue Saturation Brightness or HSB color model shown in Figure 7-1.

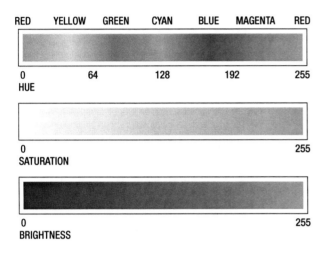

Figure 7-1. *HSB color model*

Again, we have black-and-white images of color models, but if you remember back to Chapter 2 where we discussed the RGB color wheel, HSB handles color values by specifying the colors hue with a value from 0 to 255, beginning with red and rotating through all the colors in the rainbow until we get back to red on the other end. We can also specify a color's saturation (the vividness of the color) and the color's brightness (the lightness or darkness of the color). This will work nicely in our project code because we can keep the saturation and brightness at the same level while fading through multiple colors with red at 0 on one end and blue at 170 on the other.

Hooking It Up

This basic circuit combines the BlinkM MinM smart LED with the TMP36 temperature sensor that comes in a package similar to our transistor from the last project, but with a different pin connection. It's still super-easy to hook up and, once connected to +5 volts and ground, the output pin will provide a linear reading that corresponds to the temperature measured in Celsius, as shown in Figure 7-2.

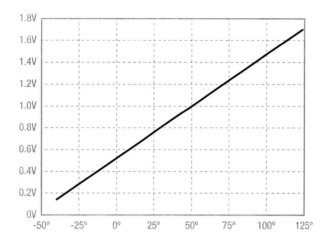

Figure 7-2. *TMP36 output voltage versus temperature Celsius*

The TMP36 has a 0.5v offset that we will have to compensate for, but because of the linearity of the output signal only a little math is needed to determine the ambient temperature to within ± 2° Celsius. There are many other temperature sensors like these that we could use or we could add additional sensors, like ones for measuring humidity or barometric pressure, but we are going to keep it simple for this project. You might also want a little more power out of your LEDs, so you could substitute one of the other varieties of the BlinkM, even connecting a MaxM to an entire string of LEDs. For more information and to download the data sheet and quick-start guide, check out ThingM's web site at `http://thingm.com/products/blinkm/`. Now, let's connect our project, as shown in Figures 7-3 and 7-4.

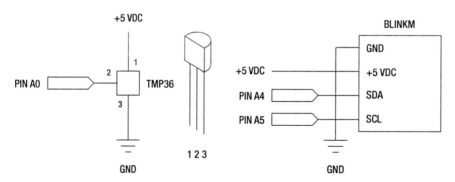

Figure 7-3. *Ambient Temps schematic*

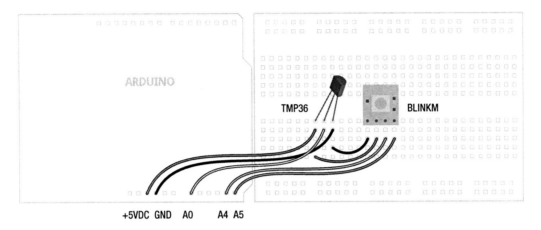

+5VDC GND A0   A4 A5

Figure 7-4. Ambient Temps illustration

Uploading the Source Code

This sketch for this project will serve as a good example of how to compartmentalize our code by writing and using custom functions, which a good part of this chapter is dedicated to. There are three main parts to this code: reading and calculating the current temperature; mapping that reading to a usable HSB color value; and then sending the appropriate commands to the BlinkM to get it to respond with the color that we want. Let's get this project wired up and the source code in Listing 7-3 uploaded, and continue our discussion from there.

Listing 7-3. Ambient Temps Source Code

```
#include <Wire.h>

const int blinkM = 0x09;
const int temperaturePin = A0;

const boolean degreesF = true;

const int hot = 100;
const int cold = 40;
const int hotColor = 0;
const int coldColor = 170;
const int brightness = 255;

void setup() {
  Wire.begin();
  stopScript(blinkM);
  setFadeSpeed(blinkM, 1);
}
```

```
void loop() {
  int hue = map(temperature(), hot, cold, hotColor, coldColor);
  hue = constrain(hue, hotColor, coldColor);
  fadeToHSB(blinkM, hue, 255, brightness);
  delay(10000);
}

float temperature() {
  float voltage = (analogRead(temperaturePin) / 1024.0) * 5.0;
  float celsius = (voltage - 0.5) * 100.0;
  float fahrenheit = (celsius * 1.8) + 32.0;
  if (degreesF == true) return fahrenheit;
  else return celsius;
}

void stopScript(byte address) {
  Wire.beginTransmission(address);
  Wire.write('o');
  Wire.endTransmission();
}

void setFadeSpeed(byte address, byte fadespeed) {
  Wire.beginTransmission(address);
  Wire.write('f');
  Wire.write(fadespeed);
  Wire.endTransmission();
}

void fadeToHSB(byte address, byte hue, byte saturation, byte brightness) {
  Wire.beginTransmission(address);
  Wire.write('h');
  Wire.write(hue);
  Wire.write(saturation);
  Wire.write(brightness);
  Wire.endTransmission();
}
```

Source Code Summary

The first line of our sketch is necessary for using the Wire library that will allow the Arduino and BlinkM to talk to each other using a protocol called I2C, discussed at length in Chapter 10. Since we don't need to worry about that for now, let's jump to the variable declarations and see what they do.

```
const int blinkM = 0x09;
const int temperaturePin = A0;
```

These first two lines set up the locations for the BlinkM and our temperature sensor. The first is an address to identify which BlinkM to talk to. This value comes as the default and if we only use one BlinkM, will not need to be changed. The second line establishes that our temperature sensor is connected to pin A0.

```
const boolean degreesF = true;

const int hot = 100;
const int cold = 40;
const int hotColor = 0;
const int coldColor = 170;
const int brightness = 255;
```

This block of code declares the variables that can be used to configure various settings in our sketch. The first of these turns on Fahrenheit temperatures using true and by using false will revert to Celsius temperatures. The variable hot and cold allows us to specify what we think is hot and cold for our location—hot in London is perhaps not the same as hot in Phoenix. With these values set, any temperature below the cold limit will remain blue while any temperature hotter than the hot value will stay red. Since it is entirely possible that hot being red and cold being blue might be too obvious for you, you can change the values for hotColor and coldColor to establish the two extreme colors in HSB values. Finally, the BlinkM can be insanely bright, so we have an option to specify a different brightness level that will dim the LED without changing its color.

```
Wire.begin();
stopScript(blinkM);
setFadeSpeed(blinkM, 1);
```

Because we are using several new functions in our sketch, the code in our setup() function is a little sparse. The first line starts the communication protocol that we will use for the BlinkM. Again, this will be covered in greater detail later in this book. The stopScript() and setFadeSpeed() functions are two of our custom functions used for setting options in the BlinkM. We'll talk about these in a moment, so let's move on to the code in our loop() function.

```
int hue = map(temperature(), hot, cold, hotColor, coldColor);
```

We begin here with mapping whatever value is returned from the temperature() function, as defined by the hot and cold endpoints, to whatever hue value will correspond to that temperature, as defined by the hotColor and coldColor variables. Because it is possible for these values to end up outside of this range, we will also need the constrain() function:

```
hue = constrain(hue, hotColor, coldColor);
```

This line will keep the LED from suddenly turning pink if the values were to get a little wonky (technically speaking). Once we have our hue value established, we need to send this out to our BlinkM as we did in the following:

```
fadeToHSB(blinkM, hue, 255, brightness);
delay(10000);
```

The function fadeToHSB() will send a command to the BlinkM, telling it to fade to whatever color is specified in the hue that we just worked out; a saturation of 255, although you could play with this number; and the brightness that we established at the beginning of our sketch. We then delay for 10 seconds just to keep the LED from flickering because of small fluctuations in temperature. Now let's look at our functions.

```
float temperature() {
  float voltage = (analogRead(temperaturePin) / 1024.0) * 5.0;
  float celsius = (voltage - 0.5) * 100.0;
  float fahrenheit = (celsius * 1.8) + 32.0;
  if (degreesF == true) return fahrenheit;
  else return celsius;
}
```

The temperature() function is a different data type than what we normally see, so it can return a value that is of the float data type. The first line of this function reads the temperature sensor and converts the values from a range of 0–1024 to a voltage from 0 to 5 volts. To obtain the degrees in Celsius we need to offset 0.5v for the TMP36, as described in the device's data sheet, and then multiply this value by 100.0, as shown in Figure 7-2. Once we have the degrees Celsius, we can convert this value to Fahrenheit by multiplying 1.8 and adding 32. The function ends by checking whether or not we wanted degrees in Fahrenheit and returns the appropriate temperature value.

Our next three functions are used to send specific commands to the BlinkM to change its default settings and output the correct color. The specific commands can be found in the BlinkM data sheet available from ThingM's web site. Our first function, stopScript(), disables the default startup script by sending it the character "o" as follows:

```
void stopScript(byte address) {
  Wire.beginTransmission(address);
  Wire.write('o');
  Wire.endTransmission();
}
```

Our next function is not entirely necessary, but it sets the BlinkM to its slowest fade speed. Each time we tell the BlinkM to change color, it will fade from its current color to the new one. This is a nice little feature and by slowing it down even more, we help make our device more ambient, slowly changing colors in the background. The setFadeSpeed() function will send the BlinkM the character "f" followed by the fade speed with a possible range of 1–255, with 1 being the slowest and 255 being instantaneous. The default speed is 15.

```
void setFadeSpeed(byte address, byte fadespeed) {
  Wire.beginTransmission(address);
  Wire.write('f');
  Wire.write(fadespeed);
  Wire.endTransmission();
}
```

The last function, fadeToHSB(), is what makes things so easy for us and is the reason for choosing the BlinkM over the standard RGB LED.

```
void fadeToHSB(byte address, byte hue, byte saturation, byte brightness) {
  Wire.beginTransmission(address);
  Wire.write('h');
  Wire.write(hue);
  Wire.write(saturation);
  Wire.write(brightness);
  Wire.endTransmission();
}
```

Using this function, we send it four pieces of information: the BlinkM's address followed by the values for hue, saturation, and brightness. The function will send the character "h" to the BlinkM followed by the HSB values, and the BlinkM will work out the math for fading from one color to another.

Well, that was a fairly lengthy overview of how the code works, but we should back up now and look at what's involved in writing and working with functions like those in our project example.

Writing Functions

So far in this chapter, we have seen some additional functions that are part of the main Arduino library, as well as some that we have written. We've also looked at how these functions can extend the capabilities of our code. Functions provide the programmer with the ability to compartmentalize chunks of code that are related by a very specific purpose. We are not limited to only those functions that are provided in the Arduino programming environment, as in fact, writing functions is the bread and butter of writing source code for C and something that any seasoned Arduino programmer will do to make their code function better, take less memory space, make the code better organized, reduce the possibilities for errors, and generally make it easier to read.

The uses for functions are really endless and we have already been using them from the very beginning. Maybe we need to perform certain arithmetic conversions on a particular analog reading. We could write a specific function to perform these tasks for us and return the finished converted values back to the main loop() function. Maybe we want to turn on a set of digital outputs all at the same time or in a sequence any time a certain condition has been met. We could make a function that we could pass a condition or value to and have the function decide what to do with it. For example, let's say we wanted to create a function that will turn on and off the pin 13 LED. That could look something like the following:

```
void blinkLED() {
  digitalWrite(13, HIGH);
  delay(1000);
  digitalWrite(13, LOW);
  delay(1000);
}
```

Now, every time we call the blinkLED() function in our sketch, the pin 13 LED will turn on and off once before returning to whatever the code was doing before. Now, let's looks at exactly what's involved in making these functions work.

Declaring Functions

To begin working with a new function, we need to first declare it. A **function declaration** involves establishing the function's **return data type**, the function's name, and any **parameters** that are being passed to the function bracketed by parenthesis. We will discuss returns and parameters in a moment, but for now you should be comfortable with what a function declaration looks like. In our last example, the function declaration is fairly simple, as follows:

```
void blinkLED() {
```

The keyword **void** is our function's return data type. The name given to our function in this case is blinkLED. This provides an understandable name for our function that tells us at a quick glance what we can expect the function to do. Since we are not talking about parameters at the moment, the parentheses are left empty. Finally, we have the first of two curly braces that enclose the code needed in the function.

Any new function that we add to our sketch must be done outside any other function that we might have, including the `setup()` and `loop()` functions that every sketch using the Arduino libraries will have. For the most part, it really doesn't mater where a function is declared within the sketch, although we often find ourselves usually declaring them after the `loop()` function, more out of habit than anything.

Calling Functions

With a function written, such as our `blinkLED()` function from earlier, we need to **call** the function when we want it to do its job. The thing is, whenever we have talked about a function in this book, we have been calling it in our code. So to call our function, we would write a simple statement like the following:

```
blinkLED();
```

And that is all there is to it. When the function is called, program flow jumps to that function, executes the block of code, and when the function has ended, program flow returns to the next line after our function call. So, building on our new function, if in our `loop()` function we only had the following:

```
void loop() {
  blinkLED();
}
```

This would effectively rewrite our blinking LED sketch by using a function. Each time through the loop, the `blinkLED()` function is called, and inside that function, the LED on pin 13 is turned on for 1 second and turned off for 1 second. When all of the statements inside the function have been executed, program flow returns to the `loop()` function and it all starts over again.

Function Returns

Our example function `blinkLED()` doesn't admittedly do all that much. To make things more interesting, we could ask our function to perform some sort of operation and give us a result back in a nice value that we could then do something with. This act of calling a function and passing a value from that function back to its calling function is known as a **function return**.

In declaring a function, the first thing we need to declare is the function's return data type. For the most part in this book, when a function has been declared, it has been done using the void data type. I know, void wasn't one of the options when we looked at variable data types. That's because it's not really that useful for variables, but when it comes to functions, it's a good idea to tell the compiler that the function being declared will have no value. In order for our function to have a value though, we need to declare a data type that matches the expected value to be returned. Take the following, for example:

```
int readSensor() {
```

Here we are declaring a new function called `readSensor()` of the `int`, or integer data type. Just as with integer type variables, this will give us an expected range of values from -32,768 to 32,767. We can pretty much use any of the data types discussed earlier for variables, including long, unsigned, or even boolean.

Now let's look at how the function can actually return a value. Let's say that we want our `readSensor()` function to not only read a sensor, but to also smooth out our sensor readings by taking 5 samples very quickly, averaging those samples, and returning that value in a format that we can use for PWM. The following is the function:

```
int readSensor() {
  int sensorValue = 0;
  for (int i=0; i<5; i++) {
    sensorValue = sensorValue + analogRead(A0);
    delay(10);
  }
  sensorValue = map(sensorValue, 0, 5115, 0, 255);
  return sensorValue;
}
```

In this function, we first create a new local variable called sensorValue. Then we start a for loop that will loop five times. Each time through the loop, it will add the current sensor reading to the running total and pause for 10 milliseconds just to get a better average. Once we have our new total, we will use the map() function to map our reading to a value with a new range of 0–255. That odd number 5115 is equal to 5 * 1023, or the total value that we could possibly get by reading an analog pin five times and adding all those values together. We could have divided sensorValue by 5 and then divided the result by 4, but the map() function gives us some options to adjust these reading later on. We end the readSensor() function with the return statement, as follows:

```
return sensorValue;
```

This line returns the value of sensorValue back to the calling function. Let's say we had the following statement in our loop() function:

```
int sensorValue = readSensor();
```

This line calls the readSensor() function and returns the final conditioned sensor reading back to the loop() function, assigning that value to the variable sensorValue. In this case, we have used the variable sensorValue twice but that's okay because if you remember, a function's scope is dependant on where it was declared. In each case here, we have declared them locally and so their scope does not extend beyond the function that they were declared in.

In addition to that, a value that is returned by a function is immediately forgotten by that function. We will need to do something with that returned value in our main loop() function or it will be lost to us.

Now we have made the assumption here that we want to use a function return to specifically return a value. We could also use the return keyword to immediately exit a function if a certain condition was met. The following is a hypothetical example:

```
if (sensorValue < 100) return;
```

Maybe we want to ignore readings that are below a certain threshold, so we could use the return keyword to exit a function without returning a value. Here we do that using an if statement with a condition that if true, will result in leaving the function and returning to normal program flow.

Function Parameters

In our last example we assumed that the analog pin being used was A0, but that might be a little shortsighted. Instead we can use **function parameters** to pass data like a pin number to the function, in this case to tell the function which pin to read from. Let's look at that function again, as follows:

```
int readSensor(int sensorPin) {
  int sensorValue = 0;
  for (int i=0; i<5; i++) {
    sensorValue = sensorValue + analogRead(sensorPin);
    delay(10);
  }
  sensorValue = map(sensorValue, 0, 5115, 0, 255);
  return sensorValue;
}
```

Function parameters are kind of like variables, but they are declared inside the parenthesis in the function declaration. Let's look at the following revised function declaration:

```
int readSensor(int sensorPin) {
```

Here we have added the function parameter of sensorPin and assigned it the integer data type. That tells the function what kind of value to expect being passed to it. Elsewhere in the function we can use the function parameter just like we would another variable. We did that in the following line:

```
sensorValue = sensorValue + analogRead(sensorPin);
```

Here, sensorPin will correspond to the function parameter being passed to the function. As long as we make sure that the specified data type matches the value being sent to the function, all should be fine. The following is what the function call would look like in the loop() function:

```
int sensorValue = readSensor(A0);
```

All we have done is given the function call the expected data inside the parenthesis, in this case the pin number we want to get our value from. With this modified function, it will now work for all six analog input pins just by specifying which pin we want to read from as a function parameter.

Now, this example only has one function parameter, but it is also possible to have multiple function parameters as long as commas separate them as we did in our project code with the fadeToHSB() function. It is also possible to specify parameters with any valid data type, not just integers. Remember though, just like a function return value, the parameters passed to a function are only temporary—they will not be remembered by that function once the function ends.

Building on this idea of writing functions, we can use a type of function that is triggered by a condition in hardware called an interrupt. This would be pretty handy for interrupting the code for a short time to perform a specific action. Let's look at a second project, HSB Color Mixer, using the BlinkM again to see how interrupts work.

Project 7: HSB Color Mixer

In this project, we've kept the BlinkM MinM, but we replaced the TMP36 temperature sensor with a pushbutton like we used in Chapter 5 in addition to a trimpot, also known as a potentiometer, although some other variable resistor could work as well. This project will allow us to cycle through hue, saturation, and brightness on the BlinkM to set a specified color. Better yet, it gives us a good excuse for using a special kind of function that uses hardware interrupts, which we will explain in this chapter.

Hooking It Up

The circuit shown in Figures 7-5 and 7-6 adds a pushbutton and trimpot, or other analog sensor, to our BlinkM to make an HSB Color Mixer. We have increased the complexity of our circuit a bit, but each of the components is fairly basic, using principles that you've seen before. We did have to make a slight modification to our pushbutton circuit by adding a small electrolytic capacitor across the positive and negative sides of the pushbutton. Electrolytic capacitors are polarized, so it is important that the white stripe attaches to the ground side of the switch. It's maybe not the best solution for hardware debouncing, but it will work for now, although other options can be found through a quick search online. While we had gotten away without using this before, the hardware interrupt happens so quickly that we need to debounce our switch using additional hardware to slow the switch down a little. This will prevent false readings without using a delay—which is necessary, as you will see in a moment.

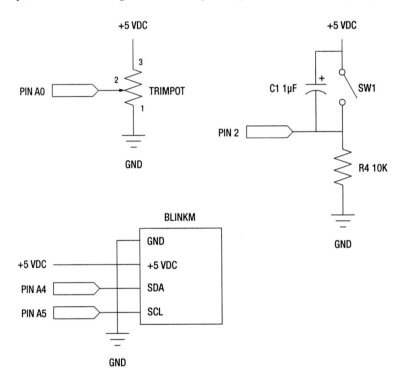

Figure 7-5. *HSB Color Mixer schematic*

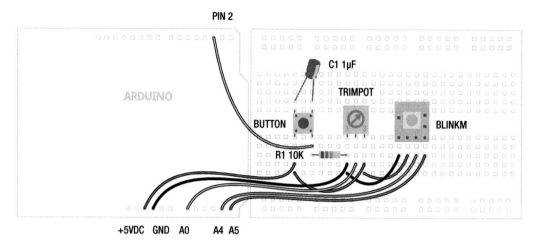

Figure 7-6. *HSB Color Mixer illustration*

Uploading the Source Code

Our sketch for this project will build from the first project code in this chapter, bringing back a few of the functions that we need to control the BlinkM. The source code in Listing 7-4 uses a hardware interrupt and a switch… case statement, so that we will be able to switch through the hue, saturation, and brightness for the BlinkM using the button and the trimpot to set each value. Let's upload the code and see how it works.

Listing 7-4. *HSB Color Mixer Source Code*

```
#include <Wire.h>

const int blinkM = 0x09;
const int buttonInterrupt = 0;
const int analogIn = A0;

int hue=0, saturation=0, brightness=0;

volatile int i = 0;

void setup() {
  Wire.begin();
  stopScript(blinkM);
  setFadeSpeed(blinkM, 15);
  attachInterrupt(buttonInterrupt, selectHSB, RISING);
}
```

```
void loop() {
  switch (i) {
    case 0:
      hue = map(analogRead(analogIn), 0, 1024, 0, 255);
      fadeToHSB(blinkM, hue, 255, 255);
      break;
    case 1:
      saturation = map(analogRead(analogIn), 0, 1024, 0, 255);
      fadeToHSB(blinkM, hue, saturation, 255);
      break;
    case 2:
      brightness = map(analogRead(analogIn), 0, 1024, 0, 255);
      fadeToHSB(blinkM, hue, saturation, brightness);
  }
  delay(50);
}

void selectHSB() {
  ++i %= 4;
}

void stopScript(byte address) {
  Wire.beginTransmission(address);
  Wire.write('o');
  Wire.endTransmission();
}

void setFadeSpeed(byte address, byte fadespeed) {
  Wire.beginTransmission(address);
  Wire.write('f');
  Wire.write(fadespeed);
  Wire.endTransmission();
}

void fadeToHSB(byte address, byte hue, byte saturation, byte brightness) {
  Wire.beginTransmission(address);
  Wire.write('h');
  Wire.write(hue);
  Wire.write(saturation);
  Wire.write(brightness);
  Wire.endTransmission();
}
```

Source Code Summary

Since a lot of this code looks the same as from earlier, we'll keep this summary limited to the new things, beginning with the following variable declarations:

```
const int buttonInterrupt = 0;
const int analogIn = A0;
int hue=0, saturation=0, brightness=0;
```

The first line sets up our interrupt pin, although as will be explained in a moment, this number is not the same as the Arduino pin number that our button is connected to. We then set up our analog input, followed by some variables to set the values for hue, saturation, and brightness. Our next variable, which follows, is a little different:

```
volatile int i = 0;
```

As we discussed earlier, a variable's value is not kept inside of a function that uses it, so we would loose track of which button state we were on unless we told the compiler to save this information for us. We've done that here with the **volatile** variable qualifier attached to our index variable, so that we can keep track of the value—hue, saturation, or brightness—we are currently adjusting.

Our setup function is the same as in our last project, except for the addition of the following line:

```
attachInterrupt(buttonInterrupt, selectHSB, RISING);
```

Here is the function that establishes which interrupt we will be using, the function to call when the interrupt is triggered, and what condition will trigger the interrupt. This will be explained shortly.

Our loop function predominately features a switch... case statement that will adjust the hue, saturation, or brightness depending on the number of button presses. So, beginning with the switch statement and the first case, as follows:

```
switch (i) {
  case 0:
    hue = map(analogRead(analogIn), 0, 1024, 0, 255);
    fadeToHSB(blinkM, hue, 255, 255);
    break;
```

The **switch** statement has been tied to the value of the variable i, which will be incremented later in the code. If i is equal to 0, then case 0 will execute. This case will read the value of the analog input pin and map that value from a range of 0–1024 to 0–255. This value is then sent to the BlinkM using the fadeToHSB() function that will also set the saturation and brightness to their highest setting while we adjust the hue. Finally, we've used the break statement to exit the switch statement without running the other cases.

Cases 1 and 2 will respectively adjust the saturation and brightness, but only when the buttons index had been incremented. Otherwise, for as long as i is equal to a value between 0 and 2, then that corresponding case will run. To increment i, we use an interrupt service routine, which is a special kind of function, as follows:

```
void selectHSB() {
  ++i %= 4;
}
```

This is the extent of our interrupt service routine. It's one and only job is to increment the index variable i by one each time the button is pressed and to keep the numbers to within four possible outcomes, 0, 1, 2, and 3. This line is a little tricky… By placing the ++ in front of the variable i, we first increment i by one before taking the modulo of i and then reassigning the new value back to i. This is a little different from the normal i++ but it's a fairly convenient way to condense a couple lines of code into one.

The rest of the functions are the same BlinkM functions that we used before, so let's skip over these to have a little closer look at how advanced functions work with hardware interrupts.

Hardware Interrupts

With an idea as to what functions can do for us, we can move on to a different kind of function—one that is driven by specific hardware in the microcontroller. The reasons for using interrupts are many; maybe we have a lot of code in our loop() function and sitting there waiting for a button press would slow things down too much or maybe we might even miss the button press all together. Or instead we might be using a photo sensor or interrupter that triggers when something gets close and it is important to stop a motor right at that exact time. These things are possible with a **hardware interrupt** that can be configured on one of two digital pins to trigger a unique kind of advanced function called an **interrupt service routine** (ISR). When the interrupt is triggered, the ISR will be called regardless of whatever the program is in the middle of. Like using one of the internal timers, monitoring of the hardware interrupt pin happens in the background and the jump to the ISR can happen within four instructions, so fairly quickly. After the ISR has been executed, program flow returns back to where it left off before the interrupt and, if done correctly, with little effect on the rest of the code.

An ISR looks a lot like a regular function but there are a few rules that we need to stick to. First, as was shown in our second project code, the ISR should be kept as short as possible, often only three to four lines of code at the maximum, so as to not overly disrupt the program flow and prevent the interrupt from being triggered again while executing the ISR. If we have a longer ISR than that, we need to disable the interrupt briefly while the ISR is running. Likewise, timing related functions would not work properly within the ISR because they use the same hardware timer. For example, millis() will not increment and delay() will not work at all. Other than that, an ISR is declared just like a normal function, but in order to use a hardware interrupt we need to first attach it in our code.

attachInterrupt()

The attachInterrupt() function enables hardware interrupts and links a hardware pin to an ISR to be called when the interrupt is triggered. This function also specifies the type of state change that will trigger the interrupt. Its syntax follows:

```
attachInterrupt(interrupt, function, mode)
```

The first parameter is the number of the interrupt. On the Arduino Uno there are only two possible hardware interrupts, 0 and 1, which correspond to digital pins 2 and 3 respectively. Note that this parameter refers to the interrupt number and not the pin number. The second parameter is the name of the function that will serve as the interrupt service routine that we will want to execute when the interrupt is triggered. Finally, we have the mode that represents the specific state change that will cause the interrupt to trigger. There are four possible modes, as shown in Figure 7-7, which include LOW, CHANGE, RISING, and FALLING.

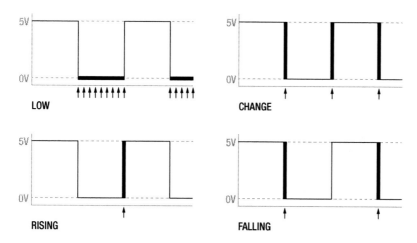

Figure 7-7. State changes

LOW triggers when the interrupt pin is in the LOW state. This mode will continuously trigger the interrupt for as long as it remains in this condition and because of this is not used as much as the other modes. CHANGE will trigger when the state of an interrupt pin changes either from HIGH to LOW or from LOW to HIGH. RISING will only trigger the interrupt when the signal goes from LOW to HIGH while FALLING will trigger on the reverse going from HIGH to LOW. Because of how our example circuit is connected, the button will send a signal of HIGH when triggered so we used the RISING mode to trigger the interrupt when the digital pin's state changes from LOW to HIGH.

Once the interrupt has been properly configured, often but not always in the setup() function, we need to write the ISR function. The function selectHSB() is a fairly good example of a short and succinct ISR. Its entire job is to increment the counter i and keep those values to a possible range of 0–3. Remember though, that in order for us to use the indexing variable i elsewhere in our sketch, we need to first use the volatile variable qualifier at the beginning of our sketch. Because the interrupt could sneak in there and change the value of a variable without the rest of the sketch knowing it, by using the volatile keyword we can tell the compiler to put the variable data in a more secure place in memory to prevent weird things from happening to our number.

detachInterrupt()

With our hardware interrupt enabled, it is possible that in a given application, we might need to change the mode of an interrupt, for example to change it from RISING to FALLING. To do this we would need to first stop the interrupt by using the detachInterrupt() function. Its syntax is fairly straightforward, as follows:

detachInterrupt(interrupt)

With only one parameter to determine which interrupt we are disabling, this parameter is specified as either 0 or 1. Once the interrupt has been disabled, we can then reconfigure it using a different mode in the attachInterrupt() function.

Summary

With that, we wrap up our discussion of advanced functions. Now we know how to create a hardware interrupt and the corresponding interrupt service routine that will cause the Arduino to drop everything and perform the code in the specified function when the interrupt is triggered. We looked at how to write our own functions, which included talking about how functions work along with function parameters and function returns. And, we even checked out a few functions for timing and randomness that we had not been able to discuss properly before now.

From here, we are going to explore a unique type of variable called an array and because inevitably arrays will begin to consume large chunks of the Arduino microcontroller's memory, we will also discuss the different kinds of memory available and how to put these storage spaces to use. This will also bring us into some areas of code not given the full Arduino treatment, so it might be a good idea to take a little breather before we keep going, but I'm sure you'll handle things just fine.

CHAPTER 8

Arrays and Memory

Arrays are an essential part of the Arduino programmer's toolbox. They are sometimes such a necessity that we have already thrown a few in our sketches and projects here and there. Arrays are essentially lists of variables that can contain multiple elements of the same data type. They can be used to store a list of pin numbers, sensor values, character strings, and even bitmaps for animations. While we could have introduced arrays earlier when we discussed variables and data types, the topic truly requires its own chapter to best understand how to use them. Because arrays can consume a large amount of the available memory on the Arduino microcontroller, we should also look at the types of memory space on the microcontroller chip and methods for how to access them, in addition to discussing how to declare arrays, accessing and using arrays, as well as using character and multidimensional arrays. But before tackling arrays in detail, let's jump in with our eighth project, Decision Machine, so that when we get to dicussing arrays in more depth you'll have already seen them in action.

What's needed for this chapter:

- Arduino Uno

- 16 × 2 character liquid crystal display HD44780 compatible

- ADXL335 accelerometer (SparkFun breakout)

- 5mm LED of any color

- 1× 220 ohm and 1× 2.2 kilohm ¼ watt resistor or similar

- Hookup wires

- Solderless breadboard

Project 8: Decision Machine

Holding our completed project in your hands, you might ask it a simple question before giving it a gentle shake and at that moment a forecast will mystically appear from the murky depths of its display. If that sounds familiar, it's because we loosely found inspiration for this project in a classic, sometimes irreverent, fortune-telling icon. Our prototype design uses an accelerometer to recreate the familiar rotate or shake to activate the device, and an LCD to provide us with the short but erudite answers to our imagined yes-or-no questions. To make it interesting, we will use arrays throughout our project to give us something to talk about in this chapter and to demonstrate how arrays work in our code.

Hooking It Up

With only few components to hook up, this project is not overly complex, although you will need lots of hookup wires. To display our fortune, we are using a 16 × 2 backlit character liquid crystal display or LCD. Ours has a black background with bright white text for effect and can display two rows of 16 characters each. This display uses the venerable HD44780 interface controller that has been around for ages, making it super easy to display text using the Arduino. Our circuit is fairly standard, using six digital pins to interface with the LCD with two little differences. First, we need to connect a 2.2 kilohm resistor from the contrast pin marked V0 in the schematic to ground. This pin controls the contrast for the LCD and is usually connected to a potentiometer to allow for manually adjusting the contrast of the screen. By using a single resistor, we keep things a little simpler. Secondly, to add theatricality, we are connecting the positive or anode pin of the LED backlight to PWM pin 11. With the `analogWrite()` function, we can fade the answer in and out of existence to simulate the smarmy answers emerging from the murky depths of the display. As usual, we could substitute many other versions of this LCD in different colors or even sizes, as long as it uses the same interface chip.

To detect the customary shake or rotation of the device after a question has been asked, we will use a 3-axis analog accelerometer, which fittingly enough is a device used to measure acceleration or the change in speed or movement along multiple axes. Our particular version is the ADXL335 from Analog Devices that provides an analog voltage corresponding to acceleration in the X, Y, or Z-axis. Because the chip is so small and not very breadboard friendly, we are using the breakout board available from SparkFun Electronics. This breakout board is the first device that needs pin headers or wires soldered to the device to work with our breadboards. For more on this topic, refer to the section on soldering in Chapter 12 With these in place, the connection is simple enough with an output from each of the three axes to three analog in pins marked A0, A1, and A2. Because this device runs on +3.3 volts we need to connect its positive power pin marked VCC to the Arduino interface board's 3.3V output pin. A number of other analog accelerometers would work just as well, but the code might need to be modified for fewer axes or if the accelerometer used some other communication protocol.

One last thing to be aware of is that to simplify wiring a little bit, we are making use of the ground bus on the side of the breadboard, usually marked by a blue line and a "-" sign. The neat thing about this row of pins is that they connect horizontally along the length of the board unlike the other pins that we have used so far. Not all breadboards have these, so you might need to adjust your wiring appropriately. Remember to take your time with the wiring to make sure the wires go to the correct pins. Figures 8-1 and 8-2 show how to hook up this project.

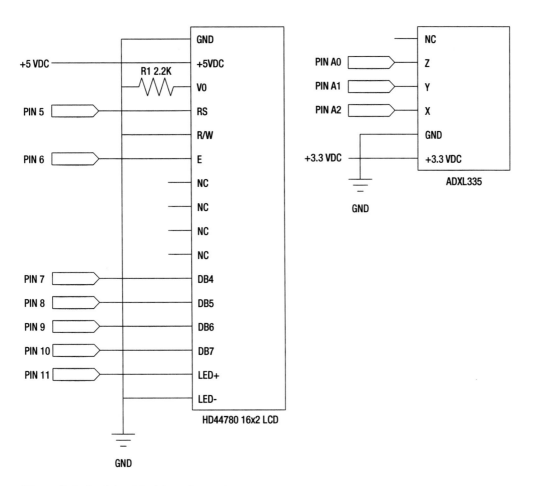

Figure 8-1. *Decision Machine schematic*

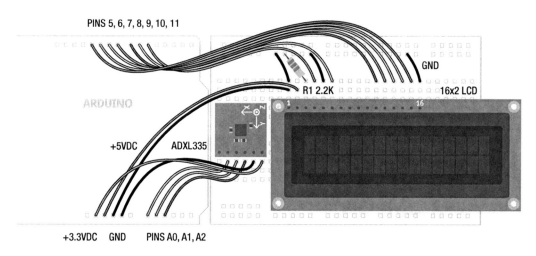

PINS 5, 6, 7, 8, 9, 10, 11

ARDUINO

GND

R1 2.2K

16x2 LCD

+5VDC   ADXL335

+3.3VDC   GND   PINS A0, A1, A2

Figure 8-2. Decision Machine illustration

Uploading the Source Code

While you might think this sketch is a bit intimidating and lengthy, in reality it's not too bad because most of it is white space. Half of the source code is tied up in listing the 20 possible answers that could be displayed each time the device is shaken or rotated. The rest builds on prior projects to come before it by using many of the functions and structures used in past sketches. We've stuck with some answers that might seem familiar as a starting point, but you should definitely make up your own answers. To get things to line up in the center of the screen, each answer is written as two lines of 16 characters using spaces as appropriate to center each line on the screen.

To compartmentalize our code a bit, we have created three new functions. The first function, named getReading(), reads the three analog inputs for each of the axes on the accelerometer. The second, oldReading(), keeps track of the last sensor readings so that we can determine if a threshold has been crossed. Finally, getAnswer() generates a random answer from the 20 possible, gets the message text to be displayed, and then sends that message out to the LCD display. To create a sense of drama, this function will also fade the display up to full brightness and then back again to darkness to simulate the response bubbling up from the aether within. Before we get into how this all works, we need to wire up the circuit, upload the source code in Listing 8-1, and see what happens.

Listing 8-1. Decision Machine Source Code

```
#include <LiquidCrystal.h>

char* allAnswers[] = {
"  As I see it,  ",
"      yes       ",

"     It is      ",
"    certain     ",
```

```
"      It is     ",
"   decidedly so ",

"      Most      ",
"      likely    ",

"     Outlook    ",
"      good      ",

"  Signs point   ",
"     to yes     ",

"     Without    ",
"     a doubt    ",

"       Yes      ",
"                ",

"      Yes -     ",
"    definitely  ",

"     You may    ",
"    rely on it  ",

"  Reply hazy,   ",
"    try again   ",

"     Ask again  ",
"       later    ",

"    Better not  ",
"   tell you now ",

"      Cannot    ",
"   predict now  ",

"  Concentrate   ",
"  and ask again ",

"   Don't count  ",
"       on it    ",

"     My reply   ",
"       is no    ",

"    My sources  ",
"       say no   ",

"   Outlook not  ",
"      so good   ",
```

```
"      Very      ",
"     doubtful    "  };

LiquidCrystal lcd(5, 6, 7, 8, 9, 10);

const int backlight = 11;
const int axisPin[] = {A0, A1, A2};

const int threshold = 60;
const int brightness = 175;

int axis[3];
int oldAxis[3];

void setup() {
  lcd.begin(16, 2);
  randomSeed(analogRead(A5));
  getReading();
  oldReading();
}

void loop() {
  getReading();
  if (abs(axis[0]-oldAxis[0]) > threshold ||
      abs(axis[1]-oldAxis[1]) > threshold ||
      abs(axis[2]-oldAxis[2]) > threshold) {
    getAnswer();
    delay(500);
    getReading();
    oldReading();
  }
  delay(125);
}

void getReading() {
  for (int i=0; i<3; i++) axis[i] = analogRead(axisPin[i]);
}

void oldReading() {
  for (int i=0; i<3; i++) oldAxis[i] = axis[i];
}

void getAnswer() {
  int thisAnswer = random(40);
  while (thisAnswer % 2 != 0) thisAnswer = random(40);

  lcd.setCursor(0, 0);
  lcd.print(allAnswers[thisAnswer]);
  lcd.setCursor(0, 1);
  lcd.print(allAnswers[thisAnswer+1]);
```

```
  for (int i=0; i<=150; i++) {
    analogWrite(backLight, i);
    delay(30);
  }
  for (int i=150; i>=0; i--) {
    analogWrite(backLight, i);
    delay(30);
  }
  lcd.clear();
}
```

Source Code Summary

With that out of they way, we should have an Arduino connected to a breadboard through a slew of wires and … nothing actually happens. That is at least until we shake the thing or turn it upside down when an answer will illuminate briefly before fading away again. Now, let's see how it does that.

Inclusions and Declarations

The first line enables the LiquidCrystal library that gives us some easy to use code for talking to LCDs:

```
#include <LiquidCrystal.h>
```

We'll get to libraries in more depth when we talk about LiquidCrystal among other hardware libraries in the next chapter. Following this line is the first of our declarations:

```
char* allAnswers[] = {
"  As I see it,  ",
"      yes       ",

"     It is      ",
"    certain     ",
.
.
.
"     Very       ",
"    doubtful    "  };
```

This page-long list of curious two-line answers is called a character array and contains all of the possible 20 answers that our Decision Machine might display. Each answer is spaced so that it will appear in the center of the LCD and some extra white space has been added to make each answer easier to read in code at the cost of extra paper. Each answer will be addressed by an index number elsewhere in our sketch. After defining our array of answers, we now need to set up the pins that we plan to use, as follows:

```
LiquidCrystal lcd(5, 6, 7, 8, 9, 10);
const int backlight = 11;
const int axisPin[] = {A0, A1, A2};
```

Like our previous sketches, these lines of code are the I/O pin numbers that we will use with our hardware. The first line tells the LiquidCrystal library which of the pins the LCD is connected to. The `backlight` pin is the built in LED on the LCD that we will fade in and out. Finally, `axisPin[]` is a numerical array that contains the three analog input pins used by the accelerometer.

```
const int threshold = 60;
const int brightness = 175;
```

These two lines are other configurable variables that determine how much movement needs to be detected before an answer is generated and the total brightness in the LCD backlight in the first and second line respectively.

```
int axis[3];
int oldAxis[3];
```

The last of our global variable declarations, `axis[]` and `oldAxis[]` are two arrays that we will use to keep track of which axis has been read and what the old values were the last time we read them. This will help to determine how much movement has been detected in shaking or rotating the device.

setup() and loop()

Our `setup()` function is fairly small:

```
lcd.begin(16, 2);
randomSeed(analogRead(A5));
getReading();
oldReading();
```

We begin with a function that starts up the LCD and tells it how big it is, in this case 16 × 2 characters. We then seed the random function with a reading from analog in pin A5 with nothing connected to it. Next, we take a quick reading from the accelerometer and set these as the old values using two of our functions, `getReading()` and `oldReading()`. We will look at these more after we talk about the `loop()` function.

```
getReading();
  if (abs(axis[0]-oldAxis[0]) > threshold ||
      abs(axis[1]-oldAxis[1]) > threshold ||
      abs(axis[2]-oldAxis[2]) > threshold) {
```

Because we have sufficiently compartmentalized our code using functions, the `loop()` function is also fairly compact. We begin with reading the sensor values first. The second, third, and fourth lines will check to see if our threshold has been exceeded on any axis by subtracting the old values from the newest values and testing the difference. We've used the `abs()` function to get the absolute value of this difference because we could have positive or negative values here, but we only want to know the difference. Using `abs()` saves us from having to also check if the old values are larger than the new values because it's only the amount the values change that we are really interested in.

```
getAnswer();
delay(500);
getReading();
oldReading();
```

If a sufficient amount of movement has been detected then we will launch our third function `getAnswer()` to generate a random message on the LCD. After that has completed, we pause for a half second to give the accelerometer a chance to calm down and then we make another reading and move the new values to the old reading just like we did in `setup()` to create a baseline for our sensor readings.

```
delay(125);
```

The last line in `loop()` is just a short eighth of a second delay to slow things down just enough. You probably have noticed that nowhere in this sketch do we know what the actual values of the sensor are. That's not really important only the amount of change, either smaller or larger, in the sensor value. So, let's look at our three new functions.

Functions

Of our three new functions, the first one that we've used is `getReading()`:

```
void getReading() {
  for (int i=0; i<3; i++) axis[i] = analogRead(axisPin[i]);
}
```

This function is a simple `for` loop that will read each analog pin as defined by the `axisPin[]` array and assign those readings to each of the 3 positions in the `axis[]` array. More on how that works briefly.

```
void oldReading() {
  for (int i=0; i<3; i++) oldAxis[i] = axis[i];
}
```

Like the last function, `oldReading()` uses a `for` loop to assign the current values in the `axis[]` array to the same index positions in the `oldAxis[]` array. This way we can keep track of the old readings so that we can detect when a sufficient amount of change has occurred.

```
void getAnswer() {
  int thisAnswer = random(40);
  while (thisAnswer % 2 != 0) thisAnswer = random(40);
```

Our final function has a lot going on beginning with choosing a random number in the range of 0 to 39. Even though we only have 20 answers, each answer is split into two lines so we want to start with an even number when displaying the first half of an answer. This means that we need to get 40 answers and then using a `while` loop, we can check to see if the random value is an odd or even number. By dividing the random number by 2, we know that we've got an even number when it is equal to 0. If it were an odd number we would start displaying our decision in the middle of our message so instead we have it try again at getting a random even number before moving on.

```
lcd.setCursor(0, 0);
lcd.print(allAnswers[thisAnswer]);
lcd.setCursor(0, 1);
lcd.print(allAnswers[thisAnswer+1]);
```

Once we have a number for our answer, these four lines will print the first line of the answer, move to the second line of the display, add one to our answer index, and then display the second line of our answer.

```
for (int i=0; i<=brightness; i++) {
    analogWrite(backLight, i);
    delay(30);
}
for (int i=brightness; i>=0; i--) {
    analogWrite(backLight, i);
    delay(30);
}
lcd.clear();
```

So far, all of this code has happened and still nothing can be seen on the screen! To actually see the answer, we need to fade the backlight from 0 or off all the way up to the brightness level determined at the top of the sketch. Once we hit the brightness level, we fade it back down to off again and clear the LCD. We could just connect the LED pin to +5v instead, but where would the fun be in that? This little addition to the code creates much more intrigue and theatricality. Try it without it and I bet you won't like it as much.

With that rather convoluted explanation out of the way, let's back up and talk more specifically about how arrays work. We will also look at some different kinds of arrays and then discuss how these arrays affect the memory usage on the Arduino microcontroller. Hopefully after looking at the way the memory works, there will be reason enough for going back to figure out how we can utilize program memory better.

Arrays

At their simplest, arrays can turn a single variable into a list of multiple variables. Another way to look at it is that an array is a collection of common data elements chosen from any of the various data types available to variables. These elements are addressed by an index number that points to a specific data element. We used both numerical and character arrays in our project code to store our answers, pin assignments, and sensor readings. To put an array to use we begin with an array declaration.

Declaring Arrays

Declaring an array is very similar to declaring any other variable. The simplest form of array declaration can be seen in this following example:

`int myArray[3];`

This basic array creates three separate variables referred to in a sketch as `myArray[0]`, `myArray[1]`, and `myArray[2]`. Declaring an array in this manner tells the Arduino compiler to set aside a block of memory that we will fill with data at some point later on. To declare an array, we need at the very least three things: the data type of the array; the name for the array; and either a number surrounded by square brackets, [ ], that is known as the **index**, or a list of values assigned to the array. The index tells the array how many individual variables, or **elements**, is a part of the array. The size of the array indicated by its index in the array declaration is collectively known as the array's **dimension**. In this case, this integer type array has a dimension of three variables that are each addressed individually by that element's index.

Arrays are 0 indexed, meaning that the first element begins at position 0 and the last element in the array has an index that is one less than the array's dimension size. That is why, in our last example in an array with three elements, the first element has an index of 0 and the last element is at index 2. Building on this, we might want to keep track of three digital pins connected to a few LEDs or maybe an RGB LED. In that case, we need to declare the array and assign values to each index in the array, something like the following:

```
int ledPins[3];
ledPin[0] = 9;
ledPin[1] = 10;
ledPin[2] = 11;
```

This example works best in a situation where we need to set up the variable at the beginning of the sketch to set aside a chunk of memory, but we won't know what the values will be until later in the sketch. Maybe we are storing multiple sensor readings and need a temporary place to put them like we did with our project code. If, however, we already know what each element should contain, we could condense the four lines of code down to one, as in this following example:

```
int ledPins[] = {9, 10, 11};
```

Although functionally equivalent, there are two things different about this declaration from the previous example. First of all, this example is missing the index number inside the square brackets that tells us the dimension of the array. That's okay though because it is only necessary to indicate the size of the array when none of the values are being initialized. In this case because we have three values listed, the Arduino compiler figures out that there must be only three elements in the array and sets the dimension accordingly. It's still okay to throw the index in there, and it might be necessary if you only want to initialize a few of the values in a much larger array, but it is not always needed.

Secondly, the three values assigned to each element in the array are declared at the same time by enclosing them in curly braces, { }, and separating each value with a comma. Because arrays are 0 indexed, the Arduino compiler assigns the first value in the list to index 0, the second to index 1, and so on until it has reached the end of the declared values. When all is said and done, ledPin[0] contains the value 9, ledPin[1] the value 10, and ledPin[2] the value 11. We should now take a moment to look at how to access arrays and how we can better use them in our sketches.

Using Arrays

By knowing how to properly declare an array and assign values to the individual elements, we can put the elements to use in a variety of different ways. To begin with, we can use the array just like any other variable except with an index number, as in this following example:

```
digitalWrite(ledPin[0], HIGH);
```

Assuming the previous array declaration with the value 9 assigned to the index of 0, this could be used to turn on an LED connected to I/O pin 9. One thing to mention is that it is possible to refer to an array without the square brackets because the name of the array points to the first element in the array. In that way, both *ledPin and ledPin[0] refer to the same value. Likewise, ledPin[1] is also the same as *ledPin+1. This little trick with the "*" symbol makes the array name into a pointer so that the compiler understands that this is a reference to an index position. Pointers are a more advanced topic that we can't really get into, but it's worth remembering because they could come in handy some time.

Anyway, instead of a number, we can also use a variable in the place of the array's index to access each element using something like a for loop. We have already snuck this in, in a previous example, with the following line of code:

```
for (int i=0; i<3; i++) digitalWrite(rgb[i], HIGH);
```

131

This line is a little tricky, so hang in there. First, we start with a `for` loop initializing a variable `i` with a value of 0 that will increment by 1 each time through the loop or three times until `i` is no longer less than the value 3, when the loop will exit. Each time through the loop we are calling the `digitalWrite()` function to turn on, or make a pin `HIGH`, as determined by the index of the array `rgb[]` that in this case is the same variable `i` as declared in the local scope of this for loop. In this way, the first time through the loop pin 9 is turned on, the second is pin 10, and the third is pin 11, when the loop will exit. This single line of code will turn on three LEDs connected to three different pins almost nearly simultaneously.

Arrays of Values

Let's say that we had previously recorded data from a sensor and now want to use these values to control the brightness of an LED or maybe alter the speed of a motor. To see this in action, let's connect a single LED with a 220 ohm resistor to digital pin 11, as shown in Figures 8-3 and 8-4.

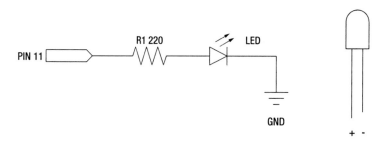

Figure 8-3. *Flicker schematic*

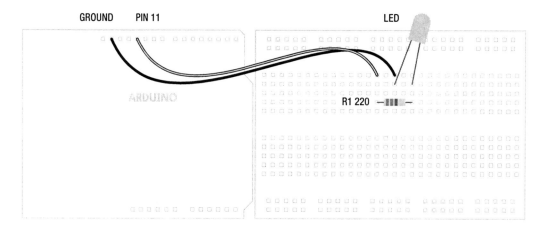

Figure 8-4. *Flicker illustration*

With this connected, Listing 8-2 provides a very simple example of how an array might work to control the brightness of a single LED connected to PWM pin 11 on the Arduino board.

Listing 8-2. Flicker Example Code

```
int ledPin = 11;
int flicker[] = {64, 22, 4, 28, 6, 130, 186, 120};
int i = 0;

void setup() {
  randomSeed(analogRead(A5));
}

void loop() {
  analogWrite(ledPin, flicker[i]);
  delay(random(100, 500));
  i++;
  if (i == (sizeof(flicker)/2)) i = 0;
}
```

This short but compact example sketch will flicker an LED at varying brightness levels as set by data stored in the flicker[] array with a delay between each value. Using the random functions discussed earlier in this chapter, this delay will be randomly determined to be between a tenth to one half of a second in length. The array flicker[] contains eight elements with values between 0 and 255 previously collected from wind speed data. More data would create a better effect but we kept it small for this example. Using actual data in this case instead of randomly generated numbers is essential to creating a more lifelike behavior that makes our flickering LED even more candle-like.

Inside the loop() function, we write the value of each element to the ledPin, in this case pin 11, beginning with the first element at index 0. By using the random() function inside the delay() function, we create a random pause of varying lengths to make things a little more unpredictable. Each time through loop(), the variable i is incremented by one to advance the array index one step moving to the next brightness level.

So our last line in this sketch will perform a simple test to check if our counter i has reached the end of our array, whatever size it might be, and if so it will reset our counter to the value 0. In this way, we start with the value at the beginning of the list, which is 64, and continue each time through the loop until we hit the last value at index 7, which in this case is 120, before starting all over again with the first value. This is pretty useful so we can add values to our array as much as we want either manually through adding extra values in our code, or through storing a multitude of sensor readings in the loop.

Array Limits and sizeof()

We should probably back up a bit here and explain a little more about the limits of an array. It is really important that we are careful to not access an array beyond the number of elements declared in the array's dimension, whether explicitly declared by us in the declaration of the array or implicitly declared by the Arduino compiler counting the values assigned to the array. For example, in Listing 8-2 if we tried to access a ninth element of the flicker[] array at index 8, which does not exist, we would be reading from parts of the program memory that might be in use by other things. Needless to say, this can cause weird things to happen. Just remember that Arduino C has no way to cross-check our array declarations and would allow us to exceed the boundaries of our arrays. It becomes our responsibility to make sure that any calls to an array stay within its dimension.

To be sure we did not exceed the limits of the array's dimension in Listing 8-2, we needed a way at the end of the main loop to know when we reached the end of the array. To do this, we brought in a nice little utility function in the Arduino library called sizeof(). This function will return the total number of bytes used in an array. Because we have an array of the integer data type, sizeof() will return twice the number of elements than are actually in the array. When we perform the operation sizeof(flicker)/2 we will get the value 8. This can be pretty handy for updating the number of elements in an array and not breaking anything in our code in the process.

Assigning Array Values

So far we have looked at various ways to pull data stored in an array using indexed elements. It's also possible to use a for loop to place multiple values into an array, very much like we did with our project source code. Take the following example:

```
int analogIn[6];
for (int i=0; i<6; i++) analogIn[i] = analogRead(i);
```

Here in the first, line we initialize an array called analogIn[] with a dimension of six elements, but we don't yet know what the values will be for each element. In the next line, we use a for loop to step through each of the six analog in pins, assigning a reading from each pin to each element in the array respectively. By placing these values into a single array, we can access those values in a multitude of ways later in our code.

Character Arrays

In the last few pages, each of our arrays has been used to store numerical data but it is also possible to store strings of text in an array, like we did earlier with the answers from our code in Project 8. A simple character array might look like the following:

```
char helloWorld[] = "Hello, world!";
```

This array is an example of C-style text strings of the char data type and contains the text Hello, world! The Arduino team has recently added a String object that offers more advanced functionality, but that's not really needed here. Essentially, the string of text is a collection of 14 elements as each letter of the string is stored as a separate element in the array. There are technically 14 elements even though there are only 13 characters, because all text strings need a final null character or 0 byte to tell any of the other functions where the string ends. Without this, functions like Serial.print() would continue to access parts of the memory that are used by other things. Fortunately, the Arduino compiler takes care of this for us adding the null character and determining the proper dimension of the array. If somehow we were to define the dimension of an array without considering this null character, the weird things will return and cause some unusual problems with our code.

Because each letter or character in a string of text is an individual element in a larger array, we could declare this array as follows:

```
char helloWorld[] = {'H', 'e', 'l', 'l', 'o', ',', ' ', 'w', 'o', 'r', 'l', 'd', '!'};
```

While functionally the same, I can tell you the second one was no fun to type. You might notice that individual characters declared in a character array use the single quotes as in 'H' where as the text string is defined in double quotes as in "Hello, world!" instead. It is even possible to create an array of text strings as follows:

```
char* helloWorld[] = {"Hello,", "world!"};
```

Because text strings are basically arrays of characters, in this example an array of strings would then be effectively an array of arrays. For this to work properly we need to bring back the "*" symbol mentioned briefly earlier for pointers in the declaration of the data type as `char*` letting the Arduino compiler know that we intended for this to be an array of strings. We used a character array in this manner in our Decision Machine project code like the following:

```
char* allAnswers[] = {
"  As I see it,  ",
"      yes        ",
.
.
.
```

With all 20 answers declared in a similar fashion, this declaration creates an array of character strings to be displayed on our liquid crystal display. Remember, the Arduino compiler doesn't care if we put our strings in a block like this or put everything all on one line—it's personal choice really. So before we bother with some of the problems with enormous character arrays, let's look at using multidimensional arrays first.

Multidimensional Arrays

While we will usually only need arrays that are one-dimensional like the ones we have discussed so far in this chapter, Arduino C allows for arrays with any number of dimensions. Think of these as arrays of arrays similar to the character arrays used in Project 8, as in the following, for example:

```
int myArray[2][3];
```

This is a two-dimensional array, where `myArray[0]` is an array of three integers and `myArray[1]` also contains three integers combined in one multidimensional array. Multidimensional arrays are declared by simply adding an additional index in square brackets for each extra dimension, just like the earlier example. To determine how many elements a multidimensional array contains, we just need to multiply the dimensions of the array, so in this case `2 * 3 = 6` total elements. These elements are as follows:

```
myArray[0][0]
myArray[0][1]
myArray[0][2]
myArray[1][0]
myArray[1][1]
myArray[1][2]
```

To assign a value to an element in a two-dimensional array, we would just need to know the position or location of each dimension to a specific element, as in this example:

```
myArray[1][2] = 42;
```

This statement assigns the value 42 to the last element in our example array, remembering that arrays are 0 indexed. We can also assign values to a multidimensional array at the time we declare it, just like the one-dimensional arrays earlier.

```
int arrayTwo[2][2] = {{1, 2}, {3, 4}};
```

Unlike one-dimensional arrays, we should specify each array's dimension even if we are assigning values in the declaration, although strictly speaking, the first dimension does not have to be explicitly declared. With this new array, called **arrayTwo**, we have two arrays with two elements each for a total of four elements. The values for each array are separated by commas and bracketed with curly braces like normal arrays, but commas also separate each individual array and the whole thing has a pair of curly braces. In this way arrayTwo[0][0] == 1, arrayTwo[0][1] == 2, arrayTwo[1][0] == 3, and arrayTwo[1][1] == 4 are all true. You can think of a two-dimensional array as a tiny spreadsheet with rows and columns of data. We can even rewrite this array declaration as follows:

```
int arrayTwo[2][2] = {
  {1, 2},
  {3, 4}
};
```

Because white space doesn't count, we can use it to lay our code out in a way that makes sense to us. In this case we put the values together in a little table. Building on this idea, two-dimensional arrays are particularly useful on the Arduino for creating patterns or animations using a row or grid of LEDs. Imagine that we have 6 LEDs each individually connected to pins 2–7 and ground. We could set up an array to declare the pin numbers like so:

```
int ledPins[] = {2, 3, 4, 5, 6, 7};
```

And then we could use a multidimensional array to create an animation pattern:

```
int pattern[3][6] = {
  {0,0,1,1,0,0},
  {0,1,0,0,1,0},
  {1,0,0,0,0,1}
};
```

Ones are used to represent on or HIGH and zeros are off or LOW. This pattern could then be used to create an animation fitting for a Cylon with LEDs that light up in the middle and expand to the outside LEDs. To make it work, we would use something like the following code fragment:

```
for (int x=0; x<3; x++) {
  for (int y=0; y<6; y++) {
    digitalWrite(ledPins[y],  pattern[x][y]);
  }
  delay(250);
}
```

Here we have two nested for loops, the first is used to increment through the three possible animations using the x counter. The second for loop increments the y counter six times and uses that counter to both increment each element in the ledPin[] array, as well as each of the six elements in the animation arrays. This way when we use the digitalWrite() function, ledPins[y] will set each of the six pins to whatever state is in pattern[x][y]. So beginning with the first loop, x == 0, then the second loop begins with y == 0, so the led at index 0 or pin 2 is set to the condition of pattern at index 0,0, which is 0 or LOW. The counter y is incremented so that y == 1, so the LED at index 1 or pin 3 is set to the condition of pattern at index 0, 1, which is also LOW. y is incremented again, turning pin 4 to the condition at pattern[0][2], which in this case is 1 or HIGH. This repeats until each of the six LEDS has been turned on or off according to the first pattern. All of this happens in rapid succession and if it weren't for the short delay to slow things down when the y loop has completed, we would only see the briefest flicker. Once the delay is over, the x loop is incremented and the y loop begins again with a new pattern.

This is only the briefest introduction to multidimensional arrays. We could use three-dimensional arrays to create a whole set of animations for an 8 × 8 LED matrix or to store the X, Y, and Z readings from an accelerometer. Maybe we could display an entire series of information on an LCD for things labeled with RFID tags. But before we find any more things to fill up the memory of the Arduino interface board we need to know more about how that memory works in the first place.

Arduino Memory

The challenging thing with arrays is that they can begin to fill up a relatively enormous amount of memory space. For example, if you look at programming arrays in C for a desktop computer, programmers will often use massive data strings in their arrays to take advantage of all of that RAM and hard-drive memory space. Unlike a computer, our microcontroller has to be programmed differently because it only has a very, very small amount of memory in comparison and arrays take up a lot of that memory space. For example, every letter in a character array takes up one byte of memory so a single 32-character message, like the ones we used in our project code, is going to take up 34 bytes of memory when it is split into two arrays. This can quickly add up and create some problems for us if we don't first know a little bit about how memory is structured on the Arduino microcontroller.

There are three separate types of memory found inside the Atmel ATmega328 microcontroller used on the Arduino Uno interface board. These are shown in Table 8-1.

Table 8-1. *Arduino Memory*

Memory	Size	Storage	Use
Flash	32,768 bytes	non-volatile	Stores the program source code and Arduino bootloader
SRAM	2048 bytes	volatile	Operating space for accessing variables and functions
EEPROM	1024 bytes	non-volatile	Permanent storage for user data like readings or settings

The largest chunk of memory on the microcontroller is flash or program memory. The ATmega328 has a total capacity of 32,768 bytes available to store program instructions, compiled from our source code, with roughly 500 bytes taken up by the Arduino bootloader. The bootloader is a small program that makes programming the microcontroller through a serial port possible rather than requiring additional hardware. Once source code has been uploaded to the microcontroller, its data is read-only and cannot be modified by the running code. It is also a non-volatile memory type meaning that the program stored in this memory is retained even when power is no longer present or the board has been reset.

The program memory is kept in a separate space from the random access memory or RAM—technically this is static or SRAM but it doesn't really matter—that is used for storing data and various microcontroller instructions like keeping track of function calls while the microcontroller is running. The ATmega328 has 2048 bytes of RAM, which gets gobbled up pretty quickly with global variables, arrays, and text strings. This memory type is volatile, so any data in RAM will be lost when the power has been turned off. During a normal operation, an instruction is fetched from the program memory and loaded into RAM to be executed. In this way, local variables are only loaded into RAM for the duration that they are needed while global variables stay in RAM for the entire running time. We will look at some of the problems this can create in a moment.

The final type of memory on the ATmega328 microcontroller is the 1024 bytes of EEPROM; short for electronically erasable program read-only memory. This memory is also non-volatile, keeping its data even when power is not present, although unlike flash memory, EEPROM has a limited life span where it can only be reprogrammed up to about 100,000 times before it becomes unusable. EEPROM is a byte addressable memory, making it a little trickier to put into use if we are not using a byte data type for our data and it requires its own library to be accessed in our code.

Now that we have an idea of what we're working with, let's count some bytes. We just mentioned how a single 32-character message when stored in an array will occupy 34 bytes of memory. When multiplied by the 20 total possible answers for our project, this single character array would consume not only 680 bytes of program memory, but when the program starts it will load this array into RAM, taking another 680 bytes of the available RAM space, as well. By the time we add in the rest of the variables and other data used by the program, we would only be left with 1043 bytes of RAM. And that's for our relatively basic example source code; as it is, by using that large of a character array, it would not have been possible to run this code on one of the Arduino Uno's predecessors that uses the ATmega168 with half as much total RAM space. Anything coded more complex with additional strings, or multiple variables, would quickly run out of RAM leading to intermittent operation and strange behavior.

Checking Free RAM

The kicker is that running out of RAM can happen at any time with absolutely no warning. When we upload our source code to the program memory on the interface board, the Arduino programming environment conveniently tells us the binary sketch size out of the maximum program memory, as in `6114 bytes (of a 32256 byte maximum)`, but we have no idea how much RAM is actually in use. Fortunately, Jean-Claude Wippler of JeeLabs wrote a small function, shown in Listing 8-3, that we can drop into a sketch to find out how much RAM is currently unused.

Listing 8-3. *freeRAM() Function Source Code*

```
int freeRAM() {
  extern int __heap_start, *__brkval;
  int v;
  return (int) &v - (__brkval == 0 ? (int) &__heap_start : (int) __brkval);
}
```

This function uses some of that ridiculous non-Arduino code that we really don't need to understand in depth, so we will just run with it. To make it work, all we need to do is drop this function into a sketch with a function call, and then open the Serial Monitor so that we can see our RAM usage. Here in Listing 8-4 is a slightly absurd example using the Blink sketch to see that even this very simple program takes 212 bytes of RAM.

Listing 8-4. *Sample freeRam() Usage*

```
int ledPin = 13;
int time = 1000;

void setup() {
  pinMode(ledPin, OUTPUT);
  Serial.begin(9600);
  Serial.println("\n[memCheck]");
  Serial.println(freeRAM(), DEC);
}
```

```
void loop() {
  digitalWrite(ledPin, HIGH);
  delay(time);
  digitalWrite(ledPin, LOW);
  delay(time);
}

int freeRAM() {
  extern int __heap_start, *__brkval;
  int v;
  return (int) &v - (__brkval == 0 ? (int) &__heap_start : (int) __brkval);
}
```

In this sample code, we tossed in the freeRAM() function at the bottom of our sketch and in our setup() function we set up serial communications and sent the text string [memCheck] followed by the value of free RAM as returned by the freeRAM() function. After uploading the source code, open up the Serial Monitor to see the unused amount of RAM. This could be a fairly useful function to have in the toolbox when using large arrays or text strings or just trying to track down some unusual problems with our code.

Armed with a basic understanding of the memory types and structure on the Arduino microcontroller and how we might check the free RAM space in our code, let's look at a couple of the libraries used to access some of the other types of memory space. We might even consider a method for rewriting our project code to save a little memory.

Using Program Memory

Instead of using a character array like we did in Project 8 that gets loaded into RAM memory, we could use the pgmspace library that is a part of the standard avr-libc library to keep read-only data stored only in program memory. The benefit to keeping large variables, arrays, or text strings in program memory is that when the program starts, this read-only data is not loaded into the RAM space.

The challenge with this library is that it has not been given the full Arduino treatment, so it's only really worth the hassle of dealing with the more difficult code when we absolutely need to store large chunks of data. It is also a two-step process that requires some extra functions to properly store the data to begin with and then again to read the data in program memory so that we can actually use it. Let's focus this all-too-brief discussion on how we could use program memory to rewrite our project code and save a little memory in the process.

To begin with, we need to let the Arduino compiler know that we want to use the program memory functions that are not a part of the standard Arduino library by specifying the following line at the beginning of our code:

```
#include <avr/pgmspace.h>
```

The easiest way to keep a string in program memory and not in RAM is to use the PROGMEM variable qualifier, like in the following example:

```
const char message[] PROGMEM =
"This message is held entirely in flash memory.";
```

This wouldn't work for our project code because we want to create an array of strings, which is not entirely supported by the pgmspace library. To get around this, we could make multiple character arrays that are stored in program memory, as follows:

```
prog_char ans01a[] PROGMEM = "  As I see it   ";
prog_char ans01b[] PROGMEM = "      yes       ";

prog_char ans02a[] PROGMEM = "     It is      ";
prog_char ans02b[] PROGMEM = "     certain    ";
.
.
.
prog_char ans20a[] PROGMEM = "      Very      ";
prog_char ans20b[] PROGMEM = "    doubtful    ";
```

You'll have to imagine the rest of the character arrays declared in a similar manner. Once this is done, we would need to create a lookup table for each one of these messages, as follows:

```
const char* allAnswers[] PROGMEM = {
  ans01a, ans01b, ans02a, ans02b, ans03a,
  ans03b, ans04a, ans04b, ans05a, ans05b,
  …
```

While we have chopped out most of the array to save paper, this part of the code looks more like the previous example array message[]. This array is set up as a pointer to each of the possible messages and would be accessed later in our code with the following line:

```
strcpy_P(buffer, (char*)pgm_read_word(&(allAnswers[thisAnswer])));
```

And here is more of that avr-libc voodoo that we are only going to briefly look at. The strcpy_P() function will copy a target string stored in program memory to a location in RAM memory. In this case we would need to declare an array named buffer[] with a dimension of 30 to temporarily store each individual line of text in RAM. This line then uses the pgm_read_word() macro to access the program memory that stores the array of messages specified in the allAnswers[] array at the location given by the variable thisAnswer to get a string of text. Dump all of that into the buffer array and it can be used by the Arduino functions, including lcd.print(), just like nothing happened. That may not make a whole lot of sense right now, but just remember that sometimes it is necessary to store large arrays of text and this is about the only way to do it without having RAM problems. There is hope because you can pretty much copy this structure verbatim and swap out the array and variable names, as well as the text strings to suit the project at hand whenever you need to.

For more on using PROGMEM on the Arduino, you can start with the Arduino web site at the top of the following list, followed by the avr-libc documentation and a helpful tutorial for putting this stuff in action.

- www.arduino.cc/en/Reference/PROGMEM

- www.nongnu.org/avr-libc/user-manual/group__avr__pgmspace.html

- www.teslabs.com/openplayer/docs/docs/prognotes/Progmem%20Tutorial.pdf

Using EEPROM

Unlike program memory, it's fairly easy to store data in the microcontroller's internal EEPROM, although we have to worry a little about the maximum 100,000 or so read/write cycles before the EEPROM stops working. EEPROM stores data in 1-byte sections with the Arduino Uno storing up to 1024 bytes. Listing 8-5 revisits that flicker sketch from earlier, but this time it puts the brightness levels into EEPROM first and reads the data from that memory instead of the array.

Listing 8-5. *Flicker from EEPROM Source Code*

```
#include <EEPROM.h>

boolean writeEEPROM = true;

int ledPin = 11;
byte flicker[] = {64, 22, 4, 28, 6, 130, 186, 120};
int i = 0;

void setup() {
  randomSeed(analogRead(A5));
  if (writeEEPROM == true)
    for (int i=0; i<(sizeof(flicker)/2); i++)
      EEPROM.write(i, flicker[i]);
  i = 0;
}

void loop() {
  analogWrite(ledPin, EEPROM.read(i));
  delay(random(100, 500));
  i++;
  if (i == (sizeof(flicker)/2)) i = 0;
}
```

To read and write data to the EEPROM, we need to use the EEPROM library. This is not included by default in our sketches so we have to use the following line to access the EEPROM functions:

```
#include <EEPROM.h>
```

We have also added the following line:

```
boolean writeEEPROM = true;
```

Since we only need to write the data once, this will allow us to upload and run the code once, then change this variable to false, re-upload the code, and this time it will only read the EEPROM data. That will keep us from using up our total read/write cycles too quickly. The values in the flicker[] array stay the same, but we changed the data type to byte because it is easiest if the information we want to store is already a byte data type. To store the data the first time, we use the following block of code:

```
if (writeEEPROM == true)
    for (int i=0; i<(sizeof(flicker)/2); i++)
      EEPROM.write(i, flicker[i]);
```

This loop, only activated when the variable writeEEPROM is set to true, increments through a for loop until the end of the array has been reached, in this case eight times, although we could easily add more elements. Each time through the loop we use the EEPROM.write() function that has the following syntax:

```
EEPROM.write(address, value)
```

The address can be a number from 0 to 1023 corresponding to the location of each byte in memory space, and the value is a number between 0–255. In our example, we start with the first EEPROM location, 0, and write the value of flicker[] at index 0. The loop increments each time, writing the next value in the array to the next space in memory until it has reached the end of the array.

```
analogWrite(ledPin, EEPROM.read(i));
```

This is the last line of code that we changed. Instead of writing the value of the `flicker[]` array to the analog pin, we instead read from each of the EEPROM addresses and write that value. The syntax for the `EEPROM.read()` is pretty simple, as follows:

`EEPROM.read(address)`

All we need to do is specify the EEPROM address that we want to read the data from, a number from 0–1023, and that value will be returned back. And that concludes the quick rundown on reading and writing data to our microcontroller's EEPROM. It's probably not the best example because our constant reading of the brightness values will potentially use up our read/write lifetime in about 10 hours, causing our EEPROM to stop working, so I don't recommend leaving the sketch running for too long.

Instead, the EEPROM is a good place to store sensor readings every minute or so over a few hours for a low-cost data logger. Because the memory is non-volatile and is not used by the Arduino otherwise, this data will remain in memory regardless of power or additional code being loaded in program memory. Only until a running program overwrites the data, the EEPROM data will persistently stick around. This is also a good reason for storing certain configuration settings that might need to get dialed in while the code is running, but if the power is reset or the program is reloaded we would still want those settings to remain. The BlinkM from the last chapter uses its EEPROM to store similar configuration settings.

Summary

If you're still hanging on after some of that less-than- friendly code, then good for you. Anytime I have to dredge through any of that fringe stuff that hasn't already been brought into the Arduino fold, I am plenty thankful for everything that has already been wrapped up for us. Arrays are a pretty useful tool in our Arduino projects and we could use two chapters to get through everything that can be done with them, but we still have more things to talk about. Arrays work to make all manner of lists of things from pin numbers, to output levels, sensor readings, and even text messages. They can be rolled into loops and functions with amazing ease because of their indexed data elements. We just need to be careful how we handle our memory usage when using them and stay on the lookout for strange behavior that might be caused by limited RAM.

Next up, we are going to look at a few more libraries written for particular hardware and devices that add functionality to the Arduino platform. We'll begin by revisiting the `LiquidCrystal` library before moving on to a couple of other libraries for different types of motors before ending the chapter with finding another way to store lots of data on a convenient memory card. What's important here is that we are now going to get back to making things move again, so the next chapter should be a lot of fun!

CHAPTER 9

Hardware Libraries

In this chapter we are going to take a bit of a breather on the lengthy code and look at some specific hardware and the appropriate libraries used to make them work. A library is a collection of functions designed to perform specific tasks that make life easier for us. Most of what we have discussed in this book so far, like the functions `digitalWrite()` or `delay()`, are a part of the standard Arduino library. These things are so integrated into the way that we write code for the Arduino that we don't even notice it.

The hardware libraries that we will discuss in this chapter are not a part of the standard, built- in functions because they would take up too much memory. Instead, each library must be added to our sketch when we want to use the extra functionality that it provides. Each library is usually written for a particular type of hardware, so in order to use each of these libraries, we need to have a lot of different hardware available. We have tried to keep our hardware selections to simple and cost-effective choices in order to make trying each of these libraries a possibility. Rather than one or two monstrous projects for the chapter, we will instead look at four smaller examples that put to use the functions described in each section. Beginning with an overview of that library, we will also have an example schematic and illustration, some sample source code, and a breakdown of the main functions in that library. Our code will be kept fairly light so that each mini-project could be used as a building block for something bigger.

This chapter is by no means an exhaustive look at every library available, as we just don't have enough paper here to do that. Instead, we will work with a few of the common libraries distributed with the Arduino software suitable for our audience. There are many more contributed libraries available to try out that you are encouraged to look into on your own. It is also possible to write custom libraries for specific hardware, but that is a bit more of an advanced topic involving principles of C++—beyond the scope of this book. Let's begin with an overview of how to use libraries.

What's needed for this chapter:

- Arduino Uno

- 16×2 character liquid crystal display HD44780 compatible

- Hobby servo (Hitec HS-322 or similar)

- Unipolar or bipolar stepper motor (approximately +5v supply)

- ULN2003 or SN754410 or similar (as appropriate for the type of stepper motor)

- Arduino Ethernet Shield (SparkFun or Adafruit SD shield or breakout also okay)

- LED and appropriate 220-ohm resistor
- TEMT6000 light sensor or other analog sensor
- Hookup wires
- Solderless breadboard

Using Libraries

To use a library in an Arduino sketch, we need to tell the compiler which library we want to use. There are two ways to do this. The first is to use a `#include` pre-processor directive at the beginning of our sketch to specify the library's file name, as follows:

```
#include <LibraryName.h>
```

`LibraryName.h` is the file name of the library that we want to use. In our last project example, we used the line `#include <LiquidCrystal.h>` to enable those functions that make it easier to use an LCD with our project. Pre-processor directives are instructions to the compiler that tell it to include the functions that we want to use at the time of compiling. They don't follow the normal syntax of statements and don't end with semicolons. We mention this here because every library listed later will need this line at the beginning of the sketch for it to work, but we will not break it out to its own section.

Another way to access libraries is through the Sketch menu and the option Import Library, and then select the library name from the menu. The programming environment will write the `#include` line to match the specific library for you. If we want to make use of a contributed library that is not on the list because it is not a part of the standard Arduino distribution, we need to properly install the library before we can access it. While this will not be necessary in any of the examples in this chapter, should you need to install a contributed library, you would need to create a folder named Libraries in the Arduino folder that contains our sketches, if there's not one already, and then copy the new library's folder into it. This library should contain at least two or three files, one ending in .h, as well as other files that could include example sketches or other documentation. Before this new library can be used, the Arduino programming environment will need to be restarted and then include or import the file as normal.

Creating an Instance

After including the library, one of the first things we will do is to either create a new instance of the library or initialize the library, depending on what the library does and how it is written. While this will be specific to each library, it is worth mentioning the basic mechanic for this now. Using our previous LCD example from the last chapter, we needed to create an instance of the LiquidCrystal library to begin working with it. This is done in the following line:

```
LiquidCrystal lcd(5, 6, 7, 8, 9, 10);
```

Theoretically it is possible to have multiple LCDs, servos, steppers, or other hardware in use by some libraries and so we could have multiple lines, like that just shown, with different instance names. Here we have created the instance named `lcd`, which is a variable name that links to the LiquidCrystal library and assigns the pin numbers to be used with it, according to the specifications of the library. Creating an instance of a library is generally only necessary when multiple instances can exist, as is the case here. If we had multiple instances of a library, for example we had multiple LCDs connected to the Arduino, then they would each need a unique name like `lcd1`, `lcd2`, and so on.

Initializing the Library

Once an instance of the library has been created, and sometimes even when we don't need to create an instance for the library, we will then usually need to initialize the library somehow. Usually this function is placed inside the setup() function, like we did with the LCD example, by using the following line:

```
lcd.begin(16, 2);
```

In this line we use a function called begin() that is a part of the LiquidCrystal library linked to the instance that we created called lcd. The instance name and function name are separated by a period. In this case, two parameters are passed to this function, which tell the library that we have a display that is 16 characters wide and 2 characters tall.

Every library is a little different and beyond this point what can be done with them begins to significantly diverge. So let's start with our first hardware library that includes a more thorough discussion of the LiquidCrystal library.

LiquidCrystal library

Earlier in this book we looked at one way to see the information coming out of the Arduino using both the Serial Monitor and code that uses the Serial library, which we will revisit in the next chapter. We can also use any of a number of different displays to show visual information and even create a simple user interface to provide visual feedback. These displays could include the simple monochrome character LCD that we used in the last chapter, a color graphical LCD, seven-segment and alphanumeric LEDs, and even text overlays for composite video or e-ink displays. Since we can't cover all of these here, we are going to go back to our character LCD that we used in the last project and look at some of the other things that the library will allow us to do with code examples, which will include displaying text, working with symbols and custom characters, and even creating very basic animations.

Obviously, to use the LiquidCrystal library we need an LCD. The schematic and illustration in Figures 9-1 and 9-2 show a simpler circuit than the one from last chapter that will be used for the next few example sketches. LCDs like these use the HD44780 driver and have a parallel interface with up to eight data bus pins, but we are only going to use four marked DB4-7. In addition, we need to connect the RS or register select pin to tell the display whether to display data or perform a command and the EN or enable pin to let the display know that data is waiting for it. The RW or read/write pin is simply tied to ground to keep the display in a read state and the V0 pin controls the contrast of the display and can be connected to the middle pin of a trimpot or to a resistor. To keep things simple, we have connected the positive or anode side of the backlight LED marked LED+ to a 220 ohm resistor that is then connected to +5v.

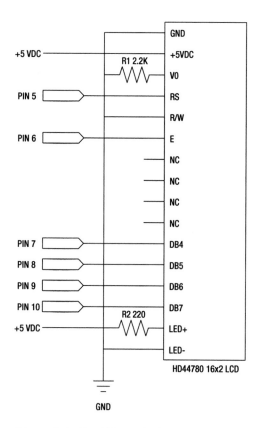

Figure 9-1. *LiquidCrystal schematic*

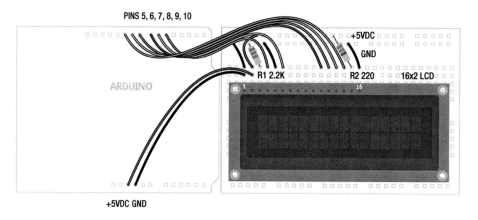

Figure 9-2. *LiquidCrystal illustration*

Example Code: Arduino Haiku

With the circuit wired up, we can get into our first source code example found in Listing 9-1 to demonstrate the basic functions of the LiquidCrystal library. For this sketch, we will display some text in the form of a haiku written by John Maeda. In short, this sketch will display four screens of text separated by a 5-second delay. After the two lines of text have been printed to the display and it has paused long enough for us to read it, the LCD is cleared removing any text from the display and then it starts over at the top left of the screen.

Listing 9-1. *Arduino Haiku Source Code*

```
#include <LiquidCrystal.h>
LiquidCrystal lcd(5, 6, 7, 8, 9, 10);

void setup() {
  lcd.begin(16, 2);
}

void loop() {
  lcd.print("All I want");
  lcd.setCursor(0,1);
  lcd.print("to be,");
  delay(5000);

  lcd.clear();
  lcd.print("is someone that");
  lcd.setCursor(0,1);
  lcd.print("makes new things");
  delay(5000);

  lcd.clear();
  lcd.print("And thinks");
  lcd.setCursor(0,1);
  lcd.print("about them.");
  delay(5000);

  lcd.clear();
  lcd.setCursor(0,1);
  lcd.print("- John Maeda");
  delay(5000);

  lcd.clear();
  delay(5000);
}
```

To understand how these functions work, we will need to examine them more closely after we get the code uploaded, beginning with the `LiquidCrystal()` function.

LiquidCrystal()

The LiquidCrystal() function creates a new instance for the library (so we can use the library in our sketches), gives it a variable name, and assigns the pin numbers for the LCD. This function must be used the first time we want to use the library. There are several different formats for the functions syntax, but we will stick with the following simple one:

```
LiquidCrystal name(rs, en, db4, db5, db6, db7)
```

In this function, name can be any unique name that we want following the normal rules for variable names, but to make things easier we will stick with the convention of using lcd in our code. To make wiring easier and to leave certain I/O pins open on the Arduino board, we will skirt tradition here and assign the digital pins 5, 6, 7, 8, 9, 10 as the pin numbers for the rs, en, db4, db5, db6, db7 pins respectively. This comes together in our source code as the following line:

```
LiquidCrystal lcd(5, 6, 7, 8, 9, 10);
```

Now that we have created an instance of the LiquidCrystal library, we will use the variable name lcd in front of each of the functions that are a part of that library, as you will see in the next function.

begin()

With the library instance created, we need to start the library and define what size LCD we intend to use. To do that, we use the function begin() inside the setup() function.

```
begin(cols, rows)
```

For a 16-character wide by 2-character tall LCD like the one we have been using, we would use 16, 2 for the function parameters. For larger or smaller sized displays we would adjust these numbers to suit, as in 20, 4 or 8, 1. The function as it appeared in our example follows:

```
lcd.begin(16, 2);
```

This statement links the begin() function to our instance lcd and specifies a 16 × 2 display. Now that we've got the library set up correctly, let's look at some of the functions that we can use with this library.

■ **Note** While LCDs of other sizes will work for these examples, the code may act a little odd or need modification.

---

print()

To actually send information to our LCD, we can use the print() function for basic character strings in one of the following two syntax formats:

```
print(data)
print(data, BASE)
```

Data can include any text strings, bracketed by double quotes (" and "), and values or variables that include `char`, `byte`, `int`, `long`, or `string` data types. Any numerical value sent to the `print()` function will be converted to a text string. For integer values, a base can optionally be specified as either `BIN` for binary or base 2, `DEC` for decimal or base 10, `HEX` for hexadecimal or base 16, or `OCT` for octal or base 8. For a simple character string like in our example sketch, we used the following statement:

```
lcd.print("All I want");
```

This statement prints the text `All I want` beginning with the current cursor position and proceeding one character at a time to the right (by default) of that position. To send an integer value, we might write a line like the following:

```
lcd.print(analogRead(A0), DEC);
```

By combining the `analogRead()` function, this statement will read the value of the analog in pin A0 and print that value to the LCD in decimal format. Because the `print()` function will keep on spitting out characters to the right of the current position each time the function is called, we need to use some additional functions to control the position of the cursor.

clear()

The `clear()` function will clear all of the contents of the display and position the cursor in the top left of the display. There's not much to the functions syntax because there are no values to pass to it, so let's look at the following example of the function as used in our code:

```
lcd.clear();
```

Like I said, not much to it. Because of the way LCDs display data, this function can be useful for clearing the screen in order to write new data to it without overwriting data or sending data off the edge of the LCD.

setCursor()

When we want to move the position of the cursor on the display without clearing the display, we can use the `setCursor()` function to position the cursor anywhere on the display. Its syntax looks like the following:

```
setCursor(col, row)
```

All we need to do with this function is provide a number between 0 and 15 for the horizontal column position and either 0 or 1 for our two-row display. A position of `0,0` for example would be the top left corner of the display and `15,1` would be the last character on the bottom-right corner. The following is a line from our example code:

```
lcd.setCursor(0,1);
```

This line is used to set the cursor to the beginning or left-hand side of the second row of the display before writing the second line of text. In our haiku sketch, we used the `clear()` function to not only clear the display, but to also return the cursor to the top left of the display so `setCursor(0,0)` was not needed.

Example Code: Symbols and Characters()

So far, we have only displayed simple characters on the LCD by using what is easily entered from our keyboard. To make more interesting symbols on the display, the HD44780 driver has a number of special symbols, like ¢, °, Ω, or π, which can be accessed using a code that tells the display what symbol to show. These character displays also have the capability of displaying up to eight custom characters of our own design. The source code in Listing 9-2 provides an example of using both the built-in symbols as well as some new ones that we will create ourselves.

Listing 9-2. Symbols and Characters Source Code

```
#include <LiquidCrystal.h>
LiquidCrystal lcd(5, 6, 7, 8, 9, 10);

byte degree = B11011111;
byte cents = B11101100;
byte sqRoot = B11101000;
byte divide = B11111101;
byte pi = B11110111;
byte omega = B11110100;
byte rgtArrow = B01111110;
byte lftArrow = B01111111;

byte symbols[] = {degree, cents, sqRoot, divide, pi, omega, rgtArrow, lftArrow};

byte smiley[] = {B00000,B00000,B01010,B00000,B10001,B01110,B00000,B00000};
byte skull[] = {B00000,B01110,B10101,B11011,B01110,B01110,B00000,B00000};
byte bell[] = {B00000,B00100,B01110,B01110,B01110,B11111,B00100,B00000};
byte note[] = {B00000,B00100,B00110,B00101,B00101,B01100,B01100,B00000};
byte heart[] = {B00000,B00000,B01010,B11111,B11111,B01110,B00100,B00000};
byte fish[] = {B10000,B00000,B01000,B10000,B01101,B11110,B01101,B00000};
byte lock[] = {B00000,B01110,B10001,B10001,B11111,B11011,B11011,B11111};
byte unlock[] = {B00000,B01110,B10001,B10000,B11111,B11011,B11011,B11111};

byte* characters[] = {smiley, skull, bell, note, heart, fish, lock, unlock};

void setup() {
  lcd.begin(16, 2);

  for (int i=0; i<8; i++) {
    lcd.setCursor((i*2),0);
    lcd.write(symbols[i]);

    lcd.createChar(i, ((byte*)characters[i]));
    lcd.setCursor((i*2),1);
    lcd.write(i);
  }
}

void loop() {}
```

This example is maybe not the most dynamic sketch we've ever written, but it gives us a sense of the types of characters that can be displayed on our display. Once we have the sketch uploaded, we can then look at the functions that we use to both display these symbols and characters as well as those that create the new characters, in order to better explain the example source code.

write()

Where the `print()` function prints strings of text to the LCD, the `write()` function is used to send a character to the display. The syntax for both functions is similar:

```
write(data)
```

The character to be sent to the display is specified in a numerical data format or through a variable name. From our example code, it is as follows:

```
lcd.write(symbols[i]);
```

This line displays whatever symbol is named at the current index in the `symbols[]` array determined by the loop counter. The `symbols[]` array is just a way to run down a list of each of the eight symbols defined in the earlier variable declarations, using a `for` loop to print them to the display. Our example code continues to print each of the eight pre-defined symbols using the `setCursor()` function to space each one out on the first line.

Declaring the address for the symbol at the beginning of our code and calling that variable name later is only one way to use the `write()` function. We can actually specify the symbol to be displayed in many different ways. For example, the symbol for cents, ¢, can be written multiple ways, as shown in the following sample fragment:

```
byte cents = B11101100;
lcd.write(cents);
lcd.write((B11101100));
lcd.write(236);
lcd.write(0xEC);
```

This block of code will display four ¢ symbols in a row on the display because each of these different values refers to the same thing. Just like our example code earlier, the first line declares a byte data type variable named `cents` and assigns it the 8-bit binary value `B11101100`. The variable `cents` is then called in the second line to print the first symbol. The second symbol is printed by specifying the binary number directly in the `write()` function. Because the value `B11101100` is not a real number so to speak, the `B` is used to tell the compiler that the following number is binary not decimal, we need to place this value in a second pair of parentheses to force the compiler to evaluate this value as a binary number. The third line uses the decimal value 236 and the fourth the hexadecimal value 0xEC for the third and fourth symbols.

To find the numerical value that corresponds to the symbol that we want to use, we need to have a look at the LCD's data sheet, a document that gives us the technical specification of the device. Figure 9-3 is a small part of the symbol set that is available to a particular LCD found in a data sheet for the driver chip, like the one hosted by SparkFun at `www.sparkfun.com/datasheets/LCD/HD44780.pdf`. These may vary depending on the chip used by the LCD, so refer to the specific data sheet for your display.

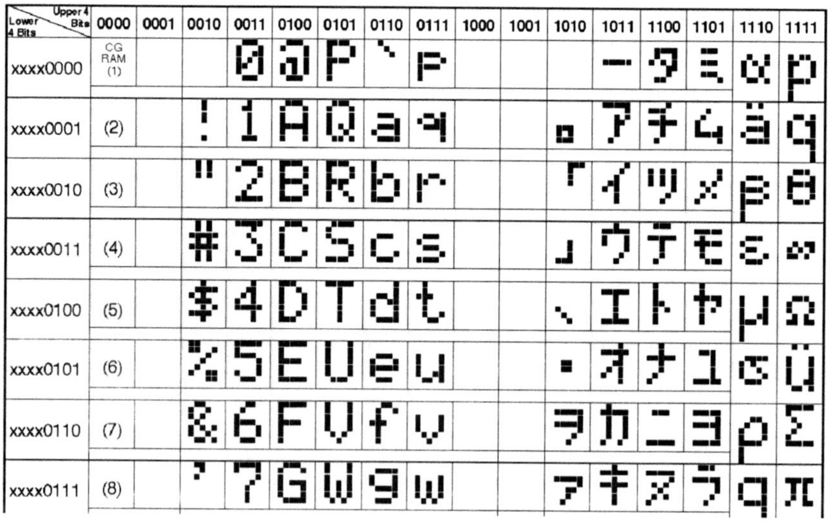

Upper 4 Bits / Lower 4 Bits	0000	0001	0010	0011	0100	0101	0110	0111	1000	1001	1010	1011	1100	1101	1110	1111
xxxx0000	CG RAM (1)			0	@	P	`	p				─	ヲ	ミ	α	p
xxxx0001	(2)		!	1	A	Q	a	q			。	ァ	チ	ム	ä	q
xxxx0010	(3)		"	2	B	R	b	r			「	ィ	ツ	メ	β	θ
xxxx0011	(4)		#	3	C	S	c	s			」	ゥ	テ	モ	ε	∞
xxxx0100	(5)		$	4	D	T	d	t			、	エ	ト	ャ	μ	Ω
xxxx0101	(6)		%	5	E	U	e	u			・	オ	ナ	ユ	σ	ü
xxxx0110	(7)		&	6	F	V	f	v			ヲ	カ	ニ	ョ	ρ	Σ
xxxx0111	(8)		'	7	G	W	g	w			ア	キ	ヌ	ラ	g	π

Figure 9-3. *Partial symbol codes from data sheet*

To use a symbol like the Greek omega, Ω, for example, we need to cross reference the first four bits, or 1s and 0s, at the top of the chart with the second four on the left. That will give us the binary number 11110100 that we can then use with the write() function to display the symbol on the LCD. Likewise, pi, π, would be the symbol at 11110111. We can then convert this value to another base if we particularly wanted to and use that as the parameter for the write() function as we mentioned earlier.

createChar()

While the LCD has many different symbols built into its driver chip, we might want to create a symbol like a smiley face, music note, or even a fish. Our character display can store eight custom characters numbered 0–7, each occupying a 5×8 grid of pixels. Creating a custom character to display on the LCD is a two-step process. First, we need to define a bitmap array that corresponds to each dot for the character and, second, we need to use the createChar() function to send our bitmap to an address in the displays memory. The syntax for this function is as follows:

```
createChar(number, data)
```

The number parameter is the number of the custom character with a range of 0–7. The data is the array name that stores the bitmap image. Before fully explaining our example code, let's look at the following hypothetical statement to make a smiley face:

```
lcd.createChar(0, smiley);
```

This line will create a new character at the number 0 according to the pattern in the array smiley[]. One way of creating this array is as follows:

```
byte smiley[] = {B00000,B00000,B01010,B00000,B10001,B01110,B00000,B00000};
```

Because each character is a collection of dots in a 5 × 8 grid, we can create an array of bytes, one byte for each row and one bit for each column. A 1 represents a pixel that is on and 0 a pixel that is off. Our example is written to save space, but it is common to write these arrays in the following format:

```
byte smiley[] = {
  B00000,
  B00000,
  B01010,
  B00000,
  B10001,
  B01110,
  B00000,
  B00000
};
```

While this way takes up more space on the screen, if you squint just right you can make out the smiley face in the code. With the array defined and the custChar() function called to assign our character to a position, we then use the write() function to display the character on the screen, like so:

```
lcd.write(0);
```

One useful utility for creating custom characters is the Character Creator shown in Figure 9-4 and found online at http://icontexto.com/charactercreator/.

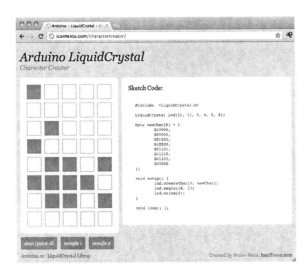

Figure 9-4. Arduino LiquidCrystal Character Creator

Simply toggle each block to draw your character and then copy and paste the generated code in the right panel into your Arduino sketch. And that's all there is to creating custom characters. The library fortunately takes on all the hard work of writing this information to the LCD's memory so that we can display this character, or even make a new character, whenever we want.

So now going back to our earlier example code that displays eight custom characters on the second row of our display, we first defined eight character arrays that included characters called smiley, skull, bell, note, heart, fish, lock, and unlock. We then made an array called characters[] to create an index of each of these individual character names. Because this is an array of arrays, similar to our discussion of character arrays in the last chapter, we need to use the "*" symbol after the data type to indicate that this is an array of pointers—basically references to places in memory where the arrays are stored.

In our for loop, we created each character in turn using the following line:

```
lcd.createChar(i, ((byte*)characters[i]));
```

Here, our character number is determined by the for loop counter and the name of the array is determined by the index of the characters[] array. To get this array to point to the correct character array, we need to remind the compiler that characters[i] is a pointer by adding (byte*) in front of the array name bracketed by parenthesis. This turns that array into a pointer that the compiler can reference, creating the appropriate character. I know I said we wouldn't talk much about pointers, but it's not that hard and plenty of reference material abounds if you want find out more.

Example Code: Fish Tank Animation

We are almost done with the LiquidCrystal library, with only one more example and a couple new functions to go. By using these new functions with some custom characters, we can create a rather low-tech 8-bit animation—maybe something like a fish swimming in a fish tank. The example in Listing 9-3 takes two strategies for creating an animation. First, it moves the character around the screen by using functions that scroll the data to the left or right. Second, it displays multiple characters at the same location with a delay in between each one to create a simple flipbook style animation.

To make this code work, we designed multiple fish characters that include different directions the fish might swim, as well as a few characters so that the fish can blow bubbles. Four functions are created to control the fish's movement: scrollLeft(), scrollRight(), stopCenter(), and blowBubbles(). By calling each function, and passing the number of steps in the case of the scrolling functions, we can get the fish to move around the LCD while keeping track of it the entire time using the variables x and y.

Listing 9-3. Fish Tank Animation Source Code

```
#include <LiquidCrystal.h>
LiquidCrystal lcd(5, 6, 7, 8, 9, 10);

byte fishLeft[8] = {B00000,B00000,B00000,B00000,B01101,B11110,B01101,B00000};
byte fishRight[8] = {B00000,B00000,B00000,B00000,B10110,B01111,B10110,B00000};
byte fishCenter[8] = {B00000,B00000,B00000,B00000,B00100,B01110,B00100,B00000};
byte fishBubbles1[8] = {B00010,B00000,B00100,B00010,B00100,B01110,B00100,B00000};
byte fishBubbles2[8] = {B00000,B00100,B00010,B00000,B00100,B01110,B00100,B00000};
byte fishBubbles3[8] = {B00100,B00000,B00000,B00000,B00100,B01110,B00100,B00000};

byte x = 0;
byte y = 0;

int time = 600;

void setup() {
  lcd.begin(16,2);
  lcd.createChar(0, fishBubbles1);
  lcd.createChar(1, fishBubbles2);
  lcd.createChar(2, fishBubbles3);
```

```
    lcd.createChar(3, fishLeft);
    lcd.createChar(4, fishRight);
    lcd.createChar(5, fishCenter);
}

void loop() {
  scrollRight(9);
  stopCenter();
  blowBubbles();
  y = 1;
  x += 1;
  scrollLeft(5);
  stopCenter();
  blowBubbles();
  y=0;
  scrollRight(10);
  delay(time*10);
  x = 0;
  y = 0;
}

void scrollRight(int steps) {
  lcd.setCursor(x, y);
  lcd.write(4);
  delay(time);
  for (int i=0; i<steps; i++) {
    lcd.scrollDisplayRight();
    delay(time);
    x++;
  }
  lcd.clear();
}

void scrollLeft(int steps) {
  lcd.setCursor(x, y);
  lcd.write(3);
  for (int i=0; i<steps; i++) {
    lcd.scrollDisplayLeft();
    delay(time);
    x--;
  }
  lcd.clear();
}

void stopCenter() {
  lcd.setCursor(x, y);
  lcd.write(5);
  delay(time);
  lcd.clear();
}
```

```
void blowBubbles() {
  for (int i=0; i<3; i++) {
    lcd.setCursor(x, y);
    lcd.write(i);
    delay(time);
  }
  lcd.clear();
}
```

This sketch uses many of the LiquidCrystal functions that we have already discussed, but it also adds a couple new ones. Let's look at these two functions before moving on to our next library.

scrollDisplayLeft() and scrollDisplayRight()

Each time these functions are called, the display will be shifted one character to the left or right, depending on which function we call. We placed these functions in for loops with a delay and a counter to track the horizontal position of the cursor. Take for example the following:

```
for (int i=0; i<steps; i++) {
  lcd.scrollDisplayRight();
  delay(time);
  x++;
}
```

This loop will call the function scrollDisplayRight() once each time through the loop for the total number of steps passed to the function. The loop will also delay for the specified amount of time and increment the horizontal position by one.

That might seem like a pretty exhaustive look at the LiquidCrystal library, but believe it or not there are even more functions to do all sorts of things that we haven't even mentioned here. However, rather than dwelling too long on this one library, let's keep moving to some of the other interesting libraries that we need to talk about.

Servo Library

Moving things around on a screen is pretty cool, but let's now look at how we can physically move material things around. The best way to move something with the Arduino is to use a motor. We already looked at a simple motor with the DC fan in Project 4, which is functionally equivalent to controlling any simple DC motor. Two other common types of motors include the hobby servo and the stepper motor. Both of these motors can be difficult to work with without the awesome libraries that are a part of the Arduino platform. The first motor that we'll discuss, the hobby servo, typically moves in 180° arcs. While initially used in radio-controlled hobby applications, the servo has quite the following in robotics and animatronics because of its integrated electronics, gearing, and positional feedback, which allow for fairly precise control.

Typically, to control the servo, a signal of varying pulse widths is sent to the servo over a regular time period and the servo moves to the position that corresponds to that pulse. As long as the signal is refreshed about every 20 milliseconds, the servo will maintain its position. On our Hitec servo, a digital pulse with a duration of 900 microseconds will send the servo arm to a position of 0°, while on the other end, a pulse of 2100 microseconds will send the servo 180° in the other direction. The drawing in Figure 9-5 illustrates the typical movement arc of our Hitec servo. Every brand of servo will be different, with typical ranges of movement exceeding 180°, and some servos even spin in the opposite direction, so always double-check the specifications for your motor. It is also important to remember that while we are in essence using a form of PWM, we do not want to try to PWM the servo signal line using `analogWrite()` or we could damage our servo motor.

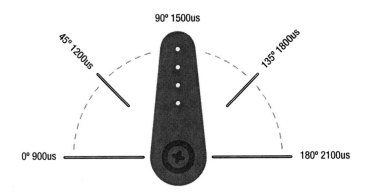

Figure 9-5. Hobby servo rotation

The Servo library can control up to a total of 12 servos on the Arduino Uno on any of the digital pins, although this functionality disables PWM on digital pins 9 and 10. Servos have three wires: signal, power, and ground. The yellow, white, or sometimes orange wire is for the logic signal and should be connected to one of the Arduino digital pins. The red wire is power and is connected to the +5v pin on the Arduino board. The black or brown wire is for ground and should be connected to the ground pin on the interface board. While we can control quite a few servos, they can consume current in excess of 100s of milliamps, so Arduino's power supply can't handle more than a few servos at a time. The supply voltage for servos should be in the +4.8v to +6v range, while the logic signal should remain within a +3–5v range. If using an external power supply, it is important that the ground wires share a common connection with the Arduino board. Figures 9-6 and 9-7 show how easy it is to connect a single servo to the Arduino board and we will then continue the discussion with some example code.

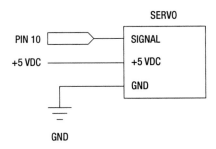

Figure 9-6. Servo schematic

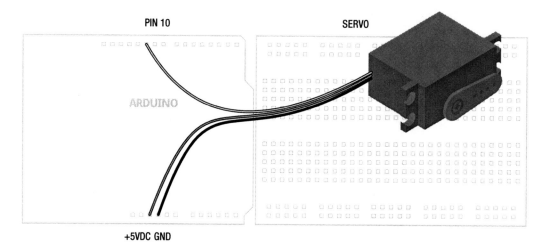

Figure 9-7. *Servo illustration*

Example Code: Reminder Bell

For our example code in Listing 9-4, we will use the servo to ring a bell. So, why a reminder bell? Honestly, it seems to me like ringing a physical bell is something that a servo would be good at. You could attach a bell with wire to the servo or maybe instead attach an arm so that when the servo moves, it will tap a bell. We might use this as the basis of a physical hit-counter or to notify us of an online-friend status or put it to use for some other nefarious means. We'll leave that up to your imagination.

Listing 9-4. *Reminder Bell Source Code*

```
#include <Servo.h>

Servo servo;

unsigned long startTime = 0;
unsigned long interval = 600000;

void setup() {
  servo.attach(10);
  servo.write(90);
}

void loop() {
  if (startTime + interval < millis()) {
    servo.write(96);
    delay(90);
    servo.write(90);
    startTime = millis();
  }
}
```

In this example code, we start with a position of 90º and jump briefly to 96º and back again each time the interval has been exceeded. Couple this movement with an event, say a timer that reminds us to get up and stretch every 10 minutes, and we have the beginnings of a really simple project. This could be adjusted to suit many applications, so rather than dwell too long on the hardware, let's look at the Servo functions.

Servo

Creating a new instance of the Servo library is quite a bit easier than with the previous library. All we need to do is use the Servo library name at the beginning of our sketch, followed by a name for our instance. In our example code this was done in the following line:

```
Servo servo;
```

And that's it for this line. Pick a name that might mean something to you whether its servo1, rightSideServo, or george—so long as the name is unique and each instance of the Servo library has been declared.

attach()

To use our servo, we need to bring out the attach() function to tell the library which pin we are using for this instance of the library. The syntax has the following two options:

```
name.attach(pin)
name.attach(pin, min, max)
```

In our example code this line took the form of

```
servo.attach(10);
```

Here we have set up servo to work with pin 10. Pins 9 and 10 seem like obvious choices because the servo function disables PWM on those pins anyway, although you are not limited to these pins.

Not all servos are created equal, however, and many will have minimum and maximum rotation angles that might be at odds with the Arduino defaults. Check the data sheet for your servo to see what these might be. If it's necessary, we can use the attach() function to define the minimum and maximum rotation angle specified in microseconds. The default minimum value is set to 544 for 0º and the maximum is set to 2400 for 180º. This will provide us with the greatest potential range of movement, but at the risk of possibly damaging our servo. If we were concerned about matching the specifications of our Hitec servo, we could specify the minimum and maximum as follows:

```
servo.attach(10, 900, 2100);
```

write()

Now with our servo set up, we need to do something with it. To make it move, we can use the write() function with the following syntax:

```
name.write(angle)
```

Simply specify an angle in degrees and the servo will move to that angle at the only speed it knows. In our sketch we wanted to start off at 90º and when the timer was triggered to move to 96º.

```
servo.write(90);
```

Because the servo only moves at one speed, when we need to slow things down we need to break large jumps in position down into smaller movements with delays between each movement. This might look something like the following:

```
for (int i=45; i<136; i++) {
  servo.write(i);
  delay(10);
}
```

This is a fairly standard sweep using a for loop that starts the servo at 45° and increments by 1° every 10 milliseconds until it has reached 135°. In order to return to the starting position at the same speed, we would need to reverse the loop. Take the code in Listing 9-5 for example.

Listing 9-5. *Double Servo Sweep Source Code*

```
#include <Servo.h>

Servo leftServo;
Servo rightServo;

void setup() {
  leftServo.attach(10);
  rightServo.attach(9);
}

void loop() {
  for (int angle=0; angle<180; angle+=2) {
    leftServo.write(angle);
    rightServo.write(180-angle);
    delay(20);
  }
  for (int angle=180; angle>0; angle-=2) {
    leftServo.write(angle);
    rightServo.write(180-angle);
    delay(20);
  }
}
```

In this sketch, two servos are used to sweep in opposite directions, maybe for a pan and tilt mechanism for a camera or sensor, or a pair of wheels for a robot. To do this, two instances of the Servo library are created named leftServo and rightServo attached to pins 9 and 10. Beginning at 0° and continuing through to 180° at 2° increments, the first loop writes this angle to the first servo while the opposite angle, by subtracting the current angle from 180, is written to the second servo. The second for loop reverses the direction at the same speed. A delay of 20 milliseconds is added in each loop to slow the servos down. To slow them down even more, we could reduce the increment or decrement to 1 and increase the delay time. Alternatively, we could speed things up by increasing the increment and decrement counter and decrease the delay.

While there are additional functions that can be used to read the location of the servo, write a position with microseconds instead of angles, and even detach the servo, but these are all somewhat situational. Let's move on to another kind of motor that is also known for its positional accuracy, but can spin 360 degrees.

Stepper Library

The servo motor is an easy motor to hook up and does what it does with ease, but what if we want that same kind of positional accuracy in a motor that can spin the full 360? For that, we need to use a stepper motor, which is a type of motor that rather than spinning continuously, rotates in a specific number of degrees or steps. The amount of rotation per step is dependent on the individual stepper; ours has a rotation of 1.8° per step while others can range from as little as 0.9° per step to as much as 30° per step or more.

To control a stepper motor, the internal coils of the motor need to be individually energized in a particular sequence, dependent on the type of stepper motor, either unipolar or bipolar. Unipolar steppers often have five or six wires with a common ground connection and the current flows through each coil in only one direction. Bipolar steppers, on the other hand, only have four wires with no common connection and the current flows through each coil in both directions.

While there are a multitude of drivers available, we are going to use one of two simple chips that only cost a couple dollars each and require no external components to get going. To control a unipolar stepper motor, we will use the ULN2003 Darlington transistor array. A Darlington array is a series of transistor pairs, where a small transistor drives a second transistor to increase its capacity, all on a single integrated circuit or IC. Four individual transistors would have the same effect, although not as convenient. The ULN2003 actually has seven transistor pairs on the chip, although we will only use four of them. By turning each transistor on in order, we can power each coil of the motor causing the motor to spin.

For bipolar stepper motors, we will use the SN754410 dual H-bridge. An H-bridge is a special arrangement of transistors on a chip that is capable of reversing the direction of the current between two pins. When used on standard DC motors, this would change the direction that the motor spins. In the case of a bipolar stepper, alternating the direction of current flow on each coil will create a step causing the motor to turn in a direction determined by the sequence.

Because every stepper is a little different, we will provide two schematics and illustrations for the two types of motor: Figures 9-8 and 9-9 for unipolar and 9-10 and 9-11 for bipolar. Pick the circuit that matches your motor type, being careful to wire the stepper motor coils as shown in the schematic. We have also used a motor that can safely operate from the Arduino board's +5v output. If you are using a motor with a different voltage or higher current requirement, then you should connect an external power supply to the +V Motor pins instead of +5v. For more information on determining the electrical characteristics of stepper motors, you might want to check out the following links:

- www.makingthings.com/documentation/how-to/stepper-motor

- www.cs.uiowa.edu/~jones/step/types.html

- www.jasonbabcock.com/computing/breadboard/unipolar/index.html

- www.jasonbabcock.com/computing/breadboard/bipolar/index.html

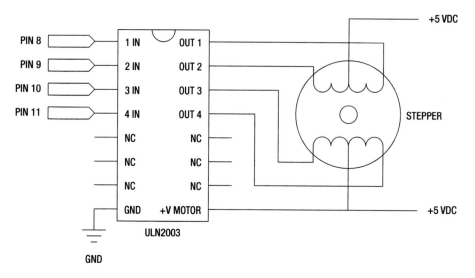

Figure 9-8. Unipolar Stepper schematic

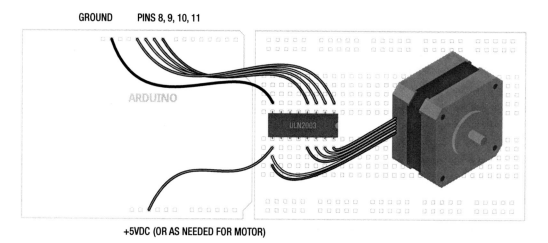

Figure 9-9. Unipolar Stepper illustration

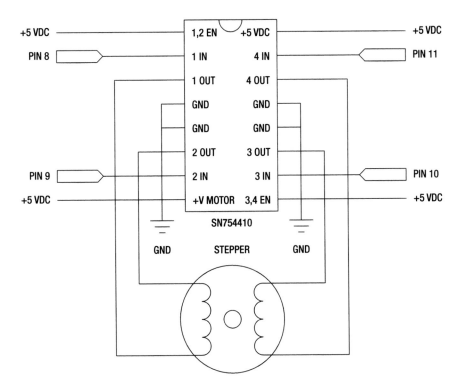

Figure 9-10. *Bipolar Stepper schematic*

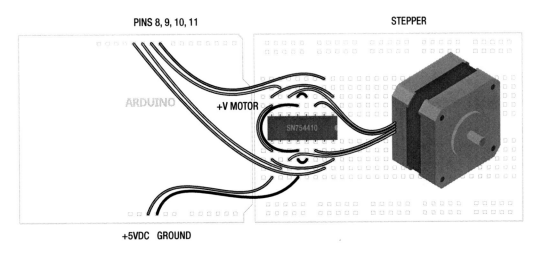

Figure 9-11. *Bipolar Stepper illustration*

Example Code: 60-Second Sweep

Have you ever wanted a clock that moves backwards? For our example source code found in Listing 9-6, we are going to create a pseudo time-keeping device that is eternally trapped in a 60-second loop. The stepper will move in a full 360º arc in about a minute. At the end of its arc, it will switch direction and spin the other way. Because our stepper moves in 1.8º steps, it's not entirely possible to have the most exacting of timepieces here, but it's close enough. Because of this, each second the stepper should move 3.33 steps, which it can't do. So we fudge the delay a little bit with a delay between steps of 909 milliseconds instead of 1 second. Because of how the two different circuits shown in the figures are designed, the single sketch provided will control either type of motor.

Listing 9-6. 60-Second Sweep Source Code

```
#include <Stepper.h>

const int steps = 200;
Stepper stepper(steps, 8, 9, 10, 11);

int stepDirection = 3;
int counter = 0;

void setup() {
  stepper.setSpeed(30);
}

void loop() {
  stepper.step(stepDirection);
  delay(909);
  counter+=3;
  if (counter > steps) {
    counter = 0;
    if (stepDirection == 3) stepDirection = -3;
    else stepDirection = 3;
  }
}
```

With our simple code in place rotating our stepper motor back and forth, let's explore the Stepper functions in greater depth.

Stepper

To create a new instance of the Stepper library, we use one of the following two syntaxes:

```
Stepper name(steps, pin 1, pin 2)
Stepper name(steps, pin1, pin 2, pin 3, pin4)
```

The syntax we use depends on whether we are using two pins or four pins to control the stepper drivers. To make our wiring a little easier and the code work on both drivers, we chose to use four pins— easier to wire at the cost of a pair of digital pins. In our example code, we created the following Stepper instance:

```
Stepper stepper(steps, 8, 9, 10, 11);
```

Our instance is named stepper although we could use almost anything for the name. The first parameter is the number of steps that our stepper motor is capable of in one full rotation. For our stepper, it has 1.8º steps, meaning that it would take 200 steps to complete a single rotation. A 7.2º step stepper motor would likewise have 360º / 7.2º or 50 total steps per revolution. In our earlier code, we declared the number of steps for our motor as the constant variable steps that we will use later in our code. The next four parameters, pins1–4, are the pin numbers connected to the drivers. Refer to the schematic for which pins go where.

setSpeed()

With our instance created, we need to set the rotational speed for our motor. The syntax for this function only has one parameter, as follows:

```
name.setSpeed(rpm)
```

The speed for our motor is set as rotations per minute. This value determines how fast the stepper moves from step to step and will naturally vary for each stepper motor. Setting this value too high for your motor may cause skipped steps or intermittent operation. Choose a speed appropriate for your application and/or motor.

Remember that the setSpeed() function does not actually move the motor—it only establishes the speed of the motor when our next function is called.

step()

The step() function is what actually makes the motor move. The syntax is simple, but there are some things we need to keep in mind.

```
name.step(steps)
```

The one parameter to pass to this function is the number of steps that we want to move the stepper motor. For example, with a 1.8º step motor, one step equals a 1.8º movement. Setting the number of steps to 50 will turn the motor 90º clockwise on our 200-step motor, or a quarter of a revolution, where -50 will turn the motor 90º counterclockwise. As you see, a positive integer will create a movement in one direction while a negative value sends it in the reverse direction.

Unlike something similar to the analogWrite() function, which you set and forget, step() will prevent the Arduino from doing anything else until it has completed its full move. This is not that big of a deal if we step the motor in small increments each time we call the step() function, but it quickly adds up. As a practical example, if we set the RPM speed to 10 RPM, our 200-step motor would take 6 seconds to complete 200 steps. In other words, if we used the statement stepper.step(200) then that would be 6 seconds that we will not be able to read inputs, communicate with other devices, or anything else. Instead it might be better to complete large rotations with a loop statement like the following code fragment:

```
for (int i=0; i<200; i++) {
  stepper.step(1);
  if (digitalRead(2) == HIGH) break;
}
```

In this example, we are incrementing the stepper motor 200 times in single-step increments to complete one revolution. Instead of calling a single 200-step movement by using a for loop, each individual step will only take 30 milliseconds and in between each step, we can, for example, check the status of a digital input pin and exit the loop using the **break** statement if a condition has been met.

With all of the Stepper library functions out of the way, let's look at one more sketch in Listing 9-7 before we move on to our next and final library for this chapter. This sketch demonstrates one way to map the values from an analog sensor to the movement of the stepper motor. A potentiometer with a giant knob on it is a good choice, or maybe better yet an accelerometer that controls the movement of the stepper through the tilt of its axes, although any analog input would work as well. Using the **map()** function, we can take an analog reading and map it to the total number of steps to indicate the level of the analog input—a full reading of 1024 will turn the stepper one full revolution.

Listing 9-7. Analog Sensor to Stepper Source Code

```
#include <Stepper.h>

const int steps = 200;
Stepper stepper(steps, 8, 9, 10, 11);
int previous, val;

void setup() {
  stepper.setSpeed(30);
}

void loop() {
  val = map(analogRead(0), 0, 1024, 0, steps);
  stepper.step(val - previous);
  previous = val;
  delay(20);
}
```

Now that we have used libraries to display text on an LCD as well as making things move with two different kinds of motors, let's take a look at how we can use libraries to store and retrieve information.

SD Library

In the last chapter, we very briefly introduced the idea of using the program memory of the Arduino microcontroller to keep large chunks of data from taking up too much room in RAM. Instead, we could use additional external hardware to read and write to an SD memory card. SD or Secure Digital flash memory cards are the very same wafer-thin memory cards used by cameras, mp3 players, and other devices. The SD library is a relative newcomer to the standard Arduino libraries and the list of functions and associated libraries would make our conversations of the LiquidCrystal library and the PROGMEM functions seem like a leisurely stroll in the park in comparison. Rather than a comprehensive analysis of the library in the few remaining pages of this chapter, we are going to take a quick look at reading and writing values to the card using as few functions as we can get away with.

To get access to an SD card, we need some hardware in the form of a breakout board or shield that will connect the card to the appropriate pins on the Arduino board. Adafruit Industries makes a nice compact microSD card breakout that can be wired up to the Arduino with only a handful of wires, while SparkFun Electronics has an inexpensive shield available that plugs directly into the Arduino board. Instead, we are going to use and recommend the Arduino Ethernet Shield, which in addition to having the hardware necessary for accessing a microSD card, also has Ethernet hardware built-in for future projects that open up the possibility for exploring Arduino Internet connectivity. The Arduino Ethernet Shield is convenient to use in that it plugs right into the pin headers on the Arduino board while still giving us access to all of the I/O pins not used by the devices on the shield.

In addition to the Ethernet Shield, we need to have a properly formatted microSD card as well. To read up not only on the procedure for formatting the SD card but also some of the differences in the hardware, check out the SD Card Notes page on the Arduino web site at `http://arduino.cc/en/Reference/SDCardNotes`. Once we have the hardware in place and a properly formatted microSD card, it's time to do something with it.

Because just storing data is not that interesting in and of itself, we will use the circuit shown in Figures 9-12 and 9-13 to create a very simple data logger to record an analog sensor input to a text file on the SD card called `data.txt`. We should start by mentioning a couple of things about the SD card on the Ethernet Shield. The Ethernet device and the SD card are both devices that use the Serial Peripheral Interface or SPI. We won't be getting into much detail with this protocol in this book, but fortunately for us, the SD library hides much of this interface from us. The Ethernet Shield connects digital pins 11, 12, and 13 to each SPI device with an additional pin needing to be tied to a hardware select pin to enable each device. The Ethernet device is connected to pin 10, the default for one SPI device, so the SD card has been connected to pin 4. In our code, we need to configure pin 10 as an output even though we are not using the Ethernet part of the shield for this example.

For the rest of our hardware, the sensor we will be using is the TEMT6000 breakout board from SparkFun to measure ambient light levels, although any other analog sensor would work as well. We will also use the Serial Monitor so that we can see the status of opening and writing to the file on the SD to tell us if something has gone wrong, what data is being written to the card, and when the file has been closed. Every time the Arduino is reset, it will open the file on the card and continue to update the values on the card for another round.

Once we know we can write files to the card, we will try out another sketch that reads values from the same text file on the card and outputs those values to a simple LED connected to a PWM pin—basically, a larger version of our Flicker Sketch from the last chapter. Because the SD card is connected to pins 4, 11, 12, and 13, and we can't use pin 10, we will connect our single LED to pin 9. Like the rest of the example code in this chapter, however, these sketches are not meant to be full-fledged projects and this is especially the case with the SD library. Think of these examples as proof-of-concept ripe for future exploration and expansion. So, let's get started.

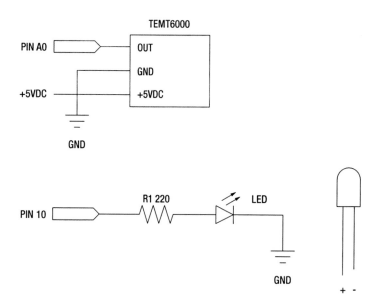

Figure 9-12. SD schematic

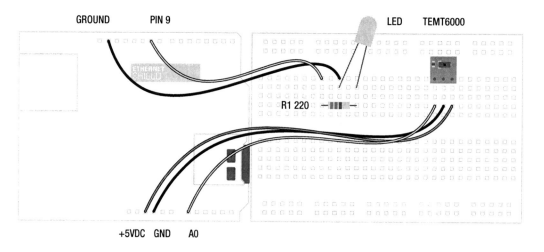

Figure 9-13. SD illustration

Example Code: SD Logger

Our first sketch for the SD library in Listing 9-8 will run entirely in the setup() function since it is not necessary to run it in a continuous loop. We start the sketch with a few settings that determine how long we want to record data, specified as `runningTime` in minutes, and the interval in between sequential readings, specified as `interval` in milliseconds. We then step through the initialization process providing feedback through the Serial Monitor at every step. Once the SD library is set up, we need to open a file to write our data to, set our clock for the running time, and then we enter a `while` loop that, for as long as the duration lasts, will print the analog sensor data to both the Serial Monitor and to the file on the SD card at an interval determined at the beginning of the sketch. After the time has expired, the file is closed and the sketch effectively ends. Each time the sketch is restarted, through reset or cycling power, it will continue to amend data to the existing values already in the file. To start over, the file will need to be deleted first.

Listing 9-8. SD Logger Source Code

```
#include <SD.h>

File file;

const long runningTime = 5;    // time in minutes
const long msMin = 60000;      // milliseconds in 1 minute
const int interval = 2000;     // time in milliseconds

const int sensorMin = 30;
const int sensorMax = 1000;
const int sensor = A0;
const int SDcs = 4;

void setup() {
  Serial.begin(9600);
  Serial.print("Initializing SD card...");
  pinMode(10, OUTPUT);

  if (!SD.begin(SDcs)) {
    Serial.println("initialization failed!");
    return;
  }
  Serial.println("initialization done.");

  file = SD.open("data.txt", FILE_WRITE);

  if (file) {
    while (millis() < (runningTime * msMin)) {
      byte value = map(analogRead(sensor), sensorMin, sensorMax, 0, 255);

      Serial.print("Writing ");
      Serial.print(value, DEC);
      Serial.print(" to data.txt... ");
      file.write(value);
      Serial.println("done.");
      delay(interval);
    }
    file.close();
    Serial.println("File closed.");
```

```
    } else {
        Serial.println("Error opening data.txt.");
    }
}

void loop() {}
```

This sketch builds on concepts elsewhere in this book, including the delay without using the `delay()` function and the Analog Serial Monitor, however, the SD library's functions are a little different from the other libraries that we have looked at.

File

The first line we will look at creates an instance of the file that we want to use. It has a very simple syntax, as follows:

```
File name
```

Where `name` is anything you want it to be. This does not have to be the actual file name on the SD card. In our example code, we used the line `File file;` because it seemed easiest although `myFile`, `dataFile`, or any other name that you like could be used here.

SD.begin()

With our file ready to go, we need to initialize the SD library using the `SD.begin()` function. It too has a basic syntax:

```
SD.begin(csPin)
```

This function will default to a CS, or chip select pin of pin 10, so in order to use this function with the Ethernet Shield or any other configuration where the CS pin on the SD card is on any other pin we need to specify that pin number. From our code it is as follows:

```
if (!SD.begin(sdCsPin)) {
```

This line contains the `SD.begin()` function and performs a test to see if the function was successful or not. If the SD card is successfully started, this function will return `true` while if there was a problem, for example the SD card is not present, it will return `false`. The `if` statement in our code will give us an error message and exit the sketch if there is any problem initializing the SD card.

■ **Note**   Even if we are using a different CS pin from the default pin 10, we need to configure pin 10 as an OUTPUT or else the SD library will not properly function.

SD.open()

To be able to write data to a file, we must open it first with the `SD.open()` function. The syntax for the function follows:

```
SD.open(filename, mode)
```

The `filename` parameter is a character string for the name of the file that we want to access. This name can also include the directory structure on the card using forward slashes, /, to separate directories. If the file does not exist, this function will create it, although the directory must already exist beforehand. This function only works with short file names from the days of yore in an 8.3 format. This means an 8-character name with a 3-character file extension separated by a period, as in `datafile.txt`.

There are two possible modes for this function: `FILE_READ` and `FILE_WRITE`. The default mode for the function when no mode is specified is `FILE_READ`. This mode will open the specified file at the beginning of the file to be read by the `read()` function explained later. The `FILE-WRITE` mode is used to write information to the file beginning at the end of the file. In other words, we read from the beginning of the file and we write to the end of a file. In our example code it is as follows:

```
file = SD.open("data.txt", FILE_WRITE);
```

We opened the file `data.txt` and set it to a `FILE_WRITE` mode so that we could write data to the file and then attributed this to the instance `file` that we created earlier. In our next few functions, the instance name `file` will be used to tell the functions what file to use.

■ **Note** Keep in mind that only one file can be opened at a time.

---

close()

When we are done with the file that we have open, or if we need to open a new file, we must first close the current file using the `close()` function to save the data that has been written to the SD card. The syntax for this function follows:

```
name.close();
```

The specified name is the name of the `File` instance that we have been working with, as in `file.close();` from our example code earlier, and has no further parameters and does not return any data. This function has been called after the data has been written to the file to save the file before moving on.

write()

Used in the sketch to write a data value to the SD card, the `write()` function has the following syntax:

```
name.write(data)
```

The name is the instance of the `File` class created at the beginning of the code and data can be a numerical value of the `byte`, `char`, or `string` data type. In our example we used the following code:

```
byte value = map(analogRead(sensor), sensorMin, sensorMax, 0, 255);
file.write(value);
```

These two lines read a value from an analog input, map those values to a range of 0–255, and assign that value to the byte named `value`. This value is then written to our file.

print()

Instead of writing numerical data to the SD card, we can use the `print()` function to print a string of characters to our file instead. This has a similar syntax to `write()`, as follows:

`name.print(data)`

Like the `print()` function for the LiquidCrystal library, data can include any text strings, bracketed by double quotes (" and "), and values or variables that include `char`, `byte`, `int`, `long`, or `string` data types. Any numerical value sent to the `print()` function will be converted to a text string, which is why it was necessary to use the `write()` function in our example so that we can use those values for our next example code.

Example Code: SD Flicker

Now that we have some data collected from our simple data logger stored permanently on our memory card, we can use that data to generate some form of output. The example code in Listing 9-9 will read each byte individually and write that value to the LED connected to PWM pin 9. To smooth things out some, we are using a `for` loop to fade from one value to the next.

Listing 9-9. *SD Flicker Source Code*

```
#include <SD.h>

File file;

const int interval = 10;    // time in milliseconds
const int LED = 9;
const int SDcs = 4;

byte oldValue = 0;

void setup() {
  Serial.begin(9600);
  Serial.print("Initializing SD card...");
  pinMode(10, OUTPUT);

  if (!SD.begin(SDcs)) {
    Serial.println("initialization failed!");
    return;
  }
  Serial.println("initialization done.");
}

void loop() {
  Serial.println("Reading from data.txt. ");
  file = SD.open("data.txt");
  if (file) {
    while (file.available()) {
      byte value = file.read();
```

```
    if (oldValue < value) {
      for (byte i=oldValue;  i<value; i++) {
        analogWrite(LED, i);
        delay(interval);
      }
    } else {
      for (byte i=oldValue;  i>value; i--) {
        analogWrite(LED, i);
        delay(interval);
      }
    }
    oldValue = value;
  }
  file.close();
  Serial.println("File closed.");
} else {
  Serial.println("Error opening data.txt.");
}
}
```

This example is a more complex version of the Flicker sketch presented in Chapter 8. Instead of using an array, we are reading sensor values from our memory card. This has the advantage that we do not need to worry so much about available memory space. Let's see how we read these values with the functions in the SD library.

available()

Because we may not know how many bytes are available in a particular file, we can use the `available()` function with the following syntax to find out:

`name.available()`

Okay, there's not much to it beyond giving it the name for our `File` instance, but it does return the amount of bytes that remain available in the file. When we open a file to read from it, we start at the beginning of the file, so we can use the `available()` function to determine when we have reached the end of the file. We used this function in the following manner:

`while (file.available()) {`

By placing the function in a `while` loop, we will continuously execute the following code so long as data is still available in the file that we are reading from.

read()

Now to get the information out of our file, we need to use the `read()` function. Like many of the other functions in this library, the syntax is minimal, as follows:

`name.read()`

When called, this function will read one byte from the file and return that value. This function will return data in whatever format it was written in. Because we used the write() function in our SD Logger example, each byte read would be a numerical value that we can use to send to the analogWrite() function later in this sketch. Considering the following line:

```
byte value = file.read();
```

Here we assign the byte obtained from the read() function to the byte variable named value. We then use this data to fade our LED according to the value stored in memory.

Summary

That pretty much wraps up our cursory glance at some of the functions available to us from the SD library for reading and writing files to SD cards and with it our discussion of a few of the standard hardware libraries available on the Arduino platform. The hardware libraries are unique in that they are generally written for very specific types of hardware, devices, or chips. Instead of presenting a comprehensive description of every function for every piece of hardware that has a library, an exhausting and expensive venture to be sure, this chapter showed some of the wide-ranging capabilities available by using libraries and some of the more universal mechanics on how libraries work. Hopefully, you've picked up a least some of the hardware presented in this chapter and have had success with the circuits and code in our examples. You might even want to try out some of the other standard Arduino libraries or some of the many community-contributed libraries, now that you have a basic understanding of how they work.

We are now going to build on our discussion of libraries by looking at some of the serial libraries used to communicate with all sorts of different types of devices. We have already used some of the Serial functions in our code throughout this book, so it's time to have a closer look and see how they work. There are also other forms of serial communication that we should look at, as well with their assorted advantages and disadvantages. These libraries are more generalized and work with a range of devices that support their protocol, so we shouldn't need as much hardware for the next chapter.

CHAPTER 10

Serial and I2C

In the last chapter, we looked at how packages of commonly used code called libraries can be useful for working with a range of different kinds of hardware. Usually, these libraries are written for very specific devices or hardware that uses particular components. In this chapter, we will look at a few more libraries for working with more standardized communication protocols that can be used to communicate between many different types of devices that speak the same language. In Chapter 6 we got a taste for using hardware serial communications for monitoring an analog input, although this was a fairly basic one-way communication.

We will revisit hardware serial in this chapter, looking at different functions that can be used to not only send but receive information as well, using Project 9 Serial to Servo, for our discussion. We will then move on to serial communications using a software library instead of the Arduino's built-in hardware to expand the number of things that we can talk to with serial, including the tag reader used in Project 10 RFID Reader. After that, we should have a look at another useful serial communication in the form of the Inter-Integrated Circuit (I2C) data bus, useful for talking with other hardware devices like sensors, displays, and the real-time clock used in Project 11 Serial Time Clock.

What's needed for this chapter:

- Arduino Uno

- Hobby servo (Hitec HS-322 or similar)

- Innovations ID-12 or ID-20 RFID reader and breakout board

- Assorted 125kHz RFID tags

- Piezoelectric speaker or LED and appropriate 220-ohm resistor

- DS1307 real time clock breakout board (SparkFun or Adafruit both make these)

- Hookup wires

- Solderless breadboard

Using Hardware Serial

Every Arduino has at least one hardware serial port. We have already used this port to send our compiled sketches to the Arduino board each time we upload our code. The single hardware serial port on the Arduino Uno is connected to both the USB to Serial convertor chip on the interface board, as well as digital pins 0 and 1. This allows us to either communicate from our computer's USB port to the Arduino board or for the Arduino board to communicate with other devices.

Serial communication is a process of sending and receiving bytes of data in a sequential manner. Two of the microcontroller's pins are needed for this communication: pin 0 is the receive pin marked RX and pin 1 is the transmit pin marked TX. These pins are also connected to two of those blinking lights that go mad each time we upload a sketch. When connecting two serial devices to each other, it is necessary to cross-connect the TX pin from Device 1 to the RX pin of Device 2 and vice versa. This also means that anytime we are using the hardware serial communications to talk to things, we cannot have anything else connected to pins 0 and 1. Likewise, if an external device is connected to the Arduino RX or TX pins, then we will not be able to upload a new sketch until those pins have been disconnected.

The serial communications protocol sends data in 8-bit chunks, or 1-byte at a time. In the hardware implementation, the serial bus has an available buffer of 128 bytes, meaning that data up to this size will not be lost if the Arduino is busy doing something else and will be available the next time the data is read. Owing to the usefulness of serial for displaying information in terminal windows and other display devices, there are two ways to send this data: as a numerical value and as a character value. As a byte data type, we can send numerical values between 0 and 255 in each transmitted packet.

Instead of using simple numerical values, we can use the char data type to send a character value that corresponds to a standard protocol called **ASCII**, short for American Standard Code for Information and Interchange. ASCII is a method of coding characters with a value from 0 to 255. For example, the character 'a' translates to the value **97**. We will revisit this shortly but for now, Table 10-1 provides a chart of the ASCII character codes and the corresponding characters.

Table 10-1. ASCII Character Codes

Code	Character	Code	Character	Code	Character	Code	Character	Code	Character
32	(sp)	51	3	70	F	89	Y	108	l
33	!	52	4	71	G	90	Z	109	m
34	"	53	5	72	H	91	[	110	n
35	#	54	6	73	I	92	\	111	o
36	$	55	7	74	J	93	]	112	p
37	%	56	8	75	K	94	^	113	q
38	&	57	9	76	L	95	_	114	r
39	'	58	:	77	M	96	`	115	s
40	(	59	;	78	N	97	a	116	t
41	)	60	<	79	O	98	b	117	u
42	*	61	=	80	P	99	c	118	v

Code	Character	Code	Character	Code	Character	Code	Character	Code	Character
43	+	62	>	81	Q	100	d	119	w
44	,	63	?	82	R	101	e	120	x
45	-	64	@	83	S	102	f	121	y
46	.	65	A	84	T	103	g	122	z
47	/	66	B	85	U	104	h	123	{
48	0	67	C	86	V	105	i	124		
49	1	68	D	87	W	106	j	125	}
50	2	69	E	88	X	107	k	126	~

The ASCII codes also contain something called escape codes. These characters have been around for a while and control things like character returns, tabs, and line feeds or newlines. Later in our example code, we use the sequence '/n', which is one of the control characters, a non-printable character that controls the behavior of a device, to signal when a line has been entered. Table 10-2 provides some of the common escape codes.

Table 10-2. Escape Codes

ASCII	Sequence	Description
8	\b	Backspace
9	\t	Tab
10	\n	Newline or line feed
13	\r	Carriage return

Finally, how fast we send our packets of information is called the data rate or sometimes the baud rate. This is a measure of how many pulses are being sent or received in one second, also known as bits per second (bps). A sort of de facto standard baud rate for the Arduino is 9600 bps although the microcontroller is capable of communications at a range of speeds up to 115,200 bps, as needed by whatever specific devices that the Arduino is connected to. Both the sending and receiving device need to be set to the same data rate to ensure that both devices are speaking at the same speed.

With the boring basics for using serial communications out of the way, let's turn our attention to the next project and some of the Serial functions available to us.

Project 9: Serial to Servo

Sending information to the Arduino board to control how it functions is as useful and almost as easy as sending information from the Arduino board. For this project, we will look at the Servo project from the last chapter so that we can use the Serial functions to send data to the Arduino board to control the servo's position. For our sketch to work properly, we need to change the communication mode from No line ending to Newline in the drop-down menu at the bottom of the Serial Monitor.

Hooking It Up

Because the circuit should be familiar, we won't dwell on it too much. Figures 10-1 and 10-2 show the standard servo schematic and illustration that we used before with nothing else needed. The following source code, however, will give us something new and fun to talk about.

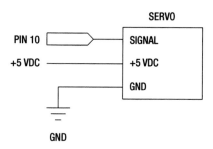

Figure 10-1. *Serial Servo schematic*

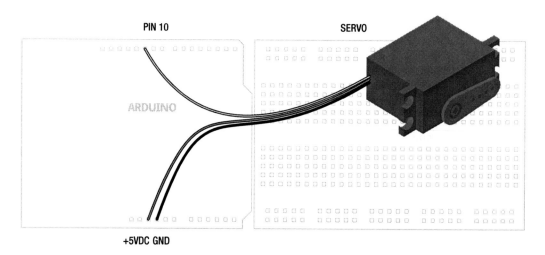

Figure 10-2. *Serial Servo illustration*

Uploading the Source Code

Where before we have used the Serial functions to send data from the Arduino board to our Serial Monitor, for the purpose of monitoring analog values, the sketch in Listing 10-1 will instead allow us to send data to the Arduino board that has been entered in the Serial Monitor. On the surface, all we need to do is type in an angle for our servo from 0 to 180, corresponding to the angle that we want to position a servo, and hit enter. When the Arduino receives this information, it will process it and move the servo to the proper angle.

We see that because serial communications happens in one-byte chunks and because of the habit of serial to send information in characters rather than numerical values (more on that shortly), we need to do a little work to get the characters that are received converted to proper numbers that can be used to position a servo. So let's upload the following code and have a look at how all this works.

Listing 10-1. Serial Servo Source Code

```
#include <Servo.h>

Servo servo;

void setup() {
  Serial.begin(9600);
  servo.attach( 10);
}

void loop() {
  int angle = 0;
  if (Serial.available()) {
    byte incomingByte = Serial.read();

    while (incomingByte != '\n') {
      if (incomingByte >= '0' && incomingByte <= '9')
        angle = angle * 10 + (incomingByte - '0');
      incomingByte = Serial.read();
    }

    if (angle >= 0 && angle <= 180) {
      servo.write(angle);
      Serial.println(angle);

    } else Serial.println("Choose an angle between 0 and 180.");
  }
}
```

Source Code Summary

Just like our example from the last chapter, at the beginning of our sketch we include and create a new instance for the Servo library. While it acts like any other library, we do not need to create an instance of Serial because it is already included as a part of our sketch as standard. In our setup() function, we have the necessary statements to establish the speed of our serial communications and attach our servo to a pin number. Our loop() function begins by starting our servo angle off at 0º and then checks to see if data is available in our serial buffer. If so, it reads the first byte and, so long as the newline escape code has not been sent, will check to see if that value of the byte represents a digit from 0 to 9. This sketch uses the Newline option in the Serial Monitor, so that each time we hit the Enter key, the Serial Monitor sends the escape code '/n' for a new line. We can test for this in our if statement like any other value to know when all of the digits for our angle have been entered.

At this point, the code will put together our angle integer digit-by-digit or byte-by-byte using a little math to convert the ASCII character into its numerical value, and then increases the angle value by a power of ten for each byte received. Once it receives the newline character or '/n' from the Serial Monitor, it will move on to check the angle value that was received to make sure it falls within the capabilities of the servo. If so, it moves the servo to that angle and sends that angle value to the Serial Monitor. If not, it will send a message letting us know to try again. Now let's look at how this is done.

Serial Library

The Serial library is a little different from the other libraries that are a part of the standard Arduino distribution. First, the library is automatically included in our sketches along with the normal Arduino library without us needing to do anything. Second, an instance of the Serial library is already created for us in the background that, on the Arduino Uno, is called Serial, and on the Arduino Mega might be Serial1, Serial2, or Serial3. So when we use one of the upcoming functions, it will be preceded by the instance name Serial and a period to separate the library name from the procedural or function name. As an aside, you might have noticed by now that many of the different libraries have similar procedures, including begin(), print(), write(), and others, so it is important that we get the instance of the library correct or who knows what will happen! Enough posturing, let's move onward with our first Serial function.

begin()

With the Serial library already included for us and an instance called Serial already created, the first thing we need to do to work with the Serial functions is to establish a data transfer speed. To do that we use the begin() function.

```
Serial.begin(datarate)
```

Again, our instance name on the Arduino Uno is Serial, so we will stick with that for our instance name. The datarate parameter is the speed measured in bits per second that, for communicating with our computer, should be one of the following speeds: 300, 1200, 2400, 4800, 9600, 14400, 19200, 28800, 38400, 57600, or 115200. Generally, you'll find that 9600 is a fairly common speed and is more than fast enough to do what we want to do. In our project sketch, this function took the following form:

```
Serial.begin(9600);
```

This sets up our communication to occur at a speed of 9600 bps. You might have a reason to set a more esoteric speed if your device calls for it, but whatever speed is set, both devices need to be set for the same speed. To do this in the built-in Serial Monitor, there is a drop-down menu in the bottom-right corner of the window where these speeds can be selected.

available()

Since we have already looked at sending data to our computer a few chapters ago, we will first talk about reading data and get back to sending it later in this chapter. Before we can read data from the serial line, we need to know if data is available or not. That's where the appropriately named `available()` function comes in.

```
Serial.available()
```

This function has no parameters but will instead return the number of available bytes waiting in the serial buffer. Remember, the hardware serial port on the Arduino microcontroller has a buffer that can store up to 128 bytes of information so that it doesn't get lost. If no data is waiting for us, it will return 0 and we can use this in an `if` statement like we did in our project code, as follows:

```
if (Serial.available()) {
```

If no data is available in the buffer, then this function will return 0 and evaluate as `false`. On the other hand, if any data is available, the function will return a value other than 0 that will evaluate as `true` and we can proceed to read from the buffer. In our example, it didn't matter how much data is in the buffer, only that there was data to be read.

read()

Now that we know there is data waiting for us in our buffer, we can use the `read()` function to do something with it. While the syntax is simple enough, there are some unusual characteristics that we will need to work through before moving on.

```
Serial.read()
```

This function simply returns the first byte of information available in the serial buffer. Because the way our serial communications are structured, each character that we send to the Arduino through the Serial Monitor will be converted to that character's ASCII character value. See, I warned you this would come up again. For example, if we were to send the Arduino the number 1, instead of receiving the numerical integer 1, the Arduino will actually receive the numerical value 49 corresponding to that character's ASCII character code. I know, this is not the most intuitive process here but bear with me.

▓ **Note** As we continue our discussion of characters, remember that the use of single and double quotes is not interchangeable. Single quotes are used for characters, as in the character 'a', while double quotes are used for strings of text, as in "Hello, world!"

When we read a byte from the serial line, we are reading one of the ASCII values from 0 to 127 that correspond to the ASCII characters, shown in Table 10-1, that are received through the serial hardware one byte at a time. We can either leave the numerical value alone by assigning it to a numerical data type, or we could store it as a character by using the `char` data type. From our example code, it is as follows:

```
byte incomingByte = Serial.read();
```

This statement assigns the numerical value of the byte that is read from the serial buffer to the variable named incomingByte of the byte data type. We used the byte data type because that is the largest data type that will be returned by the read() function. In this example, if we send the character '0' to the Arduino it will assign the value 48 to the variable incomingByte. Likewise, if we send the character '9', then the value 57 is assigned instead. While these are not the numbers we would initially expect, we can still work with them to do what we need to do. But first, let's look at what would happen hypothetically if we changed the data type to the following:

```
char incomingByte = Serial.read();
```

While the read() function will still read the incoming byte as an ASCII character code, by storing this value in a char data type, we will keep the character as a character. So rather than storing the numerical value 97, we would store the character 'a'; instead of 49 we would have the character '1'. It's important to remember that this is not a numerical value—adding two characters may not give you the expected outcome. For example the character '1' added twice is not equal to 2. Written another way, '1' + '1' != 2. Instead, it would result in a value of 98, which, if we sent that value back to the Arduino Serial Monitor would gives us the character 'b'.

To make things worse, serial communication happens one byte or one character at a time. So we would not be able to send the numerical value 180 straight from the Serial monitor. What would happen is the Arduino would receive three bytes that correspond to the characters '1', '8', and '0'. That's not going to work for the servo. If we refer back to the ASCII Character Codes chart in Table 10-1, we will see that the character '0' has the code 48, '1' is 49, and so on. So if we either subtract the numerical value of 48 from the character code for a number, or subtract the character '0' then we will end up with the actual numerical value that corresponds to the character. For example, we might write a statement like the following:

```
incomingByte  = incomingByte - 48;
```

Using this statement, we might receive the character '5' that has the ASCII code 53. Subtract 48 from 53 and we end up with 5—a number that can be used with more predictable results. That's nifty, right? We might also write the same statement as the following:

```
incomingByte  = incomingByte - '0';
```

Every time the compiler sees the single quotes it knows we are talking about the character '0'and not the numerical value 0 and so it makes the substitution for us. Now that we have converted a single digit from a character to a numerical value, we need a way to stitch them together so to speak so that we can get a value like 180. In our earlier code we used the following statement:

```
angle = angle * 10 + (incomingByte - '0');
```

The last bit of the statement should look familiar from our previous discussion, so let's look at the operation angle = angle * 10 and what happens in this statement when we send 180 from the Serial Monitor. The first time through our loop it is angle == 0, so angle * 10 will also equal 0. We then add the result of the first incomingByte after it has been subtracted by the character '0' to get its numerical value, in this case 49 - 48 for a result of 1. That's the first digit. The second time through the loop it is angle == 1; we then multiply by 10 to get a result of 10, and then add the result of the character '0' subtracted from the character '8', or 56 - 48, which is the numerical value 8, when added to 10 is 18. The third time through the loop, angle == 18, angle * 10 == 180, and then we add the value 0 and now angle == 180. If we hit the Enter key, with the Newline option selected at the bottom of the window, our sketch will quickly work all this out and send the byte value 180 to the servo function. It's not too bad if you just think it through a few times.

Now our code only has a way of converting the character of numbers to actual numerical values. For the most part it will ignore any character other than a digit from 0 through 9.

print()

Now that we know how to read various characters coming in from the Serial input, let's look at a few functions that will send information out through Serial, beginning with the `print()` function. These functions work a little differently from the `read()` function, so we will try to be thorough at the risk of putting our readers to sleep. The syntax for this function follows:

`Serial.print(data);`

The `print()` function is used for printing ASCII characters to the connected serial device. The data we specify as a parameter can take many different forms, so we need to make sure that the data we want to send is in a format of our choosing. The `print()` function makes the general assumption that if you specify a value like 33, what you really want to send are the characters `'3'` and `'3'` not the ASCII character code for `'!'`. There's another function for that, but first, Table 10-3 looks at some of the different examples of various statements and what output will be displayed.

Table 10-3. Examples of Serial.print()

Statement	Output
Serial.print(33);	33
Serial.print(3.1459);	3.15
Serial.print('A');	A
Serial.print("a brave new world");	a brave new world
Serial.print(3.1459, 4);	3.1459
Serial.print(char(33));	!

These examples begin with the default behavior of the `print()` function in that by providing a numerical value to the function, the function will display each of the characters that make up each digit of the number. It is important to note that our example does not print the integer 33 but rather the characters `'3'` and `'3'`. The second example shows that by default, the `print()` function will print to two decimal places. Characters like the letter `'a'` are enclosed with single quotes while text strings such as "a brave new world" are bracketed in double quotes. Finally, we bend the function a little by specifying additional decimal places for displaying floats and the last example shows how to force a `char` data type on a numerical value to display the ASCII character for that value.

Each time the `print()` function is called, data is displayed in one continuous line. To create spacing between multiple values we might use one of the three following statements:

```
Serial.print("     ");
Serial.print(char(9));
Serial.print ('\t');
```

The first of these three statements prints the text string of five spaces. Instead, we could use the ASCII code for the escape sequence for tab. By forcing the `char()` data type, the `print()` function will tabulate the next printed data. Alternatively, we could use the `'/t'` escape sequence to create a tab as well. Likewise, we could use escape sequences to create a new line, but to do that we usually use the following `println()` function instead.

println()

The `println()` function is short for print line. After printing the specified data, it will return to the next line and start again. Its syntax is the same as `print()`:

```
Serial.println(data)
```

This function is the equivalent to either of the following groups of two statements that print the ASCII codes or escape sequence for both return and new line:

```
Serial.print(char(13));
Serial.print(char(10));
```

or

```
Serial.print('/r');
Serial.print('/n');
```

The `println()` function is a little easier to use and helps to clean up the output that we receive with the Serial Monitor. You'll often see both the `print()` and `println()` functions used in conjunction to format the output, making the text easier to read.

write()

Where the `print()` function made one assumption about the type of data that we wanted to send, the `write()` function will make the opposite assumption. Its syntax is also similar to the `print()` function.

```
Serial.write(data)
```

However in this case, the assumption is made that if we specify the value 33 we obviously mean the ASCII character code 33, so this function will display the character ' ! '. This function effectively replaces the statements `Serial.print(33, BYTE);` or `Serial.print(byte(33));` from versions of the Arduino software prior to 1.0. As these statements are no longer valid, any time we want to display a character by calling its character code, we will need to use the `write()` function for that. Finally, the `write()` function can only send data in a single byte, limiting the values to 0–255 or the ASCII codes listed earlier.

And with that, we wrap up the last of the hardware based Serial functions that we will discuss in this chapter. There's a lot we can do with our new form of speaking to the world, but with only one serial port we are a little limited. Say we wanted to connect a new serial device, such as a reader for RFID tags that also uses serial to communicate, we would need to disconnect the device, upload our sketch, and reconnect the device to use it. Needless to say, we would not be able to fully use both the RFID reader and any other serial devices at the same time.

To get around this, we can use a new library called SoftwareSerial to create a software-based serial port on any of the Arduino's digital pins. This is hugely helpful for expanding the number of devices that we can talk to, but it's not without its limits. Our next section will look at how the Software Serial library works and use it to read data embedded in tiny little RFID tags that we can use for all sorts of things.

Project 10: RFID Reader

In this project we will use the Innovations ID-12 Radio Frequency Identification, or RFID reader to read unique identification numbers from cards, key fobs, stickers, and even little capsules. These tags have circuitry in them that when in proximity to a reader, powers up and broadcasts their unique 12-digit hexadecimal ID number. The reader transmits this data through its serial TX pin in 16-byte packets, one byte at a time. Because these tags are each unique, we can use them to inventory the beer in our fridge or to let only our cats in through our cat door.

The Innovations ID-12 is a common RFID reader that uses 125kHz tags and sends its data over a serial connection at a 9600 bps data rate. Other readers in the company's line include the ID-2 and ID-20, with similar functionality but different ranges and antenna requirements. The pins on the bottom of the device are an unusual spacing that is incompatible with our breadboard. So to make things easier for us, we are using a breakout board supplied by SparkFun Electronics that we have soldered some male pins to before soldering in the reader.

Hooking It Up

By using the breakout board from SparkFun, we can plug the reader into our breadboard easily enough, although, with only one row of open pins available, there is not much room to connect wires. So to make the connections, we are using a little area of the breadboard off to the side to connect common wires like +5VDC and Ground. Past the RFID reader, the only other part to connect is a piezo speaker that we used in our Noisy Cricket project to give us a little audible chirp whenever a card has been read, although an LED would work just as well. The wiring for this is stretching things a little, so double-check the schematic and drawings in Figures 10-3 and 10-4 to make sure the correct connections are being made.

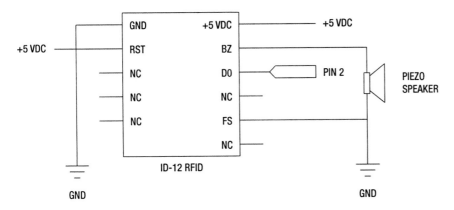

Figure 10-3. RFID Reader schematic

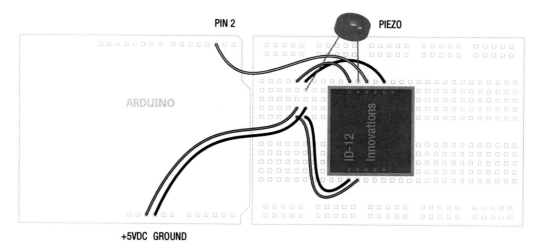

Figure 10-4. RFID Reader illustration

Uploading the Source Code

The source code in Listing 10-2 builds on the basic principals of serial communications that we have been discussing so far, but adds some new wrinkles. First, the reader sends a 16-byte stream of data in the form of hexadecimal ASCII characters each time a tag has been read, but we only really want the unique 12-digit hexadecimal ID number. Second, because this data is sent one byte at a time, we need to read each byte individually and piece it together into a single character string. Finally, we might want to know the tag's ID, compare different tags to known ID numbers, and do certain things based on the tag number. For example, maybe we want to let one cat inside but not the other, or we want our fridge to tell us when we drank the last beer. Following is our source code for this project and a discussion of how it works and the functions that we've used.

Listing 10-2. RFID Reader Source Code

```
#include <SoftwareSerial.h>

SoftwareSerial rfid(2,3);

char tag01[] = "4500B8F08489";
char tag02[] = "4500B8D36947";

char tagString[13];

void setup() {
  Serial.begin(9600);
  rfid.begin(9600);
}
```

```
void loop() {
  if (rfid.available()) {
    if (getTag()) printTag();
  }
}

boolean getTag() {
  char startByte = rfid.read();
  delay(20);

  if (startByte == 2) {
    int index = 0;
    while (index < 12) {
      char incomingByte = rfid.read();

      tagString[index] = incomingByte;
      index++;
    }
  }
  rfid.flush();
  return true;
}

void printTag() {
  for (int i=0; i<12; i++) Serial.print(tagString[i]);
  Serial.println(compareTags());
}

const char* compareTags() {
  if (strncmp(tag01, tagString, 12) == 0) return " Tag 1";
  else if (strncmp(tag02, tagString, 12) == 0) return " Tag 2";
  else return " Not recognized.";
}
```

Source Code Summary

To begin with, we need to include the SoftwareSerial library so that we can use it. If we're using a version of the Arduino programming environment prior to 1.0, we need to download and install the library from Mikal Hart's web site (provided later). We then tell the library what to name our instance and what pins we will use. The RFID reader only uses one communication pin, but the library won't let us have an RX pin without a TX pin. We then have a list of known tags that you will definitely want to replace with tags that you own, adding additional arrays as needed. We then set up a place to store the tag that we are currently reading so that we can later compare it to the known tags.

Our normal setup() and loop() functions are as simple as can be, setting up the data rate for both types of serial, and then in the loop() function, checking to see if any data is available. If there is data available, then we make the assumption that a tag has been read. At this point the code calls the getTag() function that will be used to read the incoming 16-byte packet for the tag ID. This packet begins with a start byte that is ignored by our function with the the next 12 bytes to be assigned to the character string tagString[ ]. The complete format for this packet is as follows:

Start byte (2), 12 bytes (0-9, A-F), Newline (ASCII 10), Return (ASCII 13), End byte (3)

The start of the packet will always contain the ASCII character code for 2 and the end of the packet will be the ASCII code for 3. We check for the start code by reading the first byte after serial is available and compare that to the value 2. After the start byte, we will read the next 12 bytes that will contain one of 16 hexadecimal values including 0 through 9 and the letters A through F. These are added one byte at a time to the tagString[] array, incrementing index each time through the while loop. The remaining three characters, a newline character, carriage return, and the end byte, are unimportant for our purposes and are cleared from the buffer to prevent any problems later.

If everything has been read correctly, the function will return the boolean value true, which is then used to call the printTag() function. This function will print each of the 12 hexadecimal digits to our Serial Monitor so that we can see the value of the tag before printing a call to the compareTags() function. Assuming that we want to do more than just print the value of the tag read, it might be nice to compare that value to known tag IDs. Our last function uses the C function strncmp() (discussed later) to compare the incoming ID with a list of known IDs and will then return a text string or a name for that tag. Rather than returning the text "Tag 1" or "Tag 2", we could as easily change the color of some lighting, print this information to a display, store the information somehow, or even open a door for a cat.

Most of the code should look familiar, even if it appears in a slightly different manner than you might have seen before. We will look at the specific functions of the SoftwareSerial library that are used in our example project that differ from the Serial functions discussed earlier.

SoftwareSerial Library

While Listing 10-2 could work fine with the RFID reader connected to the RX pin, or pin 0 on the Arduino board, it would be a pain to have to disconnect the reader each time we want to upload a new sketch. Or we might have a second serial device that we need to talk to in addition to the RFID reader. In order to have more serial ports than what our hardware comes with, we can use a library that will create a software serial port for us that act almost like the hardware version. To create software-based serial ports, we need to use the SoftwareSerial library, an all-new library as of Arduino version 1.0, based on the previous library formally known as NewSoftSerial, written by Mikal Hart. This new library replaces the old library of the same name and brings with it many improvements and a couple of trade-offs. At the time of this writing, the best place to find out more about the SoftwareSerial library is at the NewSoftSerial web page at http://arduiniana.org/libraries/newsoftserial.

The SoftwareSerial library will allow us to emulate the serial RX and TX pins of a serial port on any of the available I/O pins on the Arduino Uno board. (This library may only work on certain pins on other versions of the Arduino hardware.) While this "virtual" serial port lacks the buffer memory like the native hardware serial (so it cannot receive data in the background), it does share most of the same functions that the Serial library contains, with similar syntax and functionality. The newest version of this library is interrupt driven, which means that it will conflict with hardware interrupts like we used in Chapter 7, as well as the newest Servo library, which is also interrupt driven. If we absolutely must use interrupts in our code, we would either need to use a different or older version of either the SoftwareSerial or Servo libraries. Finally, SoftwareSerial also slows things down a bit, so we should avoid excessively slow data rates and generally stick with hardware serial—unless we absolutely need the extra serial port.

So, let's look at a few of the functions that make our project code work. If we don't discuss most of the functions that we used, that's because they work identically to those same functions in the Serial library.

SoftwareSerial()

To create a new instance of this library we need to use the `SoftwareSerial()` function to give it a name and specify the RX and TX pin numbers. The syntax follows:
`SoftwareSerial name(rxPin, txPin)`

The first thing we need to set is the name for our instance. We could use `mySerial`, `softSerial`, or anything else we want that's not already taken, including `George`, but it's probably a good idea to give it a name that relates to the device connected to the serial port and to avoid any confusion should we want to use the hardware Serial functions as well. In our example we used the following statement:

`SoftwareSerial rfid(2,3);`

Here, we are calling our software serial port `rfid` to remind us which device that we're talking to. While it is possible to have multiple instances of the SoftwareSerial library, we can only read from or send to one at a time. The timing of these operations could get tricky as we get more devices going at the same time. For example, if we were sending data through a wireless adapter on one serial port, we might miss an incoming tag that needed to be read from the RFID serial port.

The final two parameters that we specified in our example as 2 and 3 are the pin numbers that we will use as receive, RX, and transmit, TX, pins. These can be any of the I/O pins on the Arduino Uno, so long as they are not in use by anything else.

begin()

The `begin()` function is identical in form to the same function found in the Serial library. Give the function an instance name, in our example `rfid`, and specify a data rate in bits per second and all should be fine. Although because we are using software on an already burdened microcontroller to emulate what is often done with dedicated hardware, things don't always go according to plan. Data rates of 300 bps or 1200 bps are nearly unusable and you might be pushing your luck with 57,600 bps and over. Just keep in mind that when specifying data rates for software serial ports, if unusual behavior crops up, this data rate may be suspect.

flush()

While the `flush()` function is the same for the Serial library, we didn't talk about it before because we didn't have a good reason for it. The syntax is another simple one, as follows:

`name.flush()`

Where `name` is the name of your serial instance and beyond that there are no parameters and nothing is returned. This function's sole purpose in life is to clear the serial buffer of any waiting data or in the case of SoftwareSerial, to clear any forthcoming data on the serial line. We used this function in our most recent sketch so that we didn't need to worry about the last three characters that the RFID reader sends down the line, whether we want it to or not. We have to do something to either read this data and put it somewhere or simply get rid of it because our code is executed so quickly that these remaining bytes will be taken for tag information and consequently confuse things. Since we know there are 12 bytes that we are interested in and our communications are reasonably accurate, this gives us a way to just get rid of the extra data.

strncmp()

Our last function to talk about here is not actually a function of the Serial libraries, but is rather a part of the standard C library on which Arduino is built. The function strncmp() is used to compare two text strings and is an example of **string manipulation**. We use this function in our example code to compare the text strings from two different tags to see if they match—kind of like a lock and key. While the Arduino has a String class available with much more advanced capabilities, this function works well enough for our purposes. It has the following syntax:

strncmp(string1, string2, numberOfCharacters)

This function will compare string1 to string2 up to the maximum number of characters specified. If the two strings are identical, this function will return the value 0. Take the following hypothetical example:

if (strncmp("goodnight", "room", 4) == 0) Serial.print("goodnight moon");

In this example, the strncmp() function would compare the string "goodnight" to the string "moon" up to a maximum four characters. If these two strings were the same, then the expression would evaluate as true and the following call to Serial.print would be executed. Each of these strings needs to be specified as either the string itself or a pointer to the string. In our example code, it is as follows:

if (strncmp(tag01, tagString, 12) == 0) return " Tag 1";

Here we are using the names of the arrays tag01[ ] and tagString[ ] as pointers to the first byte in the array and are then comparing the full 12 digits of each array. If these arrays match, then we can perform an action such as printing the tag's name or some other activity. If they do not match, we can continue to compare the tag that we just read with other known tags to see if there is a match.

While not generally discussed through the official Arduino channels, string manipulation and other functions of the standard C library can be quite useful in the right circumstances. There are many more string functions as well that can be found in a good book on C programming or with a little digging in the great interweb.

From here though, we are going to look at a little different kind of serial communication called I2C that is designed to talk with other kinds of hardware. While many different devices exist, we will start with an easy-to-use, real-time clock module that keeps an accurate time and date with a battery backup for standby operation. With the right commands, it will fairly accurately tell us "when" we are.

Project 11: Serial Time Clock

The Arduino has a fairly precise internal clock, but it's not the most well-suited device to keep track of the date and time. This can be a fairly useful ability to have if we want to keep track of the time the cat comes in to the house or we want to make another digital clock. To get a reasonably accurate date and time with a little backup, we need to use a real-time clock or RTC module. For this project, we will use the venerable DS1307 RTC available on a breakout board from SparkFun Electronics and Adafruit Industries.

The DS1307 is a relatively simple device that uses the Inter-Integrated Circuit communication protocol, or I2C, or sometimes Two Wire—although these two terms are not always interchangeable—to send a 7-bit binary number for the current date and time. I2C is an interesting serial protocol that uses two wires, SDA for data and SCL for clock, to control up to 112 slave devices such as sensors, clocks, FM radios, and smart LEDs, from one master device like our microcontroller. In addition to the data and clock pins, each I2C device will also need a positive and ground connection to a power supply rated for the device. The I2C pins on the Arduino interface board, although not explicitly marked as such, are pins

A4 for SDA (data) and A5 for SCL (clock). These two pins can be connected to multiple devices on a single bus, where all the SDA pins share a common connection, as do all of the SCL pins.

For the following project, we will use the DS1307 RTC connected to the Arduino's I2C bus to display the current date and time. Because we might not want Mountain Standard Time (if you bought the version from SparkFun), we will also provide a sketch for setting the current date and time. This is also useful because, while the RTC is extremely accurate, it has a tendency to shift about ±1 minute every month. The sketches provided try to keep things as simple as possible, leaving the creative application up to the reader.

Hooking It Up

The following schematic and illustration in Figures 10-5 and 10-6 will make the assumption that the RTC is the only device connected to the I2C bus. If we needed to add additional I2C devices, we would need to also add a pair of 10 kilohm pull-up resistors connecting each line of the I2C bus to the positive supply. Otherwise, the wiring is fairly straightforward with a total of four wires needed to get our clock up and running.

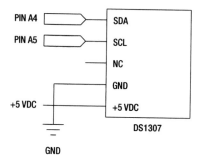

Figure 10-5. Serial Time Clock schematic

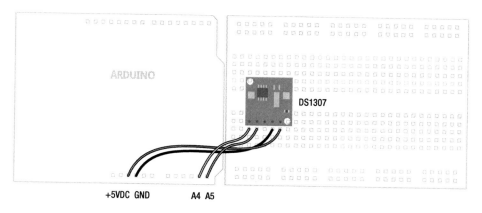

Figure 10-6. Serial Time Clock illustration

Uploading the Source Code

For this project, we have two different sketches—one to simply display the time from the RTC in a text-based, easily readable format and a second to let us set the time in the device using the Serial Monitor. The code might seem a little overwhelming at first, but the first sketch is written to be modular, allowing readers to use it for whatever nefarious means they might dream up. The second sketch is more of a utility than anything, although seeing how to set the time and date from within the code could be handy for something I haven't considered. The format for the text to be displayed should look like the following:

```
Thursday July 7, 2011 8:35 PM
```

While the RTC is a 24-hour clock by default, we have used a little `if` statement to convert this to 12-hour format rather than trying to set the 12-hour clock in the device. To read the date and time, we need to read 7 bytes of data in a row corresponding to a specific order of units, such as second, hour, minute, and so on. The data is inconveniently sent in Binary Coded Decimal or BCD format. This means that each digit is sent as a 4-bit binary number so a decimal 1 would be sent as 0001 and 5 would be sent as 0101. We don't have to worry too much about this as we have a nifty little function to convert this for us. The rest of the code consists of fairly basic `print()` functions so that we can see the data on our serial monitor.

Following in Listings 10-3 and 10-4 are the two sketches for this project. We can start with the simpler sketch to see how to read the data from the real-time clock and see what kind of data is spit back out. When we have a sense for this code, we will move on to the sketch in Listing 10-4 that really only needs to be run once to set the time for your location. This will demonstrate how to send the time to the device and all of the code that goes along with it. Listing 10-3 will concentrate the discussion on the first sketch while pointing out significant differences in the second.

Listing 10-3. Serial Time Clock Display Source Code

```
#include <Wire.h>

const int DS1307 = 0x68;

const char* days[] =
  {"Sunday", "Monday", "Tuesday", "Wednesday", "Thursday", "Friday", "Saturday"};
const char* months[] =
  {"January", "February", "March", "April", "May", "June", "July", "August",
   "September", "October", "November", "December"};

byte second = 0;
byte minute = 0;
byte hour = 0;
byte weekday = 0;
byte monthday = 0;
byte month = 0;
byte year = 0;

byte lastMinute = 0;
```

```
void setup() {
  Wire.begin();
  Serial.begin(9600);
}

void loop() {
  readTime();
  if (minute != lastMinute) {
    printTime();
    lastMinute = minute;
  }
}

byte bcdToDec(byte val) {
  return ((val/16*10) + (val%16));
}

void printTime() {
  char buffer[3];
  const char* AMPM = 0;

  Serial.print(days[weekday-1]);
  Serial.print(" ");
  Serial.print(months[month-1]);
  Serial.print(" ");
  Serial.print(monthday);
  Serial.print(", 20");
  Serial.print(year);
  Serial.print(" ");

  if (hour > 12) {
    hour -= 12;
    AMPM = " PM";
  } else AMPM = " AM";

  Serial.print(hour);
  Serial.print(":");

  sprintf(buffer, "%02d", minute);
  Serial.print(buffer);
  Serial.println(AMPM);
}

void readTime() {
  Wire.beginTransmission(DS1307);
  Wire.write(byte(0));
  Wire.endTransmission();

  Wire.requestFrom(DS1307, 7);

  second = bcdToDec(Wire.read());
  minute = bcdToDec(Wire.read());
```

```
    hour = bcdToDec(Wire.read());
    weekday = bcdToDec(Wire.read());
    monthday = bcdToDec(Wire.read());
    month = bcdToDec(Wire.read());
    year = bcdToDec(Wire.read());
}
```

Source Code Summary

This one sketch might seem overwhelming so let's focus on our first sketch in Listing 10-3 before we talk about the following version in Listing 10-4. I promise that it's not too complicated. The code has been broken down into functions, so it's not too hard to understand what each chunk of code does. To start things off, the manufacturer of every I2C device will assign it a unique address for that device. Rather than referring to the hexadecimal value 0x68, a rather confusing number for the address of our RTC, we assign the value a name that relates to our device, or in the following case DS1307:

```
const int DS1307 = 0x68;
```

We then set up a pair of character arrays to contain text strings for both the names of the days of the week and the months of the year. We also have a block of byte data type variables where we will assign data for seconds, minutes, hours, and so on.

Our setup() function uses the Wire.begin() and Serial.begin() functions to start both of these communication protocols, one for talking to the RTC and the other for talking to our computer. The loop() function shows one way that an RTC might be useful in place of long delays and in fact, there are no delays in the loop() function at all. We don't even need to display the time, instead we could have an event occur every 5 minutes, every hour on the hour, or even once daily at 7:00 a.m., like a cuckoo clock. We do this by reading the data from the RTC and comparing one of the values against a condition. For example, we decided to only update our time every minute, as follows:

```
if (minute != lastMinute) {
```

Here we are checking to see if the minute has changed or a minute has passed before reprinting the current time to the Serial Monitor. This is only one small way of using the RTC as a timer and there could be many, many more. It has the advantage of being very precise and because of the battery backup, is reliable even when the power is off. So let's look at the two functions called in the loop() function of our sketch.

The first function that we call is readTime(), which is used to read the date and time data from our I2C device. This function quite simply starts the communication with the assigned device and then reads the 7 bytes of data that is sent from the device. This is performed in a particular sequence according to the device. The readTime() function also calls another function called bcdToDec(), which nicely converts the BCD-formatted data to decimal-formatted data that we can better put to use.

The second function called is printTime(), which takes six of the seven time measurements and formats them for printing to the screen. This function jumps through some hoops that are not entirely necessary, but make the time a little easier to read. This includes fudging the array position a little, the RTC starts at 1 while our arrays start at 0, so we subtract one from the array position to get the names for the days and months, converting the 24-hour clock to 12-hour, and then buffering the minutes value with another one of those C functions, sprintf(), to create leading zeros so that instead of a time reading of 12:4 we would get the more proper display of 12:04.

So now let's look at the next sketch in Listing 10-4 to see how we can go about setting the time in our real-time clock.

Listing 10-4. Serial Time Clock Setting Source Code

```
#include <Wire.h>

const int DS1307 = 0x68;

const char* days[] =
  {"Sunday", "Monday", "Tuesday", "Wednesday", "Thursday", "Friday", "Saturday"};
const char* months[] =
  {"January", "February", "March", "April", "May", "June", "July", "August",
   "September", "October", "November", "December"};

byte second = 0;
byte minute = 0;
byte hour = 0;
byte weekday = 0;
byte monthday = 0;
byte month = 0;
byte year = 0;

void setup() {
  Wire.begin();
  Serial.begin(9600);

  delay(2000);
  Serial.print("The current date and time is: ");
  printTime();
  Serial.println("To set the date and time please select Newline ending to continue.");
  Serial.println("Would you like to set the date and time now? Y/N");
  while (!Serial.available()) delay(10);
  if (Serial.read() == 'y' || Serial.read() == 'Y') {
    Serial.read();
    setTime();
    Serial.print("The current date and time is now: ");
    printTime();
  }
  Serial.println("Goodbye.");
}

void loop() {}

byte decToBcd(byte val) {
  return ((val/10*16) + (val%10));
}

byte bcdToDec(byte val) {
  return ((val/16*10) + (val%16));
}
```

```
void setTime() {
  Serial.print("Please enter the current year, 00-99.  -  ");
  year = readByte();
  Serial.println(year);
  Serial.print("Please enter the current month, 1-12.  -  ");
  month = readByte();
  Serial.println(months[month-1]);
  Serial.print("Please enter the current day of the month, 1-31.  -  ");
  monthday = readByte();
  Serial.println(monthday);
  Serial.println("Please enter the current day of the week, 1-7.");
  Serial.print("1 Sun | 2 Mon | 3 Tues | 4 Weds | 5 Thu | 6 Fri | 7 Sat  -  ");
  weekday = readByte();
  Serial.println(days[weekday-1]);
  Serial.print("Please enter the current hour in 24hr format, 0-23.  -  ");
  hour = readByte();
  Serial.println(hour);
  Serial.print("Please enter the current minute, 0-59.  -  ");
  minute = readByte();
  Serial.println(minute);
  second = 0;
  Serial.println("Thank you.");

  Wire.beginTransmission(DS1307);
  Wire.write(byte(0));

  Wire.write(decToBcd(second));
  Wire.write(decToBcd(minute));
  Wire.write(decToBcd(hour));
  Wire.write(decToBcd(weekday));
  Wire.write(decToBcd(monthday));
  Wire.write(decToBcd(month));
  Wire.write(decToBcd(year));

  Wire.write(byte(0));
  Wire.endTransmission();
}

byte readByte() {
  while (!Serial.available()) delay(10);
  byte reading = 0;
  byte incomingByte = Serial.read();
  while (incomingByte != '\n') {
    if (incomingByte >= '0' && incomingByte <= '9')
      reading = reading * 10 + (incomingByte - '0');
    else;
    incomingByte = Serial.read();
  }
  Serial.flush();
  return reading;
}
```

```
void printTime() {
  char buffer[3];
  const char* AMPM = 0;

  readTime();
  Serial.print(days[weekday-1]);
  Serial.print(" ");
  Serial.print(months[month-1]);
  Serial.print(" ");
  Serial.print(monthday);
  Serial.print(", 20");
  Serial.print(year);
  Serial.print(" ");

  if (hour > 12) {
    hour -= 12;
    AMPM = " PM";
  } else AMPM = " AM";

  Serial.print(hour);
  Serial.print(":");

  sprintf(buffer, "%02d", minute);
  Serial.print(buffer);
  Serial.println(AMPM);
}

void readTime() {
  Wire.beginTransmission(DS1307);
  Wire.write(byte(0));
  Wire.endTransmission();

  Wire.requestFrom(DS1307, 7);

  second = bcdToDec(Wire.read());
  minute = bcdToDec(Wire.read());
  hour = bcdToDec(Wire.read());
  weekday = bcdToDec(Wire.read());
  monthday = bcdToDec(Wire.read());
  month = bcdToDec(Wire.read());
  year = bcdToDec(Wire.read());
}
```

Whew. Yeah this one is a lot longer. Although most of this sketch is just repeated from the previous version in Listing 10-3 and the rest of it is taken up in setting the date and time and providing an interface so that we can enter the details. With this sketch uploaded and the Serial Monitor opened, we should be presented with something similar to the following text:

```
The current date and time is: Thursday July 7, 2011 9:53 PM
To set the date and time please select Newline ending to continue.
Would you like to set the date and time now? Y/N
```

For anyone familiar with Zork[1], this is along the same lines with a few text prompts to enter the data to set the real-time clock. With Newline again selected in our Serial Monitor, pressing Y and Enter will start the process of setting the date and time beginning with the year and working down to the minutes. There are no time limits, so we can take as long as we need to enter each number, but there also is no error correction so the sketch will provide feedback as to what was entered. We start the process in the `setup()` function with a series of statements to print the message. From here we use a `while` loop in the following line to wait until data has been entered:

```
while (!Serial.available()) delay(10);
```

This statement will loop continuously until data has been placed in the serial buffer, signaling user feedback. Once the character `'Y'` or `'y'` has been entered, we begin with the `setTime()` function. This function walks through a series of prompts to input each unit of time. A call to `readByte()` is used to translate the incoming ASCII characters to decimal values, much like we did at the beginning of this chapter, and then assigns that value to the corresponding unit. Once this is done for all seven units, seconds is automatically assigned 0, each value is then converted using a new function `decToBcd()` to write each value to our RTC as BCD values.

When all of this has been completed, the time and date are permanently stored in the RTC, at least until the battery backup is removed or it runs out, and then we are returned to the `setup()` function, where we print the revised date and time and say good-bye. Fairly long and drawn out, at least maybe a bit, but each part of the sketch has a specific job to do to make things a little easier for us to understand. So let's now have a brief look at some of the functions from the Wire library that make all this happen.

Wire Library

The Wire library provides access to a multitude of I2C devices, not just the DS1307 real-time clock, and we used it in Chapter 8 to talk to the BlinkM MinM smart LED. Likewise, while we have typically used analog sensors for input in our projects, these could be replaced with I2C devices that would offer us many benefits that outweigh the added complexity of talking to them. I2C can be used to read from many different devices, such as accelerometers, electronic compasses, and even FM radios. Because every device will have its own requirements, we will only briefly discuss the standard functions of the Wire library here.

begin()

Like other libraries, we need to call the `begin()` function once in our code, in this case to join the I2C data bus. Its syntax depends on whether the Arduino is to be the master or slave device.

```
Wire.begin(address)
```

The address is not needed for the master device, which is usually the Arduino, but there might be reason to set the Arduino as a slave, which would need an address assigned to it. For most things, the address in this parameter is not used.

---

[1] Wikipedia, "Zork," http://en.wikipedia.org/wiki/Zork.

beginTransmission()

Because we can have so many devices connected on a single data bus, we need to identify the device that we intend to write data to using `beginTransmission()`.

```
Wire.beginTransmission(address)
```

The single parameter is the address of the slave device specified in the devices data sheet that we want to transmit data to. This function will create a queue for the `write()` function to temporarily place data into. In our example code, it is as follows:

```
Wire.beginTransmission(DS1307);
```

We defined the variable `DS1307` at the beginning of our sketch to contain the address of `0x68` for the DS1307 device. The function needs to be called to transmit data to that device and then ended before sending data to another device on the I2C bus.

endTransmission()

The `endTransmission` closes the communication with a slave device that was opened with the `beginTransmission()` function. This function will also send the data that was previously queued up using the `write()` function.

write()

After opening a connection to a slave device, we can then use the `write()` function to send bytes of data to the device. The syntax depends on the type of data that we want to send, as follows:

```
Wire.write(value)
Wire.write(string)
Wire.write(value, quantity)
```

The data to be written can include a `byte` or `char` data type and we can optionally set the number of bytes to be sent. In our example code we used this a couple of ways, as follows:

```
Wire.write(byte(0));
Wire.write(decToBcd(second));
```

The first statement is used in our examples in several places, usually to wake up the device and let it know that we are waiting to read data. It is also used in the Time Clock Setting source code to set the date and time by writing the seconds, minutes, hours, and units one byte at a time to the device. We needed to specify the data type `byte()` in the first example to avoid any problems with ambiguity in the data type.

requestFrom()

We've opened up a channel to our device and written data to it. Now let's look at how to get data from an I2C device. To start, we need to request that data be sent from the device using the `requestFrom()` function. It's syntax follows:

```
Wire.requestFrom(address, quantity)
```

All we need to do is specify the address of the device along with the quantity of bytes that the device should send. From our example code, it is as follows:

```
Wire.requestFrom(DS1307, 7);
```

Here we are addressing the DS1307 device and requesting a total of 7 bytes to be sent. Once this data has been sent, we can use the read() function to do something with it.

read()

Now that we should have data waiting for us, we can use the read() function to pull in one byte of data at a time. Since there are no parameters for this function, and it only returns the next available byte to be read, let's look at the following example from our code:

```
second = bcdToDec(Wire.read());
```

In this statement, beginning at the far right, we are calling the Wire.read() function to read the first available byte from the slave device. Because this device sends data in BCD format, we need to convert this number to decimal and then assign the value to the variable second. We will later use these variables that contain the various units of time and print their values to the Serial Monitor.

And with that, we have wrapped up our whirlwind tour of I2C and the Wire library. It would be really nice if we had to the space to look even a small percentage of the I2C devices available to us, but sadly, we have to call it a day at some point.

Summary

In this chapter we had a good look at a few different forms of serial communications, from the hardware serial port on the Arduino microcontroller; to the software emulation of serial on any of the general purpose I/O pins; and I2C, a serial communication protocol for talking to various sensors, displays, and other devices. This was only the tip of the iceberg because there are even more communication protocols, like Serial Peripheral Interface, or SPI, and OneWire among others. Hopefully, though, this chapter has shown some of the similarities and a few of the differences between these few protocols to make learning new ones easier than before.

Speaking of learning new things, in the next chapter we are going to continue on with a loose collection of ideas for new projects, new hardware, and new programming languages. We'll even show a few ways that you might contribute back to the open hardware community by sharing what you've learned. With a solid framework for programming the Arduino firmly established, we will open up our discussion to include many of the things that we haven't yet been able to cover in depth. We'll show you some neat things and how they might be put to use, hopefully to inspire even greater projects than previously imagined. No more lengthy sketches and source code summaries, instead we will provide a brief overview of some of the many directions you might want to take with your newfound Arduino knowledge, and leave the rest in your capable hands.

CHAPTER 11

Continuing On

Hopefully, at this point you might have started to think that programming can actually be a lot of fun and you might be looking for new challenges. Naturally, everything that can be done with the Arduino can't be shown in one book, however, in this chapter we will continue on with new project ideas, new hardware, and new programming languages. We will even look at a few ways that you might get involved with the Arduino and open-source communities to share what you've learned and the projects you've made.

Rather than detail complete projects in this chapter, we will look at a few directions to take your learning and experimentation. These topics are loosely related to programming the Arduino—whether it's through compatible hardware or similar ideologies. I will provide you with a general introduction to each of these topics, as well as some resources for learning more, and give you a sense of how these things can interface with the Arduino. This is the bonus round really, just enough to keep you continuing on.

Build More Projects

The first thing to do, of course, with your newfound Arduino skills is build more projects! We couldn't cover every project idea in this one book and I tried to keep what we did talk about to the very basics. So, here are a few things that I would have loved to have previously discussed in more depth that you might be able to try out.

Bonus Project 1: Make Something Tweet

Remember that Arduino Ethernet Shield I suggested was a good idea when we learned how to log data on an SD card? Well, if you have this shield, or maybe one of the new boards called the Arduino Ethernet, then you can make your next project tweet. Maybe you're inspired by the functionality of the Botanicalls shown in Chapter 1, but rather than knowing that your plants need water, you want to know instead when the coffee in the office is ready or the beer keg has been emptied, maybe you really need to keep track of the irregular hours that your cat (or teenager?) enters and leaves the house, or maybe you just want to display an updated status of your whereabouts on a display in your office no matter where you are.

What's Needed

To get started tweeting with the Arduino, we need to use a few libraries and the appropriate hardware on the Arduino, along with a Twitter account and a little utility that was written especially for this that can be found at `www.arduino.cc/playground/Code/TwitterLibrary`. To begin, we will need the Arduino Ethernet Shield, as shown in Figure 11-1.

Figure 11-1. Arduino Ethernet Shield

With that in hand, we need to plug it into the Arduino and connect it to our network using an Ethernet cable. Next up, we need to install two of the four Arduino libraries, available from the earlier link, used in this application: Twitter and EthernetDNS. The other two libraries, SPI and Ethernet, come with Arduino versions 0019 and newer. Next up, we can start with the example sketch, SimplePost, included with the Twitter library and shown in Figure 11-2.

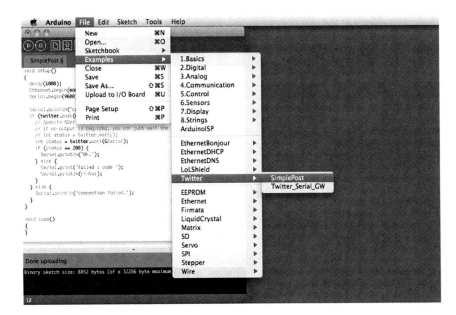

Figure 11-2. *Twitter library example*

When the libraries are placed correctly in the libraries folder, the example sketch will show up in the File ➤ Examples ➤ Twitter menu, as shown. If not, you might need to hunt down the correct library folder.

⬛ **Note** You might have noticed that we're using the 0022 version of Arduino in Figure 11-2. At the time of this writing, the Twitter library did not play nice with the 1.0 beta but the Arduino developers are working hard and I'm sure this will be fixed by the time this book is published.

Making It Work

With our sketch open, we need to set three things to make this work. The first thing to set is the MAC address of the Ethernet adapter. This is usually printed on a little label on the bottom of the Ethernet shield and entered in the array `mac[]`. Second, we need to find an available IP address on our network and enter it into the array named `ip[]`. Finally, we need to obtain an authorization token from Twitter to be able to use its services and enter this token in the `Twitter twitter()` object. To obtain this token, our example sketch uses the Arduino-tweet application at `http://arduino-tweet.appspot.com`. With all of that in place, we can upload the sketch to the interface board and then open up the Serial Monitor to see what's going on. When everything works, we should see the tweet posted by our Arduino, as shown in Figure 11-3.

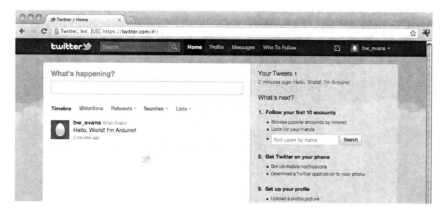

Figure 11-3. Something tweeted

Okay, so *"Hello, World! I'm Arduino!"* is perhaps not the most exciting thing to tweet, but it's a start right? With the right kind of sensors, I'm sure you can find something interesting to make tweet using these libraries. Or maybe instead, you can get the Arduino to display incoming tweets on an LCD or other form of display. For more ideas on what to do with the Arduino Ethernet Shield, check out the following tutorials from bildr, the modular tutorial site:

http://bildr.org/2011/06/arduino-ethernet-pin-control/
http://bildr.org/2011/06/arduino-ethernet-client/

Bonus Project 2: Make Something Move

We also didn't get a chance to talk much about making things move. We did have a look at connecting a small DC fan back in Chapter 6, and in Chapter 9 we discussed servo and stepper motors as way to make something move with fairly precise positioning. You might instead want to make something move using common and very popular DC motors. As explained in more depth in the next chapter, DC motors come with and without gearboxes and run at a variety of speeds with different current requirements. The following are three possible things that we can look for when connecting DC motors to the Arduino:

- The motor can run at variable speeds

- The motor can run at high currents

- The motor can switch directions

Of these three things—in a simple circuit that we are not throwing the kitchen sink at—we can usually do two of these at any one time. So for example, we can run a motor at high currents and at a range of speeds, but it's a little more difficult to get it to switch directions. Instead, we could have a motor change direction, but we would then need to decide whether a high current or variable speeds is more important.

The code to work with DC motors is fairly simple using a combination of digital and/or analog outputs, which we covered somewhat thoroughly in Chapters 5 and 6. The circuits, however, are a little more complex, and we won't be able to go into all the complexities here, but let's cover three simple ways to interface DC motors that illustrate the rule of variable speeds/high currents/switching directions with a general explanation on how to make each circuit work. We'll leave the specifics up to you for further exploration.

MOSFETs

The Metal Oxide Field Effect Transistor, or MOSFET, is one of the simpler components to use with DC motors along with the basic transistor shown in Figure 6-4 of Chapter 6. The following circuit in Figures 11-4 and 11-5 uses an IRL540 MOSFET, although others would work as well, to switch a motor with a load of up to about 20 amps. That's a pretty big motor! The IRL540 can also switch at a very fast rate of speed, so we can use PWM to control the speed of a motor connected in this circuit. This circuit also uses a 1N4001 diode connected to the positive and negative side of the motor to prevent any electrical surges from the motor damaging the MOSFET.

■ **Note** In all of these motor circuits, we have a pin that is marked +V MOTOR. While we have connected these to our standard +5 VDC supply because our motors worked on +5 volts, you may need to connect these pins to a larger power supply, depending on the needs of your motor.

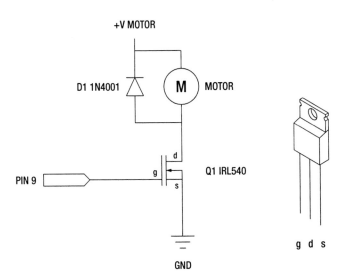

Figure 11-4. MOSFET and DC Motor schematic

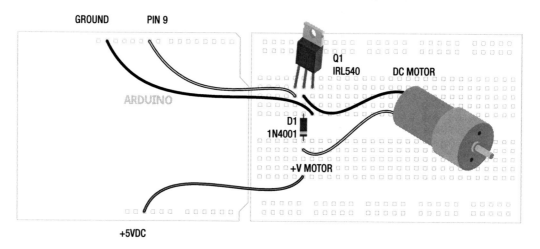

Figure 11-5. MOSFET and DC Motor illustration

When connected to pin 9 on the Arduino board, we can either control the motor digitally, meaning turn it on or off, using the `digitalWrite()` function or we could instead control the speed of the motor using PWM and the `analogWrite()` function with 0 being off and 255 being full speed forward. This high current and variable speed comes with the drawback that we can only control the motor in one direction.

H-Bridges

We have already used the SN754410 H-bridge integrated circuit in Chapter 9 to control a bipolar stepper motor, but we can also use it to control up to two DC motors, although we have only shown it with one in Figures 11-6 and 11-7. By using a couple of the Arduino's digital outputs, we can control the direction of the motor as well as its speed using one of the PWM pins. This, however, comes at the cost of the size of the motor, with the SN754410 only capable of 1-amp output capacity.

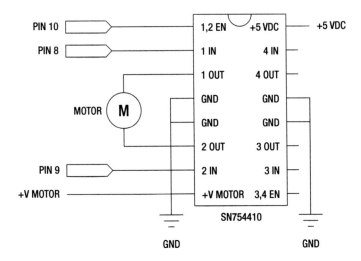

Figure 11-6. H-Bridge and DC Motor schematic

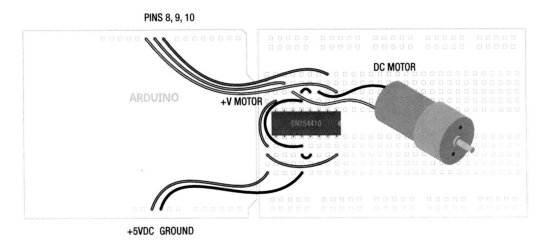

Figure 11-7. H-Bridge and DC Motor illustration

When configured as shown, pins 8 and 9 will control the direction of the motor using digital outputs and the digitalWrite() function, while pin 10 will control the motor's speed using analogWrite() with 0 being off and 255 being full speed ahead. To get a sense of how these two pins control the direction of the motor, see Table 11-1.

Table 11-1. H-Bridge Function

Input 1	Input 2	Function
HIGH	LOW	Spin motor clockwise
LOW	HIGH	Spin motor counter-clockwise
LOW	LOW	Disable motor / free spin
HIGH	HIGH	Motor brake / full stop

By writing a HIGH signal on pin 8 and a LOW signal on pin 9, then the motor will spin one direction and will reverse direction when pin 8 is LOW and pin 9 is HIGH. If both pins are LOW, then the motor will have 0 voltage and will spin freely—assuming it's not a gear motor. If both pins are set to HIGH, then current will be applied to both sides of the motor, locking the motors position just like an electronic brake.

From here, all you need to do is set the direction using pins 8 and 9, then control the speed with analogWrite() on Pin 10, and you're up and running with an H-bridge.

Relays

In this project, we will briefly look at using a mechanically switching relay to handle high currents and switch directions with a DC motor. Relays work a little like the light switches in our walls, with little metal contacts inside the switch, which are physically moved whenever the switch is activated, completing a circuit. This is done by sending a digital signal to a little magnetic coil inside the relay that activates the switch for us. In Figures 11-8 and 11-9 we are using the Axicom D2N V23105 relay with a +5v coil that can control a motor of up to 3 amps at a ridiculously high voltage of +220 volts.

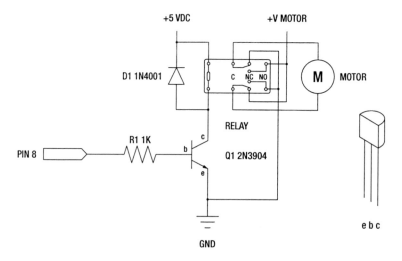

Figure 11-8. Relay and DC Motor schematic

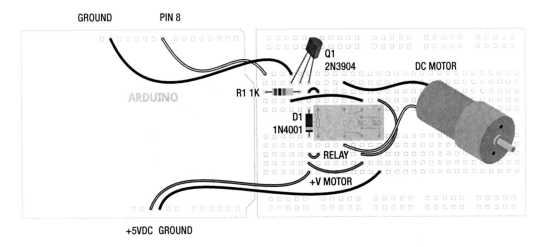

GROUND   PIN 8

ARDUINO

Q1
2N3904

DC MOTOR

R1 1K

D1
1N4001

RELAY

+V MOTOR

+5VDC GROUND

Figure 11-9. Relay and DC Motor illustration

This circuit is a little more complex, but it gives us bi-directional control of the motor using a single digital output, and we have a high amount of current to play with. Alas, this is at the cost of the ability to control the speed of the motor because the relay simply cannot switch at a very fast speed. Inside of the relay there are actually two switches with two positions each: normally open and normally closed. With the wiring as shown, when the relay is activated, the motor will be connected to the power supply in one direction and when the relay is off the motor will be connected in the opposite direction. This also means that the motor will always spin in one direction or another. This circuit doesn't quit!

While the coil of the relay is rated for +5v, I don't trust it with the microcontroller, so we've used a 2N3904 transistor to switch the relay on or off and a 1N4001 diode to protect the transistor from surges, like we did with the MOSFET. And finally, no two relays are ever really the same, so double-check the wiring for your relay before wiring this up.

That might have been a lot to take in, but the code is really simple and this brief little introduction to motors and the Arduino should be enough to send you on your way to find more information and give it a try.

Bonus Project 3: Mega-Size Something

Our final project idea isn't so much a project as it is a neat piece of hardware. Throughout this book, our projects have been written for the standard Arduino interface board, the Arduino Uno. The Uno, however, has a bigger brother called the Arduino Mega 2560, shown in Figure 11-10, and its capabilities should inspire new projects.

Figure 11-10. Arduino Mega 2560

The Mega 2560 is bigger than the little Uno in every way—it has 54 input and output pins, more than four times that of the Uno, 14 of which can be used for PWM; ten more analog inputs, for 16 total; four hardware serial ports instead of one; eight times the program memory at 256 kilobytes and four times the RAM and EEPROM space. Not only can it hold bigger sketches, it can, for example, control the speed of 14 DC motors, read from 16 different analog sensors, or even easily switch 128 LEDs with no additional hardware or tricky wiring needed. While there are always extra hardware components that can give the Uno similar levels of capabilities, the Mega 2560 doesn't need them, simplifying your wiring and your code.

Speaking of code, the Arduino Mega 2560 works pretty much just like its little brother. The pins used for I2C are in a different location and there are extra hardware serial ports, but otherwise the same code should work just fine on the Mega. The Mega is also compatible with most of the shields made for the Uno, including the Ethernet Shield, so the next time you need to blink a ton of LEDs, you might want to consider using the Arduino Mega 2560.

Learn Another Language

Now that you've got a decent handle on programming Arduino C, there is a world of new open source programming languages out there ready to be taken on. While altogether different from the Arduino's C-based language, we're going to have a quick glance over a couple of these programming languages that work really well with the Arduino platform and have complementary design ideologies. These languages will open up possibilities for using the Arduino to generate sound and images, manipulate video, and make things even more interactive. In addition to introducing the languages here, we will also have a look at a group of Arduino sketches called Firmata that make using inputs and outputs on the Arduino a whole lot easier.

Firmata

Firmata is an Arduino firmware that is loaded onto the Arduino board to allow other programming languages to easily communicate with sensors, motors, and other devices. Rather than writing a custom sketch for the Arduino each time we need to communicate with a computer, like we did in our Serial-based projects in Chapter 10, we can use the standard communication protocols that have been written for us already in Firmata, along with code that is freely available for many of the more popular programming languages. Getting started with Firmata is easy enough, as the most recent versions are included with the standard Arduino distribution. There are several different versions of Firmata available, so it might take a little experimentation to find the version that works for your purposes. All we need to do is open a version of Firmata as shown in Figure 11-11; we're using the version called `StandardFirmata_2_2_forUno_0_3`. Upload this sketch to the Arduino interface board, as usual.

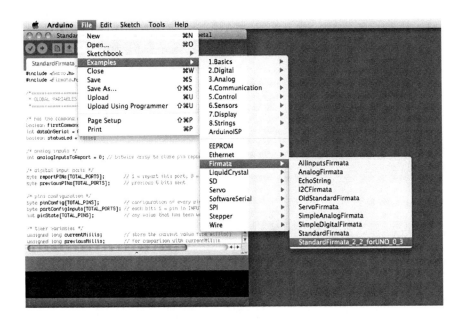

Figure 11-11. Opening Firmata

With Firmata loaded on the Arduino board, we need to find a matching object or test program for the language we want to use with it. We'll get to using Firmata with other languages in a moment, so just to test that everything works, we can use the Firmata Test Program, available from `http://firmata.org/wiki/Main_Page` (see Figure 11-12).

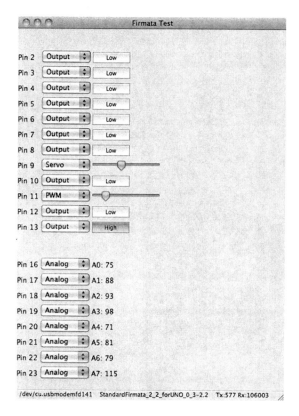

Figure 11-12. Firmata test program

With this simple program running, we can configure any of the I/O pins as Input, Output, PWM (for analog output), Servo, and Analog (for analog input). Once configured, we can toggle the state of digital outputs from Low to High, read the state of digital inputs, change the PWM value of PWM pins, move a servo to a different position, and read the values from our Analog inputs. Pretty nifty for a simple little test program, but it also shows some of the versatility in using Firmata with our computer in that it allows us to concentrate on learning a new language without getting bogged down in writing new Arduino code each time we need to do something.

While Firmata host software has been written for a range of software, including Visual Basic, .NET framework, C++/openFrameworks, C#, Perl, Python, Flash, and more, we will look at the use of Firmata on two of the more like-minded programming languages as a way to introduce these packages as candidates for where to go next.

Processing

Processing is the free and open-source programming language that in many ways started things off for the Arduino. Processing was designed by two MIT students, Casey Reas and Ben Fry, as a way to initially make programming visual design and graphics easier for the non-programmer through a text-based language used to generate images. Unlike Arduino, Processing is based off of Java, loosely related to C by lineage; however, like the Arduino, Processing gets its power and usability from carefully-written libraries of code. Processing has gained wide acclaim and has been used in commercials for Nike and Hewlett-Packard, music videos for Modest Mouse and Radiohead, and all manner of art installations everywhere. It is a really good language for visualizing data, creating immersive and interactive graphics, and generating moving images.

To get started using Processing with the Arduino, we need to download Processing and the Arduino Library for Processing from http://processing.org/download and www.arduino.cc/playground/Interfacing/Processing respectively. Figure 11-13 shows the arduino_output sketch included with this last download.

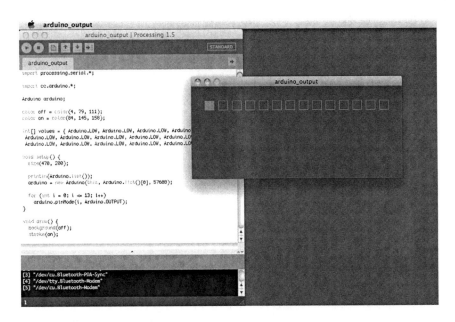

Figure 11-13. *Simple Processing sketch*

If Processing looks familiar, that's because the Processing development environment is the same one that the Arduino environment is built from. Things are a little different and the language will take some getting used to, but once you have a firm grasp of programming the Arduino, it's not overly difficult to get up to speed on Processing.

That is only the briefest introduction to working with Processing. For more information on using the Firmata, Arduino, Processing triumvirate check out the Arduino Playground site, as well as the (somewhat outdated) tutorial from Golan Levin at www.flong.com/blog/2010/installing-arduino-with-firmata-for-maxmsp-and-processing-in-osx. The creators of Processing, Casey Reas and Ben Fry, have also done outstanding jobs writing about the language with their books *Getting Started with Processing* (O'Reilly Media, 2010) and *Processing: A Programming Handbook for Visual Designers and Artists* (MIT Press, 2007). Both are great books to pick up if you are interested in learning more about Processing.

PureData

PureData, or PD, is quite the departure from the text-based programming of Arduino and Processing. PD is a graphical programming environment where lines of code and functions are replaced by reusable objects that are connected together with actual lines that link one object to another—kind of like the patches from an analog synthesizer. PD is particularly adept at audio, image, and video manipulation, and is a loosely related, free and open-source alternative to Max/MSP. If you are interested in using the Arduino to interface with sound and video generated on a computer, then PD would be a good choice. More information and downloads can be found at `http://puredata.info`.

Figure 11-14 shows a simple PD patch that reads sensor data from an analog sensor connected to pin A0 on an Arduino board with the SimpleAnalog version of Firmata loaded on it. It then uses this sensor data to control the amplitude and frequency of a band pass filter applied to a static noise signal.

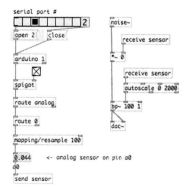

Figure 11-14. *Simple PureData patch*

This simple patch demonstrates some of the basic capabilities of PD and gives you a taste for what it's like to program in a graphical language. For this patch to work, we need to download the Pduino object available from `http://at.or.at/hans/pd/objects.html`. For some help getting started with Pduino, check out the FLOSS Manual on PureData at `http://en.flossmanuals.net/pure-data/ch061_starting-pduino`. Included with the Pduino download are several example files, including `arduino-test.pd`, shown in Figure 11-15.

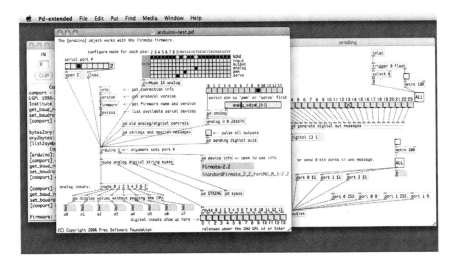

Figure 11-15. *PureData Pduino object*

This patch is a good place to start, as it shows many of the possibilities of interfacing an Arduino running Firmata and PureData. Here we can configure the various states for each of the I/O pins, toggle the states of outputs, change the PWM values or servo positions using a slider, and read the states and values of input pins. Again, the best place to read up on PD is at the FLOSS Manuals web site on PureData at `http://en.flossmanuals.net/pure-data`.

Contribute to the Community

As we discussed way back in the first chapter, the Arduino community is one of the greatest strengths of the Arduino platform and constantly drives further improvement and development of the platform as a whole. Everyone needs a question answered at one point or another so one of the easiest ways to contribute back to the community is by being there with friendly advice on various online forums. Alternatively, just sharing the types of projects that you've made using the Arduino can provide inspiration and answers to someone that didn't even know they needed help. This section will provide a few specific ways that you can contribute back to the community—each one of these communities are not only a great place to share your projects, they are also a great place for getting inspired by new project ideas.

Participate in Online Forums

There are all sorts of online forums where all manner of makers post questions, share project ideas, suggest changes to the platform, and contribute to general discussions of all things Arduino. Nowhere is this more prevalent than straight from the source itself —the official Arduino forum at `http://arduino.cc/forum/`, shown in Figure 11-16.

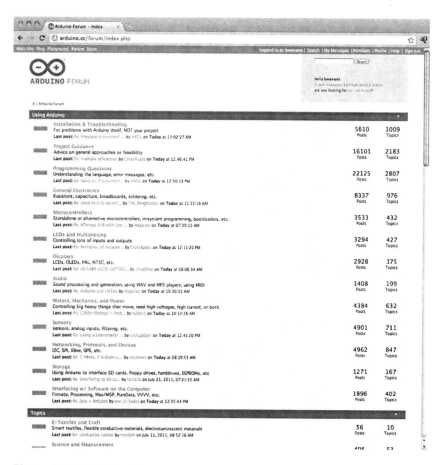

Figure 11-16. *Arduino forum*

With a multitude of categories for discussion and topics that range from electronics, programming, e-textiles, and even interactive art, there is always something to talk about on the Arduino forums. There are even international forums of a few different varieties. Sign up for a username so you can participate in the discussions and even use your username to contribute to the Arduino Playground, a wiki for contributed content at http://arduino.cc/playground/.

In addition to the main Arduino forum, two favorite retailers have very active communities in their forums as well. These include the forums of SparkFun Electronics and Adafruit Industries, listed in our Appendix. Because these forums are not exclusively limited to Arduino content, you never know what you might stumble onto. Who knows, you might find yourself drawn into making a new kind of digital clock or designing a Geiger counter. There are also forums galore for all sorts of projects that have derived from or are closely related to the Arduino project. Maybe you want to use the Arduino for 3D printing or maybe you need a little help picking up that new programming language, or maybe instead you are finally biting the bullet and want to program the AVR microcontrollers without Arduino's help. Whatever it is that you are into, these forums, also listed in the Appendix, are worthy of further investigation.

Publish Your Project

In addition to contributing to online forums, you could give back to the open-source hardware community by publishing your work in other venues. Simply blogging about your Arduino adventures or posting comments to social networking sites will help and inspire others to try out the Arduino platform. There are also other places that your projects could find a home. For example, you might want to post a how-to article on Instructables, the DIY collaboration site. The link to the dedicated Arduino channel, shown in Figure 11-17, is `www.instructables.com/tag/type-id/category-technology/channel-arduino`.

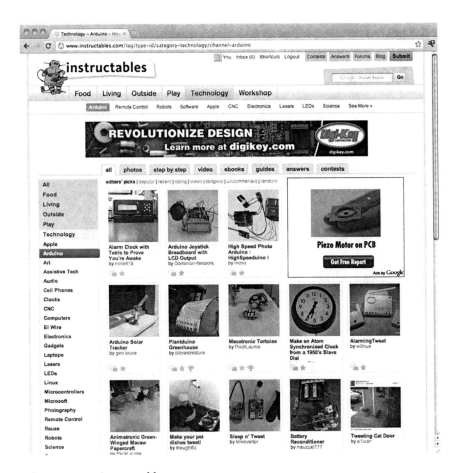

Figure 11-17. *Instructables*

Not only is Instructables a great place to share your projects, it is also pretty useful for finding answers to some unique problems. Another site for publishing and sharing projects that has gained a lot of ground especially with the 3D-printing crowd is Thingiverse, `www.thingiverse.com`, shown in Figure 11-18.

Figure 11-18. Thingiverse

Thingiverse allows you to post a page on anything you make, including images of the finished thing, design files, source code, and instructions for assembly. This allows other users to build a copy of your thing and to even create a derivative of your thing if they make changes or improvements to your design. The centrality of the derivative on Thingiverse is fundamental to a community that encourages friendly reuse and remaking of just about anything that is posted.

If you've developed a neat, simple, modular circuit and some extensible code for the Arduino that can be made into other projects, you should try writing a tutorial for bildr at `http://bildr.org` (see Figure 11-19).

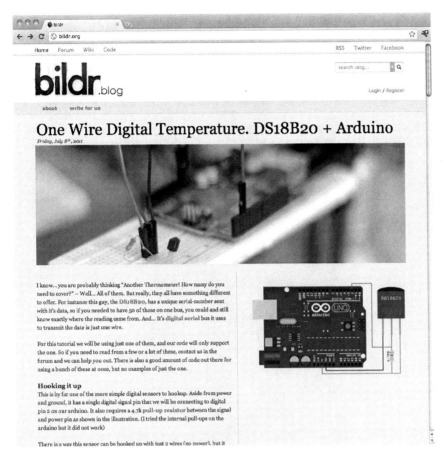

Figure 11-19. bildr.org

bildr is the place for short and simple tutorials that show how to build the parts that might be used in a larger project. It's a great resource for finding out how to connect a particular device and a little bit of code to get started with it. They are always looking for new writers, so as you learn how to connect new and interesting things to the Arduino, consider writing a tutorial to help others with that same gizmo.

Summary

Well, that pretty much wraps up our suggestions for some ways to continue on with your Arduino know-how, including some new project ideas, introductions to new programming languages, and a little encouragement for getting involved with the open hardware community. Hopefully, you've got some new ideas for projects that you can't wait to get started on. Or maybe you will pick up a new language now that you've got a handle on this one and introduce your Arduino to new capabilities it never knew before. Or maybe I'll see that you have contributed to the community in some way, like posting a project that you're working on or by answering someone's question on some forum.

We're not done with the book just quite yet. Up to now, we have really focused on the topic of beginning Arduino programming, leaving the electronics that we use as a secondary focus. For me though, what makes programming microcontrollers way more interesting than programming other things is the way that code can affect physical things—fading lights, changing the speed of motors, and firing off blenders when your cat gets on the counter. To better understand these things, we will finish our book with a review of some basic principals of working with electronics, taking a closer look at various components and what they do, how to read schematics, discussing techniques for prototyping, and a little simple soldering to better stick two things together. Armed with your understanding of Arduino programming and a fundamental grasp of basic electronics, you'll be ready for anything.

CHAPTER 12

Beginning Electronics

Normally, in a book that is primarily focused on how to program the Arduino microcontroller, it makes sense not to spend too much time on basic electronics theory. That's not to say that knowledge of electronics isn't helpful to Arduino programmers, but an honors degree in electronics theory is not an absolute prerequisite to programming microcontrollers either. That is why this chapter finds its home here at the end of our book, as a brief introduction to beginning electronics; or if you already know how to solder and read schematics, it couldn't hurt to have a refresher. Hopefully, this chapter will help to explain in more depth some of the concepts we have discussed elsewhere in the book and maybe even inspire new and interesting projects.

With that in mind, this chapter will begin with a review of the theory of beginning electronics through the use of a range of electronic hardware. We will look at the basics of a circuit, including many of the common components, how to identify them, and how we can use them in our projects. We will also cover how to read schematics to build prototypes of circuits on breadboards. With all this out of the way, we will wrap up the chapter with a little primer on the basics of soldering to help, at the very least, with attaching pins to some of the breakout boards that we have used throughout the book.

What's needed for this chapter:

- Arduino Uno

- Assorted breakout boards or things to solder

- 0.1" male pin headers

- 5mm LED of any color

- 220-ohm ¼-watt resistor or similar

- Momentary pushbutton or switch

- 9-volt battery

- Hookup wires

- Solderless breadboard

- Soldering iron

- Rosin core solder

- Sponge

Basic Electronics

When we discuss electronics, we are talking about generally small circuits using small amounts of electricity. These circuits handle electricity that is of lesser power by a great margin than that coming out of your wall outlet. Suffice to say, we won't be talking about residential electricity here. Instead we are concerned with small electrical signals used for sending information on the low end, to at the most enough electricity to spin a motor on the high end. To facilitate this conversation, we will start with a basic circuit to build from.

Circuits

The image in Figure 12-1 shows a very simple little circuit.

Figure 12-1. *Basic circuit*

This circuit has one job: to light up a lamp when the switch is closed. It has all of the prerequisites for a completed circuit that includes a power source, in this case a 9-volt battery, conductors in the form of insulated wires to carry the electricity, a load that resists the flow of current, here an incandescent lamp that produces light and a little heat in the process, and our circuit has a switch to interrupt the flow of electricity at our whim. A **power source** is needed to provide a source of electricity, whether this comes from the chemical reaction created inside of a battery or the power generated by a power plant down the road. **Conductors**, copper being an especially good one, send the electricity from the circuit's source to its load and back again, connecting each component to make a completed circuit. **Components** like our lamp create a resisting load when placed in the circuit that converts our electricity into something else, whether it's light, heat, movement, or so on. Without a sufficient load on the circuit, we would have a short circuit that would cause wires to melt, things to smoke, and other bad things to happen.

That is why it is important to remember two general rules about working with electronic circuits. The first is that electricity will follow the path of least resistance to ground. Accidently place a metal object or extraneous wire across any bare wires in our example circuit and rather than flowing through the lamp, the electrical current will jump through the metal thing instead creating a short circuit. This is also why **insulators**, materials that do not conduct electricity like plastic and rubber, are used to cover our wires.

The second thing to remember is that the available amount of energy in a circuit must all be used. This is where the smoke and bad things come in because we need to have a power source that matches the load in our circuit. If we accidentally hook the lamp up to 24 volts instead of providing it with a comfortable 9 volts, the lamp will get very bright and very hot for a very short amount of time. And then we won't have a complete circuit because the lamp will have moved on to the big place in the sky for unfortunate components.

Electricity

To make our circuit work we need to have electricity. Electrical current moves in a circle through a circuit from the point of highest potential to the lowest. For the purpose of discussion, in our circuit the current flows from the positive terminal of the battery, through the closed switch, into the lamp to produce light, and is completed when the used up current reaches the negative terminal of the battery. If we were to open the switch by turning it off, we would break the circuit and the electricity will not flow. This kind of flow is an example of **Direct Current** or DC, where the current flows though a circuit in one direction. DC is common in batteries and those black, little power transformers filling our kitchen drawers. The second way that electricity can flow through a circuit is by **Alternating Current** or AC. AC reverses polarity at regular intervals, 60 times per second in the US, and is the type of electrical current that comes into our homes and is available from our wall sockets. Figure 12-2 shows a representation of these two different currents.

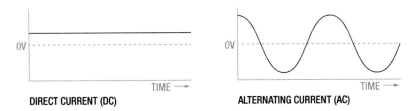

Figure 12-2. Electrical currents

There are three characteristics about our electrical circuit that are dependent on one another. The first of these is **current** or the amount of electrical energy that flows through a certain point in our circuit and is measured in **amperes** or **amps**. The second characteristic is **voltage** or the difference in potential between two points in a circuit, sometimes simply referred to as the circuit's electrical energy and is measured in **volts**. The third characteristic is the **resistance** placed on our circuit by our load is measured in **ohms**. The relationship between current, voltage, and resistance has been expressed in **Ohm's Law**, which can be summarized in the following equation:

```
Voltage = Current × Resistance
```

This equation could also be written as the following, depending on which characteristic you would like to solve for:

```
Current = Voltage ÷ Resistance
```

or

```
Resistance = Voltage ÷ Current
```

Admittedly, this may not be that important to you if all you are doing is hooking up the circuits found in this or other books verbatim, but it could come in handy sometime. Say for example that you buy an LED instead of a lamp to build our basic circuit. The LED itself has very little resistance and might only be rated for +3v at 25 milliamps. If we were to connect the LED straight to the 9v battery, we would have the closest thing to a short circuit and the poor LED wouldn't make it very long. Instead, we need to use a resistor in series with the LED to limit the current flowing through it. Using Ohm's Law, we could solve for this resistance using the following formula:

```
R = 9V ÷ .025A = 360 OHMS
```

By dividing 25 milliamps, or .025 amps, into 9 volts, we find that we need a resistor of about 360 ohms to use the entire available amount of energy. Since a 360-ohm resistor might be a little tricky to find, we can use a 330-ohm resistor instead because that's close enough, and close enough works for us. The LED and resistor in this example are two forms of components that are placed in our circuits. Let's look at others.

Common Components

While there are so many different electronic components, to discuss them all would fill a book larger than this one, so we are going to only look at a few of the very common components here. The idea is to get a sense of what these components look like and generally what kinds of things they do. That way, when you see them discussed or drawn up in a schematic, you'll have an idea of what you're looking at.

Resistors

A resistor limits, or resists, the flow of electricity. They are often useful in a circuit that would not ordinarily place much resistance on the total load, like our LED. In this way, the resistor uses up the current by producing a small amount of heat. Fixed resistors have two wires, have no polarity (so they can be placed in a circuit in any direction), and are rated in ohms, the measurement of resistance, and watts, an indication of the amount of heat the resistor can take. Fixed resistors are marked with either a series of colored bands or other printed markings that determine the resistor's value. Figure 12-3 shows many different kinds of resistors.

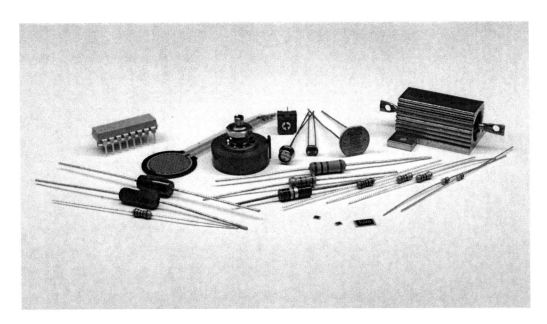

Figure 12-3. *Resistors*

In addition to resistors of the various types and sizes shown ranging from one-sixteenth of a watt to a massive 25-watt aluminum resistor, this image also shows several types of variable resistors. These resistors change their resistance depending on what kind of resistor they are. For example, a photoresistor or photocell will change its resistance depending on how light or dark it is, or how much or how little light hits the resistor. A thermistor changes resistance based on its temperature. A force sensitive resistor will respond to the amount of pressure or force applied to it. A special kind of resistor called a potentiometer will change resistance based on the position of a knob or slider.

We will use resistors for all manner of things, from limiting the current to other devices, reducing the voltage in a circuit, to measuring the change of variable resistors.

Capacitors

A capacitor will store an electrical charge when current is flowing into it only to release this charge when the current has been removed. Capacitors come in many different shapes and sizes, as shown in Figure 12-4, and are made from many different materials, but they all pretty much do the same thing. Their amount of capacitance is rated in a ridiculously large unit called a farad, although our capacitors will be a lot smaller than this, ranging from microfarads (µF) or a millionth of a farad, nanofarads (nF) a billionth of a farad, and picofarads (pF) a trillionth of a farad. These are small values indeed.

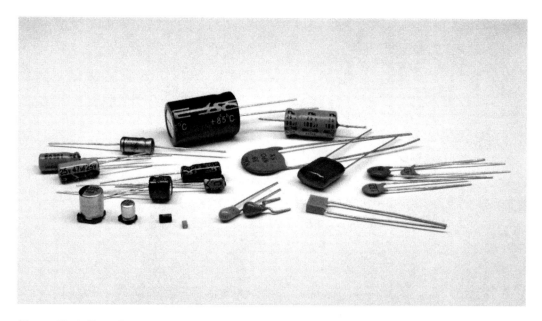

Figure 12-4. Capacitors

Inside a capacitor are two, parallel plates of conductive material separated by an insulating dialectic material. Common materials include an electrolytic oil, tantalum, ceramic, mica, and polyester. Some capacitors, like the electrolytic and tantalum capacitors, are polarized while others are not. Some circuits require one or the other, so pay attention to this as placing a polarized capacitor in a circuit the wrong way around might cause it to explode and damage other components.

We will often use capacitors to filter electronic signals, smoothing out any dips in the level of current caused by heavy or "noisy" loads. They are a necessary part of voltage regulation circuits and circuits that use motors to keep things running smoothly.

Diodes

Diodes are devices that will only allow the current to flow through a circuit in one direction. By necessity, diodes are polarized, meaning that they can only go into a circuit one way. The diode will only conduct electricity when the side called the anode (+) is more positive than the side called the cathode (-). The cathode in a standard diode is usually marked with a line. If current attempts to enter the diode the wrong way, it will be blocked and will not pass through. Figure 12-5 shows a selection of diodes.

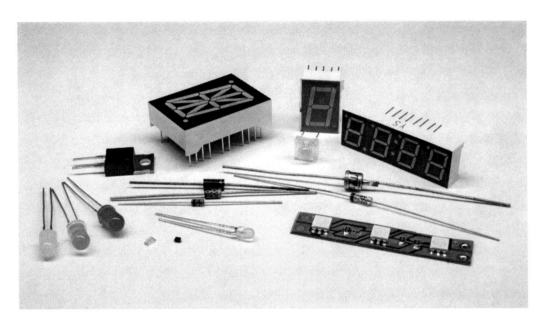

Figure 12-5. *Diodes*

There are generally two types of diodes that we will most often use. The first is a general purpose rectifier diode, such as the 1N4001. This is used for applications where we need to protect our circuit from reverse voltages that can be caused by inductive loads such as motors, solenoids, or relays.

Arguably the most common diode is the light-emitting diode that we have used many times throughout the book already. LEDs are fairly popular with the microcontroller crowd because they are so simple to connect and require small amounts of power to run. These diodes will emit light when electricity passes through them. The anode or positive (+) pin is usually the longer pin, while the cathode or negative (-) pin is the shorter one. LEDs come in many shapes, sizes, and colors, from 10mm to 3mm; miniature surface mount to large multi-watt LEDs; as well as seven-segment and alphanumeric displays for displaying numbers and letters.

Transistors

Transistors can be used just like an electrical switch. A small amount of current supplied to one pin of the transistor can switch a much greater load connected to the other pins. A bipolar transistor has three pins or wires that include the base, collector, and emitter. Figure 12-6 shows a few of the different packages available for transistors.

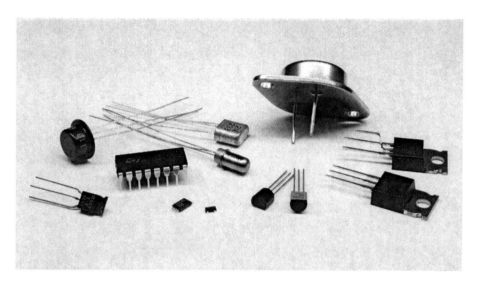

Figure 12-6. Transistors

There are two types of transistors that we are mostly concerned with. The NPN transistor, such as the 2N3904, is capable of sinking current in a circuit, allowing for current to flow from the collector pin to the emitter pin whenever current is applied to the base pin. Occasionally, we will need to use a PNP transistor, like the 2N3906, which reverses the direction of the NPN, sourcing current rather than sinking it, allowing for current to flow from the emitter pin to the collector pin whenever current is applied to the base pin. The concepts of sourcing and sinking were explained more thoroughly in Chapter 5, but Figure 12-7 provides two example schematics for how this works with NPN and PNP bipolar transistors.

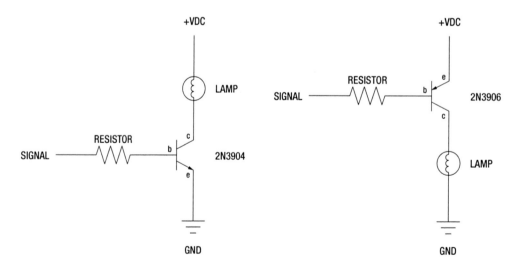

Figure 12-7. NPN and PNP bipolar transistors

We will get to reading schematics shortly, but even so, hopefully, these two schematics will illustrate the differences of the NPN and PNP transistors. We use the NPN transistor, like in the schematic on the left, to switch a load on the low side or negative side of the load. The PNP, on the other hand, like in the schematic on the right, is used to switch the high side or positive side of the load.

Another kind of transistor is the Metal Oxide Field Effect Transistor or MOSFET. MOSFETs, such as the IRF540, are available in N-channel and P-channel varieties, similar to NPN and PNP transistors. Unlike transistors though, MOSFETs are capable of handling larger currents and switch faster than our run-of-the-mill transistors. They are best used for large motors, high-wattage LEDs, heaters, or similar applications.

Switches

Switches are the human-operable, mechanical version of transistors. Their job is to interrupt or allow current to flow through a circuit. They do this with metal contacts inside the switch that either close or open when the switch is activated. There are many different kinds of mechanical switches, including momentary pushbuttons, slide switches, lever switches, reed switches, tilt switches, toggle switches, and even relays are a kind of mechanical switch. Many of these are shown in Figure 12-8.

Figure 12-8. Switches

The contacts of a switch are either normally open, N.O., or normally closed, N.C. So for example, a circuit with a normally open momentary pushbutton with two contacts will be open until the button is pressed closing the circuit. When the button is released again, the circuit is once again open. A lever switch with three contacts might have one pin labeled N.O., another N.C., and a third C. for common. When a circuit is connected to the N.O. and C. contacts, the circuit will be normally open and closed when the switch is activated. On the other hand, if the circuit were connected to the N.C. and C. contacts, the circuit would remain closed until the switch is activated, when it would open the circuit.

In addition to momentary and lever switches, slide switches or toggle switches stay in whatever position they were last left in. Slide and toggle switches are just like your vanilla, household light switch. Tilt switches, like we used earlier in the book, have a rolling ball inside that close or open the contacts depending on the angle of the switch. Reed switches have a pair of thin metal contacts inside a glass container that will close when a magnet passes near. These are often seen in alarm systems to alert when a window or door has been opened.

Relays have also been included here with other mechanical switches. The relay is a switch that is activated by a magnetic coil. When the coil is given an electric current, it closes the nearby contacts. Where transistors are only good for switching DC voltages, some relays can switch much higher AC voltages, although these relays will often need a transistor to power the larger magnetic coil to activate the switch. Many relays will also have multiple N.O. and N.C. positions available to hook up many different things.

Motors

Motors are included here because they are another common mechanical component used in many of our projects. They will either create radial motion, what we might typically associate with a motor, as well as linear motion using solenoids or other devices. Figure 12-9 shows a few of the many different types of motors available.

Figure 12-9. *Motors*

These are all DC-type motors. Motors that run on AC are as plentiful, but are also a bit more difficult to interface with microcontrollers. Radial DC motors are offered with or without built-in gearboxes.

Those motors with built-in gear boxes are called gearheads and generally run at much slower speeds, but increase the total available torque that the motor can provide. Solenoids are a type of motor that causes a shaft to contract or expand, creating linear movement when electricity is applied.

Different types of motors will have different types of characteristics. The ratings that we should be most concerned with are the motor's voltage and stall current. The rated voltage of a motor is for peak efficiency, although we can generally power a motor with a little more or less than it is rated for. The motor's stall current is the amount of amps the motor will pull when some force has caused the motor to stop moving. While the motor will generally run well below its stall current rating, our available power and switching mechanisms need to be rated for the greater stall current with a little room to spare to be on the safe side.

Radial motors are often also rated in revolutions per minute or RPM that tell us how fast the motor will spin. The speed of the motor is not as important for stepper or servo motors, which are more concerned with the positional accuracy, specified in degrees per step and total steps per revolution. Motors will also usually be rated for its pulling force or torque. This is measured by the amount of force the motor can apply at a given distance from the center of the motor's shaft. This rating is far from standard with measurements in oz/in, or ounces per inch; lb/ft, or pounds per foot; g/cm, or grams per centimeter; and even N/cm, for newtons per centimeter.

While we could continue to list category after category of components, we should probably stop here and talk about how we can use these components in our prototypes.

Reading Schematics

Let's revisit our basic circuit that we discussed earlier in this chapter from Figure 12-1, drawing it up in a type of diagram shown in Figure 12-10.

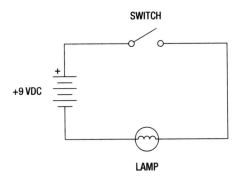

Figure 12-10. Basic circuit schematic

This drawing, an exact representation of the gadget in Figure 12-1, is a fairly standard wiring diagram called a **schematic**. We've been using them throughout this book, but you might want to know a little more about how they work. Schematics are a bit pictographic, like something out of the caves of Lascaux, but it shows us clearly how the circuit described earlier is connected. Once we know what the somewhat standardized symbols mean, in that a squiggle in a circle is a lamp, a bunch of long and short parallel lines is a battery, and a switch kind of looks like a broken line, then we can follow along with the drawing, connecting one component to another just as the lines in the schematic connect components together.

To make things easier in this book, all of our schematics have had an accompanying illustration to provide a little better sense of the completed prototyped circuit, but once you get a feeling for what all those symbols mean then it's not really all that bad. Being able to read a schematic also makes it a lot easier to wire things up. Some of the more common schematic symbols are shown in Figure 12-11.

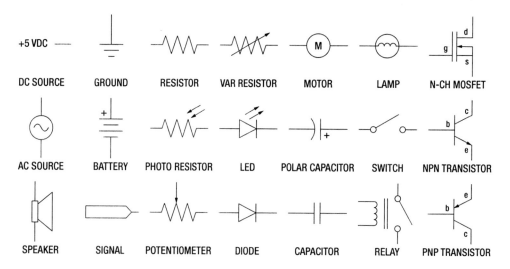

Figure 12-11. *Common schematic symbols*

While these symbols are somewhat abstract, they are also loosely based on reality. Some resistors are made by winding a long length of wire very tightly in a small package, capacitors have two plates that are sometimes separated by air, and diodes let electricity pass in one direction but block it in the other. By reading these symbols, we can use these schematics to build prototype circuits on our breadboards.

Prototyping

Prototyping is a way to quickly realize a circuit and to see if it will work or not. By prototyping a thing, we can build something without spending a lot of time and money wiring everything up from scratch. This is great for focusing our efforts and our ideas rather than getting lost in soldering wires from one component to another. One of the best things that we can use to help make prototyping even easier is a breadboard.

Breadboards

Historically, amateur radio builders would put together circuits using wires and nails quite literally on cutting boards for bread. Today, we use the solderless breadboard, shown in Figure 12-12, to quickly prototype a circuit.

Figure 12-12. *A solderless breadboard*

This image shows one of the currently popular breadboards with a clear plastic casing. On the outside there are about 244 little square holes in the face of the breadboard. Inside, you can see rows of metal clips. When a component's metal leg is placed into the breadboard, these internal clips connect that pin to others in that row. It can be a little tricky to understand exactly how these connections are made, so Figure 12-13 illustrates the hole pattern on the face of the board as well as the internal connection inside of it.

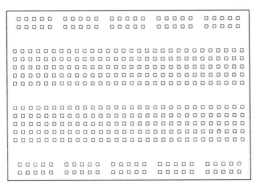

BREADBOARD HOLE PATTERN

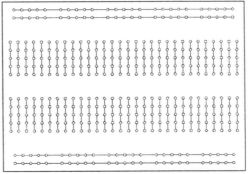

BREADBOARD INTERNAL CONNECTIONS

Figure 12-13. *Breadboard internal connections*

In this type of breadboard, two, long, power busses on both sides of the breadboard are useful for providing a + and – power supply rail that runs along the length of the board. On either side of a channel that runs down the center of the board are two rows of holes where each row of five holes are connected to each other. This center divider keeps these two sides separate and provides a place for integrated circuits that typically have two rows of pins to be plugged into the board and still be connected to other devices without inadvertently connecting the two sides of the IC together. Keep in mind that any pin inserted into one of these adjacent five positions will be connected to one another inside of the breadboard.

Now, to get a better sense for how can we use the breadboard to prototype a basic circuit, let's try one out. Figure 12-14 takes our basic lamp circuit and changes out a few of the components.

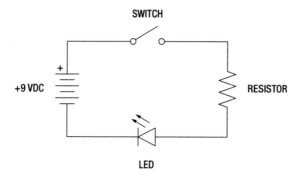

Figure 12-14. *Basic LED circuit schematic*

In this circuit, we have replaced the incandescent lamp with a light-emitting diode and the necessary current limiting resistor, but otherwise the circuit will work just the same as before. Now let's look at Figure 12-15 to see what it looks like on the breadboard.

Figure 12-15. LED circuit in a breadboard

It's important to notice here that the circuit in the breadboard does not necessarily look like the schematic. That's because schematics are not meant to be a geographical map of what the circuit looks like but rather they simply show the connections that need to be made. Connecting one pin of the LED and one pin of the resistor into any of the five holes that share a connection will connect the LED to the resistor, completing that part of the circuit. Starting at the top left-hand side of the schematic, we see that the positive side of the battery connects to one side of the switch, the other side of the switch connects to the resistor, the second leg of the resistor connects to the positive or anode pin of the LED, and the negative pin or cathode of the LED connects to the negative terminal of the battery. We could place the components in this circuit in a nearly infinite number of ways, and as long as we made the same connections, then the circuit would work fine each time.

In our example, we connect the pins of each component right into the breadboard itself. If we had a more difficult circuit to build, we would need to use hookup wires to connect one point to another. These wires can either be solid, insulated wire cut to length, we find that 22-gauge works best, or male-to-male, pre-terminated jumper wires. Keep in mind though that when building a circuit on a breadboard, or changing some of the components or wiring, it's a good idea to disconnect any power source from the board, as crossing wires while the board is powered up could damage your components.

While the breadboard provides a quick and relatively painless way to prototype a circuit sometimes soldering two wires together, or parts like pin headers to breakout boards, is just unavoidable. So let's look at what soldering is and how we can make permanent connections with reasonable success.

Soldering

We love our solderless breadboards for making our lives that much easier, but occasionally there is no escaping the need to solder. Maybe the pins on a switch don't fit in the breadboard so we need to solder wires to it. Some of the breakout boards that we have been using do not already have pins attached when we buy them, so we need to solder pin headers to them to plug them into our breadboard. Figure 12-16 shows a couple of different breakout boards that will need a little soldering.

Figure 12-16. BlinkM MinM and SparkFun DS1307 RTC breakouts

In this image are the BlinkM MinM smart LED and the DS1307 RTC breakout board from SparkFun Electronics. Unfortunately, neither of these devices comes ready to plug right into the breadboard. In the case of the BlinkM MinM, it includes the four-pin male pin header shown in the image, while the SparkFun device requires a separate purchase of the pin headers needed. Pin headers are kind of like the glue of electronics prototyping, so having a few extra on hand is always a good idea. We will make the assumption here that to complete some of the projects discussed earlier, you might want to know how to go about soldering these pins to these breakout boards.

To get started soldering you'll need to pick up a few things. The first thing, of course, is a soldering iron. On the low end, a $10–$20 pen-style soldering iron in the 30-watt ballpark is just fine for learning how to solder. A soldering stand and a sponge to clean the soldering iron tip are also good ideas. We like to use our Weller WES-51 adjustable soldering station, but other higher-end stations that run about $100 are also a good choice if you find that you'll be doing quite a bit of soldering. You will also need some solder. As long as you avoid the solder for copper pipes that you might find at the hardware store, you will probably be fine. We find .03" diameter 60/40 tin/lead rosin core solder works great for general, personal-use soldering. Other sizes and types of solders, including those that are lead-free, are also available and will work fine. It can also be tricky to hold four different things—the iron, solder, and two parts—while soldering, so some form of clamp or helper is also a good idea to have on hand.

A quick note here about safety. We are indeed recommending lead-based solder for personal use because of its ease of use and it is generally nicer to our irons. The fumes that come from soldering are mostly the rosin inside the solder burning off, but you do not necessarily want to make a habit of breathing it. Lead-free solder is not only harder on the iron, but it also uses far more toxic rosin, so you will want to seriously ventilate when using this type of solder, if you choose to use it. Either way, you should always wash your hands after handling any kind of solder.

Okay, before we start soldering, we need to get the iron good and hot. We also want a nice, clean, and shiny tip at the end of our iron. We can get this by applying a little bit of solder to the tip of our iron and then wipe the tip across a damp sponge. This is a process called tinning. It is also a good idea to clean the tip before and after each use. A clean tip will make the heat transfer better and the solder flow more smoothly. With a properly tinned tip, it's now time to solder. Figure 12-17 provides the illustrated and abbreviated version of this process.

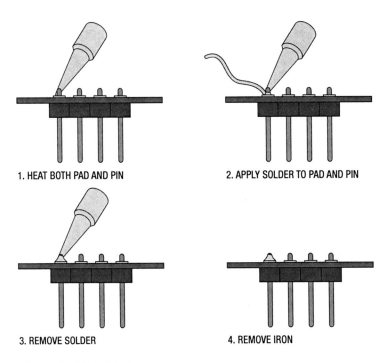

1. HEAT BOTH PAD AND PIN

2. APPLY SOLDER TO PAD AND PIN

3. REMOVE SOLDER

4. REMOVE IRON

Figure 12-17. *Soldering*

Our example assumes that you want to solder pin headers to a printed circuit board, or PCB, although this process is fundamentally the same as soldering two wires together. Generally, we want to equally heat both parts with the tip of the iron and apply the solder to the two heated parts to be soldered and not directly to the soldering iron tip. We do this by putting the two parts together so that the metal bits are in contact, and then place the tip of the iron so that it touches both of these parts. In reality, we are using both the very tip and the side of the tip to make a good enough contact with both parts. In our example, we are soldering the short side of the pin header to the copper pad surrounding the hole that the pin was fed through on the circuit board.

When the parts are sufficiently heated, solder can be applied to the parts and it should flow quickly and smoothly when there is enough heat and everything is clean. Sometimes we will touch the solder to the tip of the iron to start the flow of molten solder, but we want to keep the solder on the parts to be soldered and not the iron. Remove the solder when a nice little mountain of solder has formed, but leave the iron heating things for another second or so. Once the solder has had a chance to flow over the whole pad, we can then remove the iron allowing the joint to cool naturally.

When the joint has been soldered correctly, you should have a clean and shiny little mound of solder that completely fills the copper pad and fully encompasses the pin. Sometimes when we don't add enough solder to the joint, we will end up with a pin that is only partially attached. This might work initially, but can create problems later when you least expect it. The simple fix is to simply heat up the joint and add more solder. However, if we add too much solder, we will end up with an enormous blob that might come into contact with other nearby pins or pads on the board. To fix this, we just need to heat up the solder again and shake or tap the board to remove the extra solder. Other times, instead of a shiny little mountain, we might end up with a solder joint that is dirty and dull looking. This is what's called a cold solder joint and happens when the tip is either not clean or not hot enough for the job.

Make sure that your iron has had time to fully heat up, check that the tip is clean, and if you have an adjustable iron, set the iron to a higher temperature.

Like learning to ride a bicycle, soldering is a whole lot of fun, but it takes time and practice to get it right. The best way to learn is to pick up some electronic kits from Adafruit, SparkFun, or the Maker SHED. Electronic kits like the Minty Boost, Simon Soldering Kit, and the Atari Punk Console are all great places to continue practicing your soldering skills.

Summary

See, that was a lot of fun. In this chapter we looked at a very fundamental—maybe overly abbreviated—review of electronics theory and we got a sense for some of the more common types of components and what we might use them for. We also revisited how to read schematics and build prototypes from them using the nifty little gadget called a solderless breadboard. We even tackled how to solder pin headers to breakout boards to make some of the devices we've used more breadboard-friendly.

With that, we have reached the end of our book. By now, you should have a solid foundation of programming Arduino C; you have a working knowledge of how things like control structures, variables, functions, memory, arrays, and libraries are all handled; hopefully, you've been inspired to try out some new project ideas or get involved in the community; and you even have a basic grasp of working with electronic prototypes to make your next projects even easier.

I hope you've enjoyed reading this book as much as I've had writing it and found its content challenging but interesting, useful, and even a little fun too. I look forward to hearing from you and seeing the things that you will make.

Resources

This appendix contains a collection of various resources that you might find helpful. I've provided lists of forums, tutorials, and other useful web sites; some of the many global suppliers; and a list of all of the parts used in this book. If you had any questions about a specific part when it was needed in a particular chapter, this is the place to find out more about it.

Additional Resources

Arduino is all about the community, right? The shear volume of material published online about the Arduino platform, mostly voluntary and all free, is simply staggering. We have drawn deeply from the contributions of the community in writing this book. The following sections include some of the web sites that are useful for online discussions, additional tutorials, and other reference sources.

Forums

Adafruit Industries (`http://forums.adafruit.com`): Microcontrollers, Adafruit products, Arduino, and laser cutting

AVR Freaks (`www.avrfreaks.net/phorum`): Programming AVR microcontrollers, using GCC, AVR tutorials

bildr (`http://forum.bildr.org`): Tutorial discussion, hardware and software help

DIY Drones (`http://diydrones.com/forum`): Autonomous unmanned aerial vehicles powered by Arduino

MakerBot Industries (`http://wiki.makerbot.com/forum:start`): Arduino and 3D printing

Processing (`http://forum.processing.org`): General Processing discussion, project exhibitions, and library development

PureData (`http://puredata.hurleur.com`): All things PD—patches, libraries, and hardware

RepRap (http://forums.reprap.org): More 3D printing and other Arduino Arduino-related stuff

SparkFun Electronics (http://forum.sparkfun.com): Electronics, SparkFun products, Arduino, PCB design, and project ideas

Tutorials

Adafruit Industries (www.adafruit.com/tutorials): Beginning electronics, sensors, and other Arduino tutorials

Arduino (http://arduino.cc/en/Tutorial/HomePage): Official Arduino tutorial web site

Jeremy Blum (http://jeremyblum.com/category/arduino-tutorials): Video tutorials from Jeremy Blum

SparkFun Electronics (www.sparkfun.com/tutorials): Embedded electronics, surface mount soldering, projects, and other tutorials

Spooky Projects (http://todbot.com/blog/spookyarduino): Class notes and tutorials from Tod E. Kurt

Tronixstuff (http://tronixstuff.wordpress.com/tutorials): An ever-expanding series of Arduino tutorials from John Boxall

Wiring (http://wiring.org.co/learning/basics): Tutorials for the Wiring platform, similar to and mostly compatible with Arduino

Other Stuff

Arduino Shield List (www.shieldlist.org): Summaries of hundreds of Arduino compatible shields

Freeduino Index (www.freeduino.org): Index of all things Arduino and Freeduino compatibles

MAKE Magazine (http://blog.makezine.com/arduino): Arduino coverage, tutorials, and crafty projects

Selected Suppliers

Arduino and electronics prototyping is a worldwide phenomenon. To complete the projects in this book, you will need to draw on a variety of suppliers to find all of the parts that you might need. Following is an incomplete list of selected suppliers that carry the Arduino products, as well as many of the additional components that you will need. Undoubtedly there are more suppliers out there than listed here, many of them in your own neighborhood, but I've only listed some of the retailers that we've had experience with. For a more complete list, visit www.arduino.cc/en/Main/Buy.

Adafruit Industries, www.adafruit.com, United States

Arduino Store, http://store.arduino.cc/eu, Italy

Cooking Hacks, www.cooking-hacks.com, Spain

DFRobot, www.dfrobot.com, China

Earthshine Electronics, www.earthshineelectronics.com, United Kingdom

Farnell, http://uk.farnell.com, United Kingdom

Little Bird Electronics, http://littlebirdelectronics.com, Australia

Maker SHED, www.makershed.com, United States

Modern Device, http://shop.moderndevice.com, United States

Mouser Electronics, www.mouser.com, United States

.:oomlout:., www.oomlout.co.uk, United Kingdom

Parallax, www.parallax.com/Store, United States

Pololu Robotics & Electronics, www.pololu.com, United States

RobotShop, www.robotshop.com/eu, France

Seeed Studio, www.seeedstudio.com/depot, China

ServoCity, www.servocity.com, United States

Solarbotics, www.solarbotics.com, Canada

SparkFun Electronics, www.sparkfun.com, United States

Parts Used in This Book

For the projects discussed in this book, we have drawn from many different sources to obtain our parts. As we discussed in Chapter 1, a starter kit from one of the many retailers listed in that chapter is a great beginning point, because they contain many of the smaller fiddly parts needed to make things work. Some of the parts, like the ADXL335 accelerometer breakout board from SparkFun that we used in Chapter 8, could be substituted with other boards from Adafruit, Modern Device, or many others.

Table A-1 is a list of all of the parts used in this book, with the supplier, a part number, and an approximate price in US dollars for each item, along with the chapter number that the part was first mentioned. Part numbers are from the listed supplier, although many of our selected suppliers sell the same or similar items. This is just to give you a reference so that you can see what we were looking at.

Table A-1. *Parts Used in This Book*

Part Description	Supplier	Part Number	Price	Chapter
Arduino Uno interface board	SparkFun	DEV-09950	$30	1
Solderless breadboard 240 tie points	SparkFun	PRT-09567	$6	2
Premium male-to-male jumper wires	Pololu	1708	$11	2
5mm RGB LED common cathode	SparkFun	COM-09264	$2	2
220 ohm ¼-watt resistor	Mouser	291-220-RC	$.05	2
330 ohm ¼-watt resistor	Mouser	291-330-RC	$.05	2
10 kilohm ¼-watt resistor	Mouser	291-10K-RC	$.05	4
Tilt switch	SparkFun	SEN-10289	$2	4
PIR motion sensor	Parallax	555-28027	$10	5
Piezo buzzer	SparkFun	COM-07950	$2	5
Mini pushbutton switch	SparkFun	COM-00097	$.35	5
1 kilohm ¼-watt resistor	Mouser	291-1K-RC	$.05	6
Wind sensor	Modern	MD0550	$17	6
2N3904 NPN transistor	SparkFun	COM-00521	$.75	6
DC brushless fan 5v 50mm	SparkFun	COM-09648	$5	6
10 kilohm photocell	SparkFun	SEN-09088	$1.50	6
10 kilohm trimpot/potentiometer	SparkFun	COM-09806	$1	7
1 microfarad capacitor	Mouser	URZ1H010MDD	$.13	7
TMP36 temperature sensor	Adafruit	165	$2	7
BlinkM MinM smart LED	SparkFun	DEV-09904	$13	7
5mm LED assorted colors	SparkFun	COM-09592	$.35	8

Part Description	Supplier	Part Number	Price	Chapter
2.2 kilohm ¼-watt resistor	Mouser	291-2.2K-RC	$.05	8
16 × 2 character LCD 5v	SparkFun	LCD-00709	$16	8
ADXL335 triple axis accelerometer	SparkFun	SEN-09269	$25	8
Arduino Ethernet Shield	SparkFun	DEV-09026	$46	9
Hitec HS-322HD standard servo	Servo City	33322S	$10	9
200 step bi-polar stepper motor	SparkFun	ROB-09238	$15	9
Darlington transistor array	Mouser	ULN2004A	$.88	9
H-bridge	Mouser	SN754410NE	$2.30	9
TEMT6000	Mouser	SN754410NE	$2.30	9
Innovations ID-12 RFID reader	SparkFun	SEN-08419	$30	10
125kHz RFID tag	SparkFun	SEN-09417	$4	10
DS1307 real-time clock module	SparkFun	BOB-00099	$15	10
Arduino Mega 2560 interface board	SparkFun	DEV-09949	$65	11
N-channel MOSFET	Mouser	IRL540PBF	$2.82	11
DPDT relay 5v	Mouser	V23105A5001A201	$2.14	11
1N4001 diode	SparkFun	COM-08589	$.15	11
.1" breakaway headers	SparkFun	PRT-00116	$2.50	12

Index

CPSIA information can be obtained at www.ICGtesting.com
Printed in the USA
LVOW121906140312

273104LV00002B/10/P

9 781430 237778